# China Boys

# ADST-DACOR DIPLOMATS AND DIPLOMACY SERIES

*Series Editor:* MARGERY BOICHEL THOMPSON

Since 1776, extraordinary men and women have represented the United States abroad under all sorts of circumstances. What they did and how and why they did it remain little known to their compatriots. In 1995 the Association for Diplomatic Studies and Training (ADST) and Diplomatic and Consular Officers, Retired, Inc. (DACOR) created the Diplomats and Diplomacy book series to increase public knowledge and appreciation of the role of American diplomats in world history. The series seeks to demystify diplomacy through the stories of those who have conducted U.S. foreign relations, as they lived, influenced, and reported them. NICHOLAS PLATT's *China Boys*, 38th in the series, fulfills these aims brilliantly.

OTHER TITLES IN THE SERIES

HERMAN J. COHEN, *Intervening in Africa: Superpower Peacemaking in a Troubled Continent*

CHARLES T. CROSS, *Born a Foreigner: A Memoir of the American Presence in Asia*

WILSON DIZARD JR, *Inventing Public Diplomacy: The Story of the United States Information Agency*

BRANDON GROVE, *Behind Embassy Walls: The Life and Times of an American Diplomat*

PARKER T. HART, *Saudi Arabia and the United States: Birth of a Security Partnership*

JOHN H. HOLDRIDGE, *Crossing the Divide: An Insider's Account of Normalization of U.S.-China Relations*

CAMERON R. HUME, *Mission to Algiers: Diplomacy by Engagement*

DENNIS KUX, *The United States and Pakistan, 1947–2000: Disenchanted Allies*

JANE C. LOEFFLER, *The Architecture of Diplomacy: Building America's Embassies*

WILLIAM B. MILAM, *Bangladesh and Pakistan: Flirting with Failure in Muslim South Asia*

ROBERT H. MILLER, *Vietnam and Beyond: A Diplomat's Cold War Education*

DAVID D. NEWSOM, *Witness to a Changing World*

RONALD E. NEUMANN, *The Other War: Winning and Losing in Afghanistan*

HOWARD B. SCHAFFER, *The Limits of Influence: America's Role in Kashmir*

ULRICH STRAUS, *The Anguish of Surrender: Japanese POWs of World War II*

JAMES STEPHENSON, *Losing the Golden Hour: An Insider's View of Iraq's Reconstruction*

NANCY BERNKOPF TUCKER, *China Confidential: American Diplomats and Sino-American Relations, 1945–1996*

# China Boys

## How U.S. Relations with the PRC Began and Grew

### A Personal Memoir

NICHOLAS PLATT

An ADST-DACOR Diplomats and Diplomacy Book

NEW ACADEMIA PUBLISHING · VELLUM

Washington, DC

New Academia Publishing/VELLUM Books, 2010

Printed in the United States of America

Library of Congress Control Number: 20109221730
ISBN 978-0-9844062-2-7 paperback (alk. paper)

To my marvelous, adventurous wife, Sheila,
who rode with me the whole way

Sheila Maynard Platt, Hong Kong, 1965

From now on, you China Boys are going to have a lot more to do.

—*Richard M. Nixon, Shanghai, February 28, 1972*

# Contents

# Prologue

I spoke with Richard Nixon for the first and last time on February 28, 1972, the night the Shanghai Communiqué was signed.

I arrived early for the meeting at the official guesthouse. The president was sitting in a flowered silk dressing gown over an open-collar shirt and trousers, a long, fat cigar in one hand and a tall scotch and soda in the other. He looked drained but satisfied with what he had accomplished. What an extraordinary-looking man he was up close! Huge head, small body, duck feet, puffy cheeks, "about three walnuts apiece," my notes indicated, and pendant jowls hanging down, the entire combination exuding authority.

Secretary of State William P. Rogers, my boss, came in. H. R. Haldemann was already there, hair close cropped, yellow legal pad and sharp pencils close to hand. Henry Kissinger was nowhere to be seen. Assistant Secretary Marshall Green and John Holdridge from Kissinger's staff arrived a bit later, and the discussion began. These men, the leading Asia experts in the U.S. government, were leaving on a tour of Asian capitals the next day to explain what Nixon had accomplished in China the past week.

The president did virtually all the talking. He shaped the individual approach our experts would take with each leader at every stop, based on his own knowledge and personal relationship with him. "Tell [Philippine President] Marcos I said . . . " "Make sure [Korean President] Park understands . . . " "[Japanese Prime Minister] Sato should bear in mind that . . . " The president had a personal message for each.

Nixon predicted a generally favorable reaction from Asia's leaders. Only Taiwan had reason for disappointment, he said. However, Chiang Kai-shek could be confident that we would maintain our security commitment. Our 9,000-man force stationed in Taiwan was not important in the grand scheme of things, especially when compared with the 450,000 we had in Vietnam. Anyway, Nixon concluded, where else could he turn? The president implied from his remarks that he was also well aware of the difficulties his China visit would cause the Soviets.

Nixon's performance was a tour de force, close-up confirmation of his repute as the great foreign policy president of his time. The experts were not advising him what they should say. He was telling them. As the meeting came to an end, he made a point of thanking each of us for our work. Secretary Rogers introduced me to him as one of the new China specialists in the State Department. I told Nixon that I had spent ten years preparing for this trip and was grateful to him for making it happen.

He accompanied me to the door of his suite, placing an avuncular flowered arm on my shoulder as we went. "Well," he said, as we reached the door, "you China boys are going to have a lot more to do from now on."

This book is the personal account of how I came to be in that room, what happened later in the pioneer days of U.S.-China relations, and my role in the growth of our relations after I left the government and joined the Asia Society. It is dedicated to the other "China Boys"—those professionals from State, the CIA, and the Pentagon who built the US.-China relationship link by link over the years since Richard Nixon and Henry Kissinger laid the foundation. Dramatic accounts by the president and his national security advisor document the early groping that removed the daggers drawn between China and the United States. Journalists, and now historians, daily add more critical analyses of the events that started the key international tie of the twenty-first century. It is time for the working level to weigh in—to enrich the grand narratives and answer questions about the evolution, the texture, and the consequences of events.

President Nixon and Henry Kissinger cut the State Department out of their balance-of-power diplomacy with the Chinese in the period leading up to the Beijing breakthrough and during the Liaison Office years that followed. The bureaucracy grumped that we had been relegated to deal with the "nuts and bolts" of the relationship: trade, investment, sports, culture, education, and scientific exchange. In fact, my colleagues and I were happy to be in Beijing at all, fascinated with domestic Chinese politics, life in China, and the dynamics of the first interactions between Americans and Chinese, whether Olympic athletes, orchestra maestros, members of Congress, airplane manufacturers, bankers, scientists, or inner city youths.

Over the years, our "nuts and bolts" fastened together the structure of U.S.-China relations, in the process creating an economic imperative that replaced the original strategic rationale after the Soviet Union collapsed in 1989. The size of the structure has become enormous. Two-way trade exceeds $400 billion, unbalanced in China's favor. By 2007, U.S. direct investors had pumped more than $60 billion into China, and the Chinese have begun buying into our economy. The year Nixon went to Beijing perhaps fifteen hundred Americans visited China. Now, every day, five thousand people are in the air traveling to and from China. U.S. universities have trained hundreds of thousands of Chinese students. Chinese composers write operas for U.S. companies and hit scores for American and Chinese films. Hundreds of millions of Chinese watch their stars on National Basketball League Television each week. In August 2008, millions of us tuned in to the Beijing Olympics.

These practical daily ties bind the two peoples, societies, and economies. They also give the relationship a weight and a depth that help prevent lasting damage from domestic politics in either country and from the accidents of history. These ties are the contribution not only of the prime movers, Nixon and Kissinger, but also of the early managers of the "nuts and bolts" issues—Secretary William P. Rogers, Ambassador David Bruce, and the Foreign Service professionals who served them. This book will describe how it all began.

It will also address other questions. What possessed a youth from New York's Eurocentric Upper East Side to study Chinese in the post-McCarthy era? How does one learn an Asian language? What do we know about China during the Cultural Revolution, and how did we learn it? Does the Cultural Revolution mean anything now? Were Foreign Service professionals aware in 1969 of the impact that fighting between the Chinese and the Russians was having on U.S.-China relations? What role, if any, did Secretary of State Rogers, so openly and painfully disrespected by Nixon and Kissinger, play in preparing and accompanying the president to Beijing? What were the pressures on Americans and their families living in China in the early seventies? On a personal note, did a fatal road accident near Beijing also kill a promising career? When the People's Liberation Army and the Pentagon sought each other out after Mao's death and the Soviet invasion of Afghanistan in 1979, what issues and emotions were involved? Finally, how do we build on the structure in place to keep both the United States and China secure in the years to come?

# Notes on Sources

This memoir is based on a lifetime of notes taken, diaries written, and letters home preserved by careful parents and returned after their deaths. Taking good notes was part and parcel of many of my Foreign Service assignments, and I became addicted to the practice, finding even now that I cannot listen carefully unless my hand is moving on paper. Dutifully, I destroyed or handed in notes that were truly sensitive; but I kept many others in the belief that someday I might write some history, the subject I loved the most as a child and still do now.

The result is this volume, peculiarly my own to answer for. No one else bears responsibility of any kind. I drew on a number of books to make sure I had the context right and my facts straight. Brandon Grove's riveting *Behind Embassy Walls* helped me capture the first weeks as an A-100 Foreign Service trainee. We were classmates, and his example also helped me persevere with this memoir. John Holdridge's *Crossing the Divide* and Marshall Green's contribution to *War and Peace with China* were solid reference points by former bosses who supervised my work during years in Hong Kong, Washington, and Beijing. *Window on the Forbidden City: The Beijing Diaries of David Bruce, 1973–1974* was especially helpful in documenting Liaison Office days. The *Diaries* quote fully from reports that I wrote for Bruce's signature, placing them in the public record and obviating the need for me to get them cleared. Naturally, I had to read the memoirs of Richard Nixon and Henry Kissinger, if only to assure that the ant tracks I traced did not wander too far off the broad paths set forth by those who had moved the world. I read *Nixon and Mao: The Week That Changed the World* to make sure that Margaret MacMillan had not written my book. Happily, my perspective is totally different, although I was pleased by the extent she drew on oral histories from key colleagues like Winston Lord, produced by the Association for Diplomatic Studies and Training. *About Face* by James Mann helped me with background on military relations during the post-Nixon years.

Other key sources first and foremost included my wife Sheila, a devoted diarist herself, who shared the life of which I write. The Three Tigers, sons Adam, Oliver, and Nick Jr, added pungent comments of their own about my writing skills and our family experience in Mao's China. Mary-Hart Bartley, my executive assistant during Asia Society days and still, helped me put together the final chapters of the China Boys saga. Peter Frost, the notable Asia studies professor at Williams College and the University of Mississippi, who won perseverance awards for reading not only one, but two of my drafts, provided scholarly insight and encouragement. I am also grateful to Columbia University's Rachel DeWoskin, author of *Foreign Babes in Beijing*, who saw an early draft and added a valuable, younger-generation New China perspective.

This volume draws only on material relevant to my experience with China. There is more, much more about experiences in Washington, Africa, the Philippines, and Pakistan. I will get to them if I live long enough among people who are interested.

The Association for Diplomatic Studies and Training deserves my special thanks for choosing this memoir as part of their ADST-DACOR Diplomats and Diplomacy Series, allowing me to join treasured colleagues and bosses in the telling of their tales. I am indebted to their caring and careful editor, Margery B. Thompson, for her patient guidance.

# China Boys

# 1

# Choosing Diplomacy

## Early Asians

I met my first Asian at St. Paul's School in Concord, New Hampshire. A chubby, homesick new boy, who still sang soprano, I reported for football practice on the lowest club team one day in mid-September 1948. Placed with the heavies in the middle of the line, I found myself standing next to a young Asian man, older and smaller than I. We eyed each other warily, both looking ridiculous in the football equipment of the day: leather helmets with drooping doglike earlaps, high-winged shoulder pads, and bulging pants. He announced quietly that he was Ben Makihara from the Seikei High School in Tokyo, then blurted out, "I don't understand this game at all! I just don't know what to do."

"Well, our job here in the middle of the line is to knock people down," I replied helpfully. "There are three ways to do that. We can just charge straight ahead, or you can lie down on the ground and I can knock someone over you, or I can lie down on the ground and you can knock someone over me."

"Oh," said Ben.

We used all three methods during the season, becoming lifelong friends in the process. Makihara went on to become the chief executive officer and chairman of Mitsubishi, one of Japan's largest conglomerates, and a key figure influencing U.S.-Japan relations. We have joked together since that ours was the real beginning of U.S.-Japan security cooperation.

Nestled in the New Hampshire countryside, St. Paul's, a strict, private Episcopalian boarding school patterned after English models, had within three years of Japan's surrender pioneered an exchange program with Seikei, a counterpart school in Tokyo. Two years later Tatsuo Arima, destined to become a top diplomat, joined my class. We were to work closely almost thirty years later in Washington, where he headed the Political Section of the Japanese embassy in Washington and I was in charge of the Japan desk at the State Department. Together we dealt with the problems of the day, boasting that the class of '53 at SPS managed U.S.-Japan relations from both sides of the Pacific.

## School Influences

St. Paul's shaped me. My Japanese friends provided a look beyond the swarm of WASPs (slang for white Anglo-Saxon Protestants) who were my classmates. I learned to love history under the gruff, incisive discipline of a teacher named Carroll McDonald. The chance to observe history in the making would later pull me into diplomacy. So would the SPS connection with a Peace Corps forerunner in England called the Winant Volunteers.

John Winant, the revered U.S. ambassador to the Court of St. James's during World War II, had been a master at St. Paul's before becoming governor of New Hampshire. He committed suicide at the end of the war, as much a casualty of the conflict as any battlefield death. His friends in Britain, led by a spellbinding evangelist named Tubby Clayton, organized in Winant's memory a summer program for college- and high-school-age volunteers to help rebuild London's war-damaged East End. Clayton's first recruiting stop was SPS in the late 1940s. I remember sitting in the school's chapel, a callow choir boy, mesmerized by Tubby's descriptions of London ravaged, of Winant's craggy appearances at blazing scenes during the Blitz (firefighters reported seeing Abraham Lincoln), and the need to rebuild. I told myself I just had to join the Volunteers. Several years later I did.

The summer before my sophomore year at Harvard, I was sent to work as a Winant Volunteer at the Brady Boys' Club, the world's oldest Orthodox Jewish Boys' Club, in the heart of East London. I learned to communicate in their patois of English, Yiddish, and Cockney rhyme slang. (I nearly lost my newfound status as an honorary Jew when I tried to put mayonnaise on chopped liver.) Living abroad turned out to be fun and fascinating. Explaining the United States and its policies to kids from a different culture was a challenge. Persistent nagging by my Cockney kids to tell them what I planned to do with my life set me searching for an adult analog to my current work. I returned to college with my cap set for the Foreign Service.

In addition to intellectual rigor, SPS served up an exhausting array of things to do. I sang, boxed, rowed, and was part of the student government. The impact of these activities on the way I operated later in life, particularly rowing, was huge. My management style as an ambassador and a bureaucrat, which treasured teamwork and measured progress one stroke at a time, was formed in a racing shell.

## Maiden Aunts of Influence

I was fifteen when I took a summer job at "Naumkeag," the estate of my great-aunt Mabel Choate in Stockbridge, Massachusetts. Mabel had inherited the large summer "cottage" in the Berkshires. Architect Stanford White had designed it for her father, Joseph H. Choate, the New York lawyer who made his name opposing the graduated income tax and became U.S. ambassador to the Court of St. James's (1899–1906). Mabel added what became a famous array of gardens to the working farm that served the estate. At 75 cents an hour, I weeded bricks, mowed lawns, milked cows, and did whatever the farm manager instructed. I was proud of my Social Security card, whose early number I carry to this day, and moved seamlessly between "Upstairs" and "Downstairs" at the big house.

Mabel Choate was amply sized. She strongly believed that good health depended on the vital organs being surrounded by a layer of fat. Witty and quick, responsible and philanthropic, she made herself easily accessible to all ages. Mabel had suffered from a number of ailments in her life, and apparently kept on taking every medicine ever prescribed for her. One of these was Argyrol for sinus problems. As a result, over time she turned a distinctive color. The children in our family referred to her fondly as "our navy blue aunt." A more accurate description would be a light battleship gray. She wore a set of silver bracelets that tinkled loudly when she walked and announced her presence from a distance. My mother adored Aunt Mabel, her father's younger sister, and so did we.

Aunt Mabel had traveled extensively in the "Orient" as a young woman. She fell in love with the arts and architecture of China and brought home, brick by brick, an entire ancestral temple, which she reconstructed at Naumkeag. As an employee during the day, I would sweep the dragon walk and clean the spirit gate. In the evenings I would sit on the temple porch and listen to her traveler's tales and the lore she had absorbed. The spirit gate, she told me, was placed to block the direct approach to the temple, forcing visitors to detour around it. Evil spirits could fly only in straight lines and were thus denied entry.

Mabel imported other Chinese practices valuable to teenage boys. It was the height of politesse in old Peking (as Americans then called Beijing), she reported, to belch loudly in appreciation for a delicate dish or a fine meal. She had mastered the technique and taught it to me, empowering me to disrupt school study halls for years to come. At the time, I had no conscious sense of pull toward China. Seeds Mabel Choate sowed would sprout later.

The source of another early family link with Asia was my father's Aunt Lina, his mother's sister. Mary Caroline Hardy graduated from Radcliffe College in 1902, one of the original "Blue Stockings." The years had bowed her legs and placed wisps of moustache under her hatchet nose, but left her sharp and wise. Sunday dinner at her walk-up apartment on Sparks Street in Cambridge was a regular feature of my years at Harvard. She cooked us toothsome dishes with odd names—"Cry Like a Child," roast chicken basted with 7- Up, was so delicious you did just that; and "Train Wreck," a beef stew with sour cream and red wine, was chaotic in appearance but equally good. Sunday nights were a haven for family. My cousins Charley and Frank and my sister Penny all overlapped with me at college and were regulars at table. Literary people like John Updike also enjoyed Aunt Lina's company and the victuals and steady flow of sherry from S.S. Pierce.

Aunt Lina's Hardy family photograph album showed pictures of nineteenth-century Bostonians, large males in frock coats with muttonchop whiskers and ladies in elaborate dresses shaped by whalebone corsets and bustles. Among them was a small Asian gentleman.

"Who was this?" I asked Aunt Lina, as we sat on her sofa going through the album one Sunday evening.

"That was your Japanese relative, Joseph Hardy Neesima," she replied, and told me the story that Japanese, as I discovered years later, remember and repeat to this day. His name was Nijima Jo, a twenty-year-old Samurai who stole out of Japan in 1864, four years before the Meiji Restoration. Under the Tokugawa Shoguns, his country had been closed for 250 years, and emigration was a capital crime. But Admiral Perry's black ships had appeared in Japanese waters ten years before, bringing evidence of a different world, new technology, and strong Christian beliefs that Nijima and other young Japanese were not permitted to study. So frustrated that he became physically ill, Nijima had to escape. With the help of a Russian Orthodox priest and an American packet-schooner skipper, he made his way to Shanghai. There, in the roads of the Whampoa River, he found an American clipper ship, the *Wild Rover*, owned by Alpheus Hardy, Aunt Lina's grandfather. Nijima, an extraordinarily focused young man, made straight for the vessel and found a job as cabin boy.

By the time *Wild Rover* reached Boston a year later, stopping in Hong Kong and Manila among other Asian ports, Nijima had learned English, translated portions of his Chinese Bible into English, and made strong friendships with key members of the crew, most notably the captain, who arranged for him to meet the boss. In 1865, Alpheus Hardy, a handsome, imposing, and deeply religious man, received Nijima in his Boston office, standing next to a large rolltop desk.

"Why did you come here?" he asked, simply.

"This is why I came," Nijima replied, and placed on the desk several pages of the New Testament he had translated. Hardy, impressed, asked him to write an essay that described his feelings and motivations. In Nijima's quaint but passionate prose, he told Hardy and his wife that he had felt like a "rat in a bag" in Japan. Originally thinking to hire him for the household, they were so moved that they adopted him as their son.

Nijima became a close member of the Hardy family for the next ten years, calling himself Joseph Hardy Neesima. Under Alpheus's patronage and guidance, he studied with characteristic intensity and graduated from Phillips Academy Andover, Amherst College, and Andover Theological Seminary. In 1875, he returned to Japan to found the country's first, and still largest and most successful, Christian university, in Kyoto. He called it the Doshisha (Society of Friends). Every year Mary Caroline Hardy received an engraved invitation to attend graduation. Nijima's story fascinated me. Like Aunt Mabel's Chinese temple tales, the early Japanese connection would echo in later years. With great fanfare, my father and I attended the Doshisha centennial anniversary in 1975, while I was serving in our embassy in Tokyo.

## Choices at Harvard

Asian inklings aside, my focus at Harvard remained on preparing for a Foreign Service career in Europe. Diplomatic history and German language training were main subjects. My honors thesis traced the passage of the Marshall Plan through Congress. During my undergraduate years, Eisenhower was president, the role of the United States as leader of the West solidified, and the lines of battle for the Cold War hardened. U.S. interest in world affairs was strong and growing. University teaching began to reflect these realities. Courses I took from McGeorge Bundy and Arthur Schlesinger and lectures I audited by Henry Kissinger lent intellectual life and shape to my choice of calling.

Having decided early what I wanted to do, I began unconsciously searching for someone to do it with. Deep down, the idea of launching into a complicated international life without a mate terrified me. Sheila Maynard was a year behind me at Radcliffe. We had both been born in 1936, midway between the Great Depression and World War II, in the same Upper East Side New York hospital. We did not know each other then, but our parents did. They were members of a socially cohesive group of professionals—lawyers, architects, and investment bankers—thus assuring that, one day, we would meet. We found each other in February of my junior year at a ghastly, smoke-filled, post-exam party in a crowded dormitory room, drinking gin out of Styrofoam cups. We sat down and started talking. Three hours later we were astonished to find that we had not run out of things to say. The conversation has lasted more than fifty years. I gave up rowing my senior year in order to court her. In the winter of 1957, my senior year, I startled Sheila and myself by proposing, out of the blue, that she come with me on my chosen adventure and be the mother of my children. Equally startling, she agreed. We married just after graduation.

## Convincing the Family

Diplomacy was an unorthodox choice, particularly in a family whose professional traditions were architecture and law. My grandfather, Charles A. Platt, had been a leading architect. He designed the Freer Gallery, Deerfield Academy, and Phillips Andover as well as a host of grand residences for the tycoons of his time. My father, Geoffrey, had a distinguished career of his own, which culminated as New York City's first Landmarks Commissioner. Happily, my father had no preconceived notions of what I should become. On the contrary, when I asked him early in my teens whether I should become an architect, he responded in the kindest manner, "If you have to ask, you should not be one." He advised me to go with my own passion.

My mother had doubts about a son "in the Diplomatic," but history helped her get used to the idea. Her grandfather's successful stint as U.S. ambassador to the Court of St. James's from 1899 to 1905 had provided rich nuggets of family lore. Joseph H. Choate's skirmish with the Argentine foreign minister during a reception at Claridge's Hotel is still famous. The minister, decked out like a Roxy Theater doorman in an elaborate court uniform with epaulets and frogs, mistook Choate for a waiter. This was a common occurrence in those days, as American diplomats, representing an egalitarian republic, wore only black tie or white tie and tails on formal occasions.

"My man, call me a cab," the minister exclaimed. A crowd gathered, knowing Choate was fast on his feet.

"You are a cab, sir," he replied.

In his early twenties, my mother's father, Joseph Jr., served two years as Ambassador Choate's private secretary. He was the duty officer on August 14, 1900, the day the Boxer Rebellion ended and the Siege of Peking was lifted. The U.S. Embassy in London was the telecommunications center for information about the international expeditionary force sent to rescue the foreign legations. Official London and royal London were all at the annual garden party at Buckingham Palace. My grandfather put on his striped pants and frock coat, took a hansom cab to the palace with the fateful telegram, and found himself the instant man of the hour. A reticent and self-effacing person, Pa Choate told me later this was the highpoint of his life. His story also made it easier for my mother to accept the idea of a son in the Foreign Service.

My father-in-law, Walter Maynard, a leading Wall Street investment analyst and banker, had little time for government officials and told me so in the most genial way. Assistant secretaries were a dime a dozen, he said. Wall Street had a comfortably clear and quantitative way of measuring performance. The more money you made, the better you were. Even though I was only twenty-one and painfully green (he tactfully diverted me from asking for Sheila's hand as we stood side by side in a downtown club men's room), Walter respected my judgment in choosing his daughter. We liked each other from the beginning. He knew that my mind was made up and simply advised me to consider his profession as a fallback, should my plans fail to work out.

## Convincing the U.S. Government

His advice was well taken. I may have decided to join the Foreign Service, but the service had hardly decided to join me. The entrance exams were notoriously competitive. In 1957, the first year I applied, 240 officers were chosen from a field of 14,000. Failure was common, and many subsequently successful diplomats had flunked several times. I took my first set of exams before graduating from Harvard in 1957 and fell short. The examiners said I knew nothing about economics and had to fix that. They encouraged me to try again once I had. A solid commitment to the career was rare in someone so young, they said, implying that I needed to go away and grow up some.

That afternoon, I went to call on Paul Nitze at the Johns Hopkins School of Advanced International Studies (SAIS). The father of a classmate at college (as well as Walter Maynard's Harvard roommate), he was a founder of SAIS, former head of the State Department's Policy Planning Staff under Dean Acheson, and a respected member of the Washington foreign policy establishment. I had consulted him earlier on the benefits of graduate school for a Foreign Service career. A blunt and friendly mentor, he had advised that I take the exams first. If I got in, the Foreign Service would train me on the job. If I did not pass, come and see him. Graduate school could help.

The two years at SAIS were stimulating and eventful. We lived in a tiny house in Georgetown and fell in love with the city that was to become our headquarters for the next thirty-five years. The school, now renamed after Nitze, was the perfect place to start learning the Washington ropes. Small then, with a student body limited to seventy-five by the size of the two converted townhouses in which it was housed, the teaching was done by international figures with years of Washington knowledge, like Hans Morgenthau, and experienced practitioners, like Roger Hilsman and Nitze himself. Papers were graded on the quality of the interviews students conducted with working officials, rather than books cited.

SAIS taught us the mechanics of Washington. My formal academic focus remained on Europe. I studied advanced German, economics, history, psychological warfare, and the balance of power. But we were lucky to get a look at loftier levels of life in the capital. The columnist Joseph Alsop, an admirer of Sheila's mother, befriended us when we arrived in Washington. He liked to sprinkle his guest lists with younger people and included us in some of his famous Georgetown dinner parties, where he gathered the top personalities and policy makers of the day. At one of these, his cousin, Alice Roosevelt Longworth, snapped my head back with the catty observation that the vain General Douglas MacArthur hid his baldness with an "armpit comb-over."

Paul and Phyllis Nitze took us under their generous wings and included us in weekend activities at their spectacular farm on the Potomac in Maryland. Sheila and I were close to the Nitze children and later our boys to their grandchildren. The weekends at the farm were a cozy mix of family, policy talk, and sport, featuring ferocious tennis games between people like the CIA's Desmond Fitzgerald, Stewart Alsop, and a variety of admirals and generals. I remember asking Paul at one of these events what he thought of Secretary of State John Foster Dulles. "Foster Dulles was a bore and a fart!" Nitze replied, never one to mince words.

We started our family. Adam was born in July 1958. His first month of life was marked by a severe case of pneumonia, which almost killed him and taught his parents more about the fragility and value of life than anything that had happened before. Taking the advice of my father-in-law, I spent the summer of 1958 as a trainee at the Baltimore investment banking firm of Alex Brown and Sons, working in all their departments for a dollar an hour. We bought our first house, in the old town of Alexandria, and moved there.

I took the Foreign Service exams again. The Board of Examiners, noting that I had showed up once more, this time a year older, married, and a father, and with some real-world economic experience under my belt, decided to let me in. It took another year to complete the security and medical clearances (obtaining urine specimens from an infant was a challenge) and for the Congress to appropriate the money to bring in another class of new Foreign Service officers.

The call came in April 1959 to report to the A-100 course at the Foreign Service Institute, the State Department's equivalent of boot camp. The choice was made.

# 2

# Choosing China

## A Rude Shock

In 1959, the State Department's Foreign Service Institute, now located on a handsome Virginia campus named after Secretary of State George P. Shultz, occupied the garage of an ugly brick apartment building across the Potomac River named Arlington Towers. There, in hastily assembled, mostly windowless, wallboard compartments, our training as junior diplomats began. I reported to the "A-100" indoctrination program for new recruits, a gentle, dull survey course on the infrastructure of American diplomacy, the organization of the State Department and its constituent embassies and consulates abroad, and the roles and relationships of other government agencies involved in foreign policy. The eagerly awaited climax of our training came toward the end of the twelve-week course, when we learned where our first posts would be.

Eligible for assignment anywhere in the world, we were invited to state our preferences. A European history major from Harvard with a Johns Hopkins masters degree in international relations and tested German language skills might be considered for work in Europe. Right? Wrong! My orders were for the U.S. Consulate in Windsor, Ontario, where I was to serve as vice consul in the visa section. A quirk of geography had placed this Canadian border city due south of Detroit on a peninsula, the Foreign Service Post Report told us, of "poorly drained soil, whose principal crop is rutabagas." Windsor produced cars and Canadian Club whiskey in flat, prosaic surroundings totally at variance with the dreams of a brand new diplomat bent on seeing the world and witnessing history.

My A-100 classmates, including future ambassadors Brandon Grove and Allen Holmes, thought my assignment was hilarious and razzed me incessantly. They had received orders for glamorous sounding places like Isfahan, Iran, Yaoundé, Cameroon, and Paris. I felt crushed and humiliated. State Department Personnel insisted I go, arguing that Canada was in the European Bureau and a good place to start. Three other applicants had wriggled out of the assignment, one because, he argued, his mother-in-law lived in Detroit.

**A New Idea**

Roaming the halls of FSI in shock and despair, I ran into Herbert Levin, an older friend from Harvard who had joined the service a few years before. What was he doing at the Institute? I asked. Studying intensive Mandarin Chinese, came the answer. Why? There are no posts there, I continued. Well, there will be, came the reply. History is on our side. The Far Eastern Bureau of the State Department, he added, is free of prejudice toward Jews, an important factor in his own decision.

Having never given a single thought to China, I was intrigued. The year was 1959. Mao's Great Leap Forward was failing, and news of the resulting turmoil and starvation was filtering into the Western press.

I was influenced by the example of Charles E. "Chip" Bohlen, ambassador to the Soviet Union, France, and the Philippines and later under secretary of state. Bohlen had fashioned a famous career in the Foreign Service by choosing to study Russian at a time when the United States had no relationship with Moscow. He calculated that the time would come when U.S.-Soviet relations would be paramount and he would be in the thick of things. Chinese was clearly the current analog. My father had roomed with Bohlen at Harvard and introduced me to him the summer I went to college. He endeared himself to me instantly by telling how he had survived in life despite being expelled from St. Paul's School five days before graduation (the legend was that he had inflated a condom in the library).

Levin, who already knew the ways of the bureaucracy, recommended that I put in a strong application for Chinese language training before I left for Canada, and then do the research during the two years in Windsor to determine if I really wanted to proceed. The State Department would not force a hard language on unwilling officers. The process was simply too expensive.

I pondered Herb's advice and consulted Sheila. The hard language option provided a rudder for Foreign Service careers. There were few jobs in Europe for young officers and lots in Asia, provided you learnt a core language. Senator McCarthy had purged the Foreign Service of many competent China specialists. Chinese was culturally relevant to more Asian countries than any other language. Personnel officers, I had learned the hard way, did not care what you knew before you entered the Foreign Service. But if they made their own investment in training you, they had to justify your onward assignments to congressional watchdogs. In cold blood, I decided that Chinese language training represented the perfect combination of interest, expense, and opportunity. I applied for a training slot two years hence. The officer in Personnel told me to forget about it. An untried junior FSO with no Asia background had little chance. I urged him to remember my face, because I would keep coming back until he approved my request.

Three months later, after passing a grueling FSI course on immigration law and visa procedures, we left Washington for Windsor, Sheila, infant son Adam and I, stuffed into a small German car. The plan was to issue visas by day, read about China at night, and see where that would lead.

### The First Call

The Consulate in Windsor was a four-man post where Foreign Service officers traditionally began or ended their careers. I was by far the most junior, the only vice consul in a section that issued eight thousand visas a year to immigrants, Canadian commuters, and visitors from all over the world. The offices were on one floor of an old office building on the Detroit River, with the skyline of the Promised Land shining through the window. A 23-year-old novice, I was to decide who got to go there and who did not.

The new principal officer arrived a month after we did. He was replacing a consul of long tenure, locally known for his skill at the poker table, and more so for entertaining guests in his office barefoot. He suffered from a psoriasis condition made worse by wearing shoes. Colleagues reported that he would put his scaly feet on the desk when meeting others with whom he felt at ease.

The new boss had spent years as a clerk in debilitating posts along the Mosquito Coast in Central America. He had become a Foreign Service officer in the late 1950s under the Wriston program, which sought to integrate into one officer corps all the different components that made up the service, including the Foreign Service Staff and the Civil Service. Fresh from an assignment heading the visa section in a large embassy in Latin America, Windsor was his first command.

Sheila and I prepared meticulously for our formal first call on the consul and his wife. Carefully following the guidance from "Social Usage in the Foreign Service," a State Department manual which we had been told to consult for all such occasions, we dressed in our best, she wearing hat and gloves, and I a dark blue suit. My calling card was turned down at the corner, with the appropriate initials penciled in as instructed.

Walking down the flagstone path to the modest brick suburban house that served as the residence of the ranking American official in Windsor, we were apprehensive about our first official occasion as a Foreign Service family abroad. The consul met us at the door, dressed in a pair of khaki shorts and nothing more. Bald, with knobby knees, bunions, and undisciplined sprouts of chest hair, he greeted us affably and invited us out onto the back porch to meet his wife and enjoy a glass of iced tea.

Also dressed in khaki shorts, but with a halter-top, she welcomed us warmly. We sat stiffly on the porch glider, which had not been oiled for some time and squeaked with every movement back and forth.

The women carried the burden of the small talk that followed, with Sheila asking the consul's wife about her life and work. In soft tones from her native Virginia (the boss was also from there), she told us that she had been trained as a nurse, a profession that had served her well in the unhealthy climate of coastal Central America.

"I set great store by enemas, Sheila," she said. "Whenever I'm feeling a mite puny, I just bend over and take a quart."

The glider squeaked loudly as it moved back and forth in the dead silence that followed.

"How was your trip up to Windsor?" Sheila asked, alertly filling the void.

"Oh, we had a horrible time with our medical exam in Washington," came the reply. "You see, neither me nor my daughter [a sallow 21-year-old who accompanied the new top couple] could produce the stool specimen required. It was Friday, and we thought we'd be stuck the whole weekend."

The glider squeaked back and forth.

"So, what did you do next?" Sheila asked, helpfully.

"Well, my husband never suffered from this complaint. He produced a big one. We just cut it in three pieces and went on our way. That's how we got to Windsor, Sheila!"

After a few more squeaks of the glider, we took our leave, walked to the car, drove around the corner, stopped, and broke down laughing. What have we gotten into, we wondered? Was this the same Foreign Service that produced Chip Bohlen?

Composing ourselves, we drove back to our hotel in silence. "Bend over and take a quart" became a secret family motto. But hilarity aside, our first call troubled and even shamed us. It took years before we told others of the conversation.

## Management and Diplomatic Training

My colleagues were weak. The leadership example set by the new principal officer included driving the official car home each afternoon to watch *Queen for a Day*. The head of the visa section, a cultured and fastidious Europeanist, turned out to be an alcoholic who binged when his domineering wife was away, drinking vodka out of a paper bag in his desk drawer between visa applicants. I had not expected as the most junior of officers to have to send my supervisor home. The Consul kept the situation at arm's length. "You handle it," he said.

I did, and, in effect, ran the visa section. The staff, eleven smart polyglot Canadian women from Ontario, Quebec, Serbia,

Montenegro, and Italy and a dignified, soft-spoken Pakistani man with long experience in the Consular Service, kept me from making mistakes. I had much broader responsibility than most of my contemporaries working on one specialized kind of immigration problem in the huge visa assembly lines in Toronto, Montreal, and Rome. With immigration lawyers crossing from Detroit to push their cases, and congressional staffs a mere phone call away, I had to know the law and the procedures cold.

The flow of applicants provided endless variety. The Australian female bullwhip champion, a Polish spy, Cuban baseball players, Japanese chicken sexers, suspected Lebanese marriage frauds, and midget wrestlers were among my "clients." I learned early one of the basic skills of diplomacy—imparting difficult news in a positive way. The cherry-cheeked grandmother had to be told that she had failed the Wasserman test for syphilis, but could get a visa after a big shot of penicillin. The middle-aged couple who had never formally wed despite twenty years together had to be told to go get quietly married during the lunch hour, lest their teen-age daughter find out she was illegitimate. The Iranian student who married an American prostitute from the pits of Detroit had to be told that this relationship would not get him into the United States or her out of jail.

Sheila and I, insular New Yorkers by birth, learned a lot about the American Middle West (two of our daughters-in-law are Michiganders). I found out how the United States and Canada manage their peaceful 4000-mile-long border, knowledge still relevant in the current age of borderless terrorism. We made lifelong friends. Our family grew, with the birth of second son Oliver in 1960. Inspired by a great folksinger named Odetta, I took up the guitar and sang to my boys, a practice that turned into a semiprofessional passion in later years.

My supervisors, such as they were, appreciated what I did for them and wrote glowing efficiency reports, which in turn convinced personnel in Washington to take a gamble and assign me to Chinese language training. We were thrilled when the word came through at the end of 1961. Reading the five-foot shelf on China during long Windsor evenings had implanted a fascination that was to last a lifetime. Two years of intensive Mandarin—one in Washington and one in Taiwan—would start us down a new path after a grim, if instructive start in the Foreign Service.

# 3

# Learning the Chinese

**Dr. Ma's First Lesson**

"You should know something important about Chinese feelings as you start your study of our language. Americans may think we are yellow, but we think you are purple." Dr. Ma was sitting in his office under the fluorescent lights at a drab steel table that was standard Government Issue for classrooms. He wore a shawl, a scholar's wool cap, and calligrapher's gloves (with the fingers free) to protect against the fierce air-conditioning blast in Arlington Towers. An elderly, exiled editor of a major Catholic newspaper in Peking before the revolution, Ma was a fund of lore on Chinese attitudes, beliefs, and history. He had suffered when the Communists took over in 1949, was in poor health, and died a few months later.

Ma's jolting description of the wide gap in perceptions that Americans and Chinese have of each other, of course, applies more widely than to mere appearance, but the sense of how strange Chinese think we look was a good place to start a long journey of learning. Later, when traveling in Taiwan and provincial Mainland cities where huge crowds would gather in the streets to ogle my family and me, I already understood that they saw us as odd zoo animals from another world.

**Infant Formulas**

World War II had transformed Asian language teaching. The urgent need for speakers and readers of Japanese and Chinese gave rise to a two-track system patterned after the way children learn to speak from their mothers and to read from their schoolteachers. Return to infancy was another rude shock for a twenty-five-year old.

Back in the garage at Arlington Towers at the beginning of 1962, we spent the first three weeks of our course mindlessly hearing and mimicking noises. Our mother was a language lab tape recorder. For six hours a day we drilled in class the four hundred distinct sounds that Mandarin Chinese uses to differentiate meaning. (English has twelve hundred such sounds). It was important to get the tones right. These are really directions of sound, rather than notes. The syllable *ma* pronounced with a high steady tone means "mother," with a falling tone means "scold," with a low dipping tone means "horse," with no tone at all denotes a question mark, and so on. More dangerously, *bi* means "pen" with the low dipping tone and a rude word for "vagina" when pronounced high and steady.

The weeks of mime gave way to months of drill on meaning, patterns of grammar, and increasingly complex dialogues that dealt with social interaction, survival in daily situations, and later, history and economics. Seven weeks into the course we started the second track, learning to write Chinese characters, constructing them in the proper stroke order and making them look right. We were responsible for "active" knowledge of about eight hundred characters, which meant we had to know how to replicate the calligraphy precisely. The thousands of characters and combinations we studied later we learned passively, which meant we could recognize them in a text and know what they meant. Our goal was to read the media with speed and competence, rather than draft correspondence.

The pace was a language marathon—six hours of class and three to four hours of homework each weekday for eleven months. My three classmates—Roger Sullivan (later deputy assistant secretary of state for East Asian affairs), Stan Brooks (later consul general in Shanghai), and Tim Manley (who served at our Embassy in Taipei)—were talented, hard working, and humorous. We became fast friends. (The process has been known to create lifelong enemies, too.) Happily, we moved along at more or less the same pace.

Our teachers were skilled and versatile. Mr. Li Tsung Mi was an erudite linguist who knew the origins of the words and ideograms and how they related to one another. Miss Ouyang Chao was an inventive discussant, who forced us to build our halting child vocabularies into real conversations. When we could say and comprehend more, Dr. Ma added substance to our education.

Dr. Ma performed another valuable service. He gave me a real Chinese name. Normally, when naming purple foreigners, the Chinese choose characters that are phonetically as close to the sound of your surname as they can find. They sound all right but don't mean anything, and identify you clearly as a barbarian outsider. Under that formula, my name would combine three characters with the sounds *pu*, *la*, and *te*. Dr. Ma wanted all of us to have names that sounded roughly right but meant something to Chinese. *Pu* was a regular surname with only two easy-to-write strokes. To that he added *li*, to force or propel, and *de* virtue. So I have gone through life as "Self-Propelled Virtue Pu." Chinese have always liked the name and invariably ask me how I came by it.

## Singing for Kennedy

Vivid glimpses of Washington's glitterati enlivened the plain daily grind of language learning. The advent of the Kennedy administration brought columnist Joe Alsop to the height of his influence. A World War II veteran of a Japanese internment camp in Hong Kong and service in Chungking with Flying Tiger General Chennault, Joe had strong opinions about China. He also believed he had influenced my decision to study the language and kept in close touch when we returned to the capital.

One summer morning, he telephoned to say that he was organizing a dinner for "the Young Man." Would we join him, bring the guitar, and provide the entertainment? Sheila took the call sitting on the staircase with Windsor-born two-year-old Oliver behind her, a bottle of shampoo in his hand, poised over her head. As she struggled to guess which "young man" Joe had in mind, Oliver began to pour. Quelling him, she realized Alsop was talking about the President of the United States. The idea of singing for John F. Kennedy terrified us both (by now duets with Sheila were our best numbers), but we accepted immediately.

Georgetown was bathed in a lovely summer evening light as we approached Alsop's house on Dumbarton Avenue, guitar case in hand, shadowed along the street by discreet well-dressed men with hearing aids. They closed in as we moved to enter the house and thoroughly inspected the guitar in the decorous Secret Service manner. Once inside, we found Joe's closest friends, people like the British ambassador, Phil and Katharine Graham of the *Washington Post*, the Chip Bohlens, all straining to create a natural atmosphere for the "Young Man," who was relaxed and cordial. Jacqueline Kennedy was in Newport, so the gorgeous Mary Meyer (later tragically murdered while jogging on the Georgetown Canal) kept the president company on this occasion. As normal for Washington parties, the talk covered all the issues of the day, particularly Medicare, which had that day failed to pass in Congress. At Joe's after-dinner roundtable, the president voiced his disappointment in no uncertain terms. Phil Graham kindly asked me if I had anything I wanted to say, in which case he would arrange for me to get a word in edgewise. I demurred, having no view on the topic.

Later in the garden, Sheila and I sang "St. James Infirmary," "I'll Fly Away," and "John Henry." The president listened politely. Attorney General Robert Kennedy, arriving late from a trip to Michigan, chinned himself in a nearby tree.

### Taiwan at Last

The prospect of living and communicating in a real Chinese place had buoyed us through the long months of drudgery in Arlington Towers. We were itching for the final phase of our formal training, a year at the FSI Field School in Taiwan. Our teachers thought we were ready, too. After eleven months training in Washington, my classmates and I qualified at level 2 (out of 5). This meant that we could operate safely in a Chinese environment, but were not yet able to work professionally (level 3). We infants had become teenagers.

Sheila was eager, too, having studied the spoken language at her expense with FSI teachers in the evenings during our months in Washington. The State Department provided no money to train wives.

We had never been to Asia. The long flight to Taiwan via Hawaii and Japan with two small sons, Adam and Oliver, was a major passage for our family. We fought jet lag and culture shock in Tokyo, our sense of strangeness compounded by staying at the Imperial Hotel designed by Frank Lloyd Wright. This massive pile of scratchy yellow masonry, earthquake-proof by virtue of its thickness, made its inhabitants feel like ants in a hill. After two days of peering sleepily through misty pollution at the famous sights of Japan's capital, we took off for Taiwan. Arriving at the airport in Taipei, we found instant comfort because we could actually communicate. The long hours of training began to pay off.

In 1963, the Republic of China on Taiwan, like the People's Republic of China across the Straits, was a single-party police state under an authoritarian ruler. But in contrast to the economic stagnation and starvation on the Mainland, rapid growth in agriculture under a land reform program designed by American and Chinese economists and enforced by the strict government was beginning to spur the entire economy. Nationalist Mainlanders under Generalissimo Chiang Kai-shek and his wife, the fearsome, accomplished Wellesley graduate Soong Mei-ling, dominated politics, the army, and the police. Native Taiwanese, who had received higher education as doctors and agriculturalists under Japanese rule (1895–1945), were taking charge of the economy and the underground political opposition.

The FSI Field School was located in the city of Taichung, nearly ninety miles down the coast, happily removed from the distractions of embassy life, the demands of the ambassador, and the grim, drizzly weather of the capital.

Today Taiwan's largest city, with a population of several million and a bustling port on the Taiwan straits, Taichung was then a much smaller, slower place, where 600,000 people dwelled. The city limits ended long before one reached the sea. Electricity was limited and nights were dark. Motorbikes and cars had yet to replace bullock carts and pedicabs, though the process had begun. Water buffaloes plowed the green rice paddies under sunny skies, framed by wrinkled, blue mountains in the background. We rented a Japanese-style house in a walled compound at the end of a dirt road, a short bike ride from the school, and settled in happily.

"It is a shock to find oneself a curio," I wrote my parents. "Yesterday I was downtown engrossed in bargaining for a balloon for the boys. Nearing the end of this exhilarating process, I looked up and found myself surrounded by a crowd of at least fifty people. Sheila, on the other hand isn't just a curio, she's a phenomenon!

Walking in the park the other day, clad in her rather full blue overcoat (the one that makes her look like a six-foot tea cozy), the Chinese crowded around exclaiming "*Tai da*" ("too big"). The reaction, far from being mirthful, was one of awe and amazement. It was Queen Liliakulani walking in their midst." (She was also carrying our third son.)[1]

Sheila wrote:

> The boys are really thriving, and they've made a clutch of Chinese friends in the neighborhood. Yesterday Adam sailed forth bright and early, dressed in blue overalls, a red shirt, cowboy hat jammed down over his nose, red bandanna around his neck, and a flashy Hong Kong cap pistol and holster low on the hips. He was met by a horde of admirers outside the gate, and they escorted him to their stomping ground under a bush, where they placed him on a bamboo stool, seated themselves on stones in a circle around him and proceeded to admire him. Adam thought this was great, especially when they gave him some caps for his pistol, and he had a fine noisy time for the rest of the morning. . . . Adam and Oliver are known as "Big Tiger " and "Tiger Number Two."[2]

Every school-day morning, pressed handkerchiefs pinned to their clean shirts, the boys were carted off to a missionary kindergarten in a yellow pedicab bus filled with neighborhood Chinese.

## Back to School

At the start of the 1963 school year in February, some twenty students and their families from the State Department and the U.S. military made up the population of FSI Taichung. Last year's class, soon to graduate, welcomed us new kids (the Platts, Brookses, Sullivans, and Tim Manley). The "old boys" included Morton Abramowitz, Harry Thayer, and Don Anderson, who would later make big names in Asia and Washington. In a few months, they and their families would proceed to assignments in Hong Kong, Taipei, Singapore, and Malaysia.

The school was a two-story building, honeycombed with small classrooms, all of which had windows. The teachers were all Mainlanders with pure Beijing accents, led by a soft-spoken American linguist named Gerardus (Gerry) Kok, whose academic bloodline included Monterey and Yale.

The infants had grown up. The routine of six hours of class and four hours of homework remained the same, but instruction was now one-on-one, beyond intense. Live materials, newspapers, radio broadcasts, oral discussion, and debate replaced the pablum of elementary texts. Still shy, and fenced off as foreigners, we did our best to practice in the street and on the trips we took with teachers at the end of each term. These travels broadened our experience with Chinese, enriched our vocabulary, and placed us in some ridiculous situations.

Sheila's letter home that April describes one inadvertent sojourn in a hot-spring brothel. There were seven of us, including Roger and Margie Sullivan and three Chinese tutors from the school. We had been driving for days over the mountains of northern Taiwan in a Chevrolet Apache van. Exhausted and hungry, we arrived in the town of Beitou just after dark.

Our travels that day brought us down out of the mountain to a hot-spring resort north of Taipei, where we discovered that all hotels are dual-purpose affairs, partly for travelers, but mostly for good time Charlies. Each had a staff of young ladies to assist the Charlies in having a good time. The gents picked an establishment called the "New Life Hotel," and we were helped to our rooms by clouds of young ladies, one called "Goldie" in Chinese. The tutors thought the whole thing fairly amusing but not too far out of the ordinary. But we thought it a scream, especially when Goldie wanted to help N. & me take a bath. We managed to get rid of her, and had a lovely time wallowing around the hot spring water, from which we emerged much refreshed, but smelling strongly of sulfur. As we were going to bed, the door was practically broken down by young "misses" as they are called, who wanted, to use the local euphemism, to "rest a bit" with Nicky, who said no thank you. We were the only Americans in this establishment, so maybe we got special attention. Anyway, the giggles, door slamming, and other activities during the night were formidable, but we rather enjoyed, in a surrealistic way, the idea of sleeping in a brothel!

Our Chinese really benefited in the process. We are on really cozy terms with those particular tutors now—our first Chinese pals. They are humorous, jolly people and real artists at enjoying themselves. During the trip, each new bit of scenery, dish of food, or whatever, was greeted with sighs and cries of delight, Chinese style, and we have become quite good at being delighted ourselves.[3]

## Studying the Chinese

Like Dr. Ma in Washington, our teachers in Taiwan yielded a wealth of lore on how Chinese think. One morning, I was studying the word *duifu*, an all-purpose term that means to "deal with," "cope," or "handle." The teacher asked me how I would "deal with" a Chinese visa applicant who had no chance of getting into the United States. I answered that I would inform him right way, saving him time and effort. The teacher shook his head. The Chinese approach to *duifu* was completely different. It would involve inviting the applicant to fill out forms and return every few weeks. Each time he returned you would invent a new excuse; the case had to be referred to Washington; word had not yet been received from the State Department, and so on. After several visits, the applicant would realize on his own that he would never get a visa. He would, however, be grateful that you had not "poured cold water on his head."

"In our society," I replied, "That's called 'giving a person the runaround.'"

The teacher noted with delight this new American slang term, and replied, "Our society has different, indirect ways of 'dealing with' people and situations." Later on when dealing with Chinese, I knew when I was being given the *duifu* treatment. I also turned the tables, to good effect.

The teachers also taught us the art of *yanjiu*, which means to "study" or "analyze." In practical terms it means examining from every angle any contemplated action and constantly revisiting your conclusions, right up to the time of the action itself. It could take up to two hours, for example, to decide what to eat or where to stay. Time was plentiful in the Taiwan of the sixties, and everybody seemed to enjoy the process. Later, in the Mainland, I found Chinese just as prone to interminable *yanjiu*, though for different reasons. Fear of making a mistake rules in a tense, competitive society. Even now, anyone trying to organize a conference, plan an event, or introduce a new policy in China will run into hours, even days of *yanjiu* and the changes and delays that result from the process. Irritating though it may be to people from the West, I benefited from grasping the practice early on.

## Breakthrough to Fluency

I finally achieved genuine fluency during a weekend with a brilliant and eccentric teacher named Zhang Damu, who moonlighted as an instructor of Chinese composition at elementary schools throughout central Taiwan. He had refused my invitations to tour together down-island, suggesting instead that I take him on his teaching rounds in my car. He asked me to prepare a five-minute introduction of myself—who I was, where I came from, why I wanted to learn Chinese, and so forth—which he would then ask me to present in Chinese to the students of each of his classes.

The prospect—imagine a purple adult six-footer, making his maiden speech in Chinese to a classroom full of tittering Taiwanese sixth-graders!—was alarming. But I did it, and got better each time. In two days we visited six schools, three classes at each school. By the eighteenth session, I was teaching the entire hour, answering questions about America ("Does everyone wear six-guns?") and asking the students about their own lives. Zhang, who knew exactly what he was doing, would disappear from each class after introducing me and make me fend for myself. After that weekend, I was confident that I could finish any sentence I started. The inhibitions were gone.

When the FSI course ended in early 1964, I qualified with the rest of my class at the 3+ level, which meant I was ready to work professionally in Mandarin Chinese. Our command of the language was still rudimentary, we found. It would take years on the job, as well as constant practice, for all the material that had been stuffed into us to settle.

## Meeting Generalissimo and Madame Chiang

One day that spring, while we were on the road with some tutors, an ornate invitation arrived at the school from the capital, Taipei, requesting the presence of Mr. and Mrs. Nicholas Platt at the annual garden party hosted by President and Madame Chiang Kai-shek. The teachers were impressed and the students envious. How had this happened? Why were we singled out?

It turned out that my uncle Joseph H. "Sandy" Choate III had written a letter about us to Madame Chiang's close confidant and assistant, Pearl Chen. Sandy was a lawyer in New York who for decades had managed the financial affairs of Chang Hsueh-liang, the notorious "Young Marshal." Hsueh-liang, a Manchurian warlord turned Nationalist general, had made history by kidnapping Chiang Kai-shek at a hot spring near Xi'an in 1936. After surrendering himself and his boss, the Young Marshal was placed under house arrest for most of the rest of his life (he was released at age 89 in 1990). The Generalissimo did not touch Hsueh-liang's private wealth. Under Sandy's management his portfolio swelled.

The Chinese loved Sandy Choate. Huge (six feet five inches and 250 pounds), with a prominent nose and flaming red hair, patches of which covered his entire body, Sandy was everything the Chinese thought a foreign devil should be. Witty and smart, he made many friends during periodic contact with the Nationalists. Madame Chiang and Pearl were among them.

Sheila wrote home the authoritative account of this meeting:

When we arrived, tired and dirty, at the Embassy in Taipei, we found the invitation to tea with the Generalissimo and Madame Chiang waiting—very elegant and formidable. We had no proper clothes with us, of course (white gloves were necessary), but friends in Taichung kindly sent some up, and the whole school was in an uproar because the President's office had called about the invitation! It turned out to be a very large tea indeed. We were all delivered in big black cars, and sorted out on arrival into categories: Diplomatic corps, A.I.D., U.S.I.S., and something called "Others." We were "Others," placed at the very foot of the line with some Fulbright professors. We all snaked through the residence and shook hands with Madame (fierce) and the Generalissimo (old and rosy) and then were herded to the "Others" tables in the garden. Soon, an elderly Chinese lady rushed up. She was Miss Pearl Chen, Madame's American secretary for 28 years, who urged us to get something to eat. We did, whereupon she urged us to eat it. We did, in front of her eyes. Then she said, "Good, now I can go and tell Madame you have had something to eat," and hotfooted it off to do so. We were walking around admiring the garden (lovely with fat pots of daisies, snapdragons, verbena, palms & Korean grass, all marvelous and healthy) when up panted Miss Chen, perspiring heavily, and said that Madame wanted to see us and would we please follow her, which we did, galloping after her through the surprised guests.

Madame and the G. were sitting in a pavilion, and we were charmingly greeted, seated on pillows, talked to, and given tea, while the Embassy people stood around with their eyes out on stalks. Needless to say, this was all due to Sandy, whom she really likes. She is expecting to see him when he comes out, asked fondly after him, and really made a royal fuss. We were impressed, charmed, and generally bowled over by all this, and really had a lovely time on the reddest carpet you've ever seen. The Generalissimo speaks no English, but we were able to murmur appropriate politenesses in Chinese to him, which was lucky. The crowning touch occurred on the way out. As the Madame and the Generalissimo made their way through the crowd, she said loudly to me, "Goodbye, Mrs. Platt," which practically finished the Embassy people.[4]

An event of no substantive importance whatsoever, Sheila and I valued the encounter later. It made us one of the very few couples of our generation to have met Chinese leaders from both sides of the civil war, Zhou Enlai and Madame Mao in the People's Republic of China, President and Madame Chiang Kai-shek in Nationalist Taiwan.

Another far more significant development in the diplomacy of China marked our time in Taiwan. General De Gaulle announced that France would recognize the Communist government in Beijing. Washington was dismayed, but my classmates and I gathered in the garden of our house in Taichung to offer a private toast to Le Grand Charles. The logjam of history was breaking.

Tying a loose end in our family history, we made a brief side trip from Taiwan to Kyoto, Japan, to reestablish the relationship with Joseph Hardy Neesima's university. As a fifth-generation direct descendant of Alpheus Hardy, and the first family members to visit the Doshisha in more than fifty years, we were treated royally. The chancellor of the university, the president of the student body, and the head of the Alumni Association were waiting on the tarmac at the airport and whisked us in limousines to the college administrative offices. There, under a stained glass window depicting the clipper ship *Wild Rover*, we were asked to fill in the blanks in the family tree since the last visit two generations ago, a daunting task completed by my father, who came a month later. This was to be the first of many visits, and an important connection when fate later shifted our career path to Japan.

# 4

# Watching China

## Newspapers Wrapped around Fish

The Mainland Section of the American Consulate General in Hong Kong was the China Watching headquarters of the world during the 1960s. Without diplomatic relations for more than ten years, all Americans could do was watch and listen. The three-story office building on Garden Road (still there, and larger) housed a staff of several hundred, many of whom were assigned to collecting and assembling data on the People's Republic and guessing what it meant. Other sections did consular work, facilitated U.S. trade with Hong Kong and Macao, and took care of American citizens.

A newly minted language officer, I showed up for work at Garden Road in February 1964. As luck would have it, a shortage of analysts gave me a rare opportunity to choose the field I wanted to cover. China's external affairs were hot. These were the peak years of Sino-Soviet polemics, month after month of propaganda broadsides exchanged between Moscow and Beijing, richly detailed and highly insulting barrages of invective between rival approaches to Communism (Khrushchev's "revisionists" and Mao's Stalinists). Dirty laundry about the relationship, collecting since the Soviets pulled their technical experts out of China in 1960, was now washed in the public media.

By comparison, domestic politics seemed cool and dry, but I was attracted by the opportunity to learn the names of China's players and the system that they had built. I wanted to get the most out of Chinese language capability so arduously acquired over the past two years. My choice of internal affairs turned out to be momentous.

The process of watching China was, and still is, labor intensive. My colleagues and I read every newspaper we could get our hands on, including provincial publications smuggled into the colony wrapped around fish. Native linguists listened to every radio broadcast, from every province. Refugees were debriefed and their stories written up.

I was to sit each day at the end of a conveyor belt of such data, tasked to convert it into meaning. More than 90 percent of the material we analyzed was in the public domain. Clandestine sources and methods existed, to be sure, but their yield was limited. Our starting points were the prevalent slogans and the jargon of daily political discourse in the official media. Any deviation or repositioned language meant something. We felt like subscribers to a dull and repetitive orchestra that played the same pieces day after day. We listened for squeaks from the oboes or sour notes from the horns, changes of rhythm or volume, all potential indicators of debate or shifts in policy.

The reading skills I had acquired worked as a rough strainer. I could scan *People's Daily* editorials quickly, moving smoothly through the set rhetoric. The formulations I could not understand right away signaled what was new and needed analysis. The Consulate General had a staff of translators I could consult, as well as a towering Manchu-language teacher named Tang Hung (also a fine painter), with whom I could discuss new terminology.

## The Importance of Being Literate

Chinese literature provided a crucial code to political expression and debate in the Mainland. Editorials were shot through with references to figures and stories from great classical novels of Chinese literature. The plots and characters of *The Three Kingdoms, Dream of the Red Chamber, Water Margin*, to name a few, were embedded in the upbringing of every educated Chinese, whatever his or her politics. In particular, *The Three Kingdoms*, a fourteenth-century novel of struggle and statecraft set around 200 AD, represented an encyclopedia of every political and military ploy in the Chinese lexicon, as well as many of the plots in Chinese opera. If you had not read this book, you simply could not decipher the editorials. Other classics, including Confucius' *Analects* and Sun Zi's *Art of War*, also helped. These had been assigned reading during our training years. The time we had spent in Taiwan acquiring and reading pirated English translations of these works—one could buy the entire Encyclopedia Britannica for $18—turned out to have been invaluable.

In this most closed of systems, all serious political attacks were masked in cultural allegory. As we will see later, the opening shot of the Cultural Revolution was fired in a Shanghai editorial panning the revival of an opera lionizing an official fearless enough to criticize his emperor. The reviewer was aiming at contemporary political leaders who had crossed Chairman Mao.

In 1964 and most of 1965, the China we were watching was quiet on the surface. I wrote learned dispatches, called "airgrams," sent by diplomatic pouch to Washington each week on some aspect of the domestic political scene, from party politics to population control. I learned the traditional tools of the China-Watching trade and the names and histories of the leadership.

## The Politics of Night Soil

Culture was an important part of my portfolio. One of my reports covered the Festival of Peking Opera on Revolutionary Themes, which took place in Peking during the summer of 1964. In June, Madame Mao, under wraps for decades, made her first public speech at this event. "Do you eat?" Madame Mao asked her audience of theater professionals and officials from the Ministry of Culture, as reported in the *People's Daily*. "That food came from the farmers! So serve the farmers in your plays and operas."

One work that drew rave notices in the *People's Daily* was a one-act opera called *The Bucket*. Here's how it went:

> The curtain opens. A bucket sits center stage, nothing else. It contains night soil, the contents of the family chamber pots and privy, a valuable commodity in rural China.
>
> Enter stage left the virtuous wife (cymbals, squealing strings, and woodwinds), who sings a fervent aria describing her plans to spread the contents of the bucket on the communal fields to increase production for the benefit of the revolution. Cheers.

Enter stage right the husband (Chinese Communist theater conventions, like our TV sitcoms, usually portray the male in the buffoon or bourgeois villain role). His aria describes the advantages of dumping the bucket on the family private plot to improve vegetable yields and their personal earnings. Boos, hisses.

The husband and wife sing a competitive duet, each grasping their side of the bucket. A tug of war ensues (drums, cymbals, gongs, flutes).

Enter center stage rear the mother-in-law, who casts the deciding vote in favor of fertilizing the communal fields. Curtain, applause.

Though the allocation of human fertilizer was a real issue in the Chinese countryside, I found this grungy debate in classical opera form ridiculous, even hilarious, a view shared by Seymour Topping, the *New York Times* Hong Kong bureau chief, who wrote it up after I briefed him. So did a number of Chinese officials, we later learned. This turned out to be a big mistake, probably the biggest of their lives. For Madame Mao's revolutionary operas, plays, films, and ballets—works like *The Red Detachment of Women*, *White-Haired Girl*, and *Red Lantern*—would be the only sanctioned entertainment for years to come. She had convinced Mao that this was a vital way to purify the thoughts of the Chinese people.

The festival turned out to be a harbinger of big trouble, of which we had no inkling then.

### A Collegial Rumor Mill

China Watching was intensely and competitively collegial. Visiting diplomats whose governments had embassies in Beijing became treasured sources and friends. Journalists with special knowledge and good contacts as well as scholars with relevant research projects were courted for what they knew. No passing traveler to or from China had to worry about where his next meal was coming from. It did not matter who or what you were, whether government official, newsman, or trader, if you had some knowledge or connection to offer, you were welcome at the table, literally. At regular lunches, organized by my colleagues and me, we chewed over different lines of analysis and traded bits of intelligence.

Members of the group included people who went on to earn big reputations in journalism, government, and academe. The chief of the Mainland Section, FSO John Holdridge, the convener of the club, went on to play a key role in the opening to China as Henry Kissinger's aide on the National Security Council Staff and later became U.S. ambassador to Singapore and Indonesia. Other prominent members of the group included Stanley Karnow of the *Washington Post*; Harvard University's Ezra Vogel, Richard Solomon, then a professor at Columbia and later a key staff member of the National Security Council; legal scholars like Jerry Cohen from the Harvard Law School and Stanley Lubman from Berkeley; and Michigan professor Michel Oksenberg, who later served with me at the National Security Council.

Other China hands from the American Consulate General included William Gleysteen, later ambassador to Korea, and Burton Levin, who became ambassador to Burma and, later, the Asia Society's man in Hong Kong. Although he kept his distance from government officials, we all revered Father Laszlo LaDany, an indefatigable Hungarian Jesuit with decades of experience, as the high priest of Hong Kong's China analysts.

Rumor was a staple of the community. China's public information system was clamped tight, but its word of mouth grapevine was one of the world's busiest and most efficient. We all listened hard for real news in the buzzing clouds of gossip. To test the speed of the system, I once told a visiting diplomat that the reason the mayor of Shanghai had not been seen for more than a month (true) was due to liver cancer (false). One week later a Norwegian journalist, just in from Beijing, whispered in my ear that the mayor of Shanghai had—guess what?—liver cancer. Beijing residents reported that juicy items would travel from one end of the capital to another within a day.

## Motley Mighty Visitors

We sang for our supper to touring media moguls like Katharine Graham and Osborn Elliott, and megapundits like Joseph Alsop, who passed regularly through Hong Kong on the way to Vietnam, where the war was heating up. Joe had strong, often wrong, views on everything, including what was happening in China. I discovered that the only way to change his thinking was to reverse the normal procedure and interview him. I would ask him questions and add my own data to his answers, which often showed up in the stuff of his articles. The relationships we formed with such figures turned out to be important during later assignments in Washington.

Visiting congressmen, also on their way to and from Vietnam, were a plague. They came to shop, hundreds of them each year, and had little real interest in China per se, though we briefed them all. One exception was the tyrannical Armed Services Committee chairman, Mendel Rivers, who was deathly afraid he would be kidnapped in Hong Kong and spirited across the border into Red China. We assured him and his staff that this was totally unlikely, but to no avail. He demanded special security measures.

As his "control officer," the official assigned to meet, greet, and manage each congressional delegation, I was also responsible for Rivers's peace of mind. The British authorities would have laughed me away if I had approached them for a special police detail. The manager of the Hilton Hotel, an inventive Australian, solved the problem by stationing all the uniformed Pinkerton guards in the hotel, twenty in all, on Rivers's floor for the first two hours of his stay. When the elevator door opened upon his arrival, a long line of tall Chinese from Shantung province (where the British traditionally recruited their police) in full uniform with side arms holstered, snapped to attention. Rivers's shoulders sagged in relief.

## Tales from Prisoners of War

Returning American Korean War defectors provided unique sources of insight and information about life in China during my time in Hong Kong. Three of these, William White, Morris Wills, and Clarence Adams, left the People's Republic in 1965 and 1966. Originally, twenty-one POWs refused repatriation at the end of the Korean War and settled in China. All but five had gone back to the United States. These men were among those who had adjusted best to life in China, married, had families, and taken jobs. We were interested in what they could tell us about their lives and treatment.

As they left China, I met each of the defectors and their families on the Chinese side of the border at Lowu, the modest farming village that has since become part of the huge economic zone at Shenzhen. Consular ritual required that I ask some pro forma questions to determine whether any of the POWs had taken actions that might have lost them their citizenship. After making sure that I got the right answers, I walked them across the railroad bridge and took them to Hong Kong by car. Being the first American official they met created a bond that eased for me the debriefing process to follow. They were expecting a sterner welcome than I gave them.

The bucolic farmland of the Hong Kong Colony's New Territories we drove through was only a more prosperous version of the Chinese side of the border. But the new arrivals went into shock when, suddenly rounding a corner in the mountain pass, they got their first sight of bustling downtown Kowloon and the glittering island of Victoria across Hong Kong's great teeming harbor. Foreign visitors getting their first look at the instant mega-skyscrapers of the Pudong development zone in Shanghai have much the same reaction today.

When I asked the former POWs why they had left China, all responded that their families would have a better future in the United States. Their decade plus in the PRC had convinced them that children of "mixed blood" would have little chance in Chinese society. Seamier considerations drove the departure of some, White and Adams in particular. The Beijing authorities had cracked down on black market activities and implicated both.

All three had something to tell. White, who was African American, in particular, was a brilliant linguist, who had spent years as a top government translator. We learned from him, for the first time, how carefully the Chinese Communist Party kept up with developments at home and abroad. White described a layered system of confidential party publications containing the latest news and articles about China in the foreign press.

The most closely held and voluminous of these, *Mei Ri Bao,* literally translated as the *Every Daily,* printed every item on China that appeared each day. Only the top leaders were allowed access, and probably only one of them, Mao himself, had time to read it. It was in this publication, we learned later from Zhou Enlai, that Mao read Richard Nixon's 1967 *Foreign Affairs* article calling for rapprochement with China.

The next level of publication, called *Reference Materials* (*Can Kao Ziliao*), contained important foreign articles and internal party documents for distribution to senior officials throughout the government and the provinces. The lowest-level periodical was the better-known *Reference News* (*Can Kao Xiaoxi*), which was circulated to all party members.

Morris Wills, also known for his mastery of the Chinese language, had studied at Beijing University and ended up working on the publication *China Pictorial*. He gave us a sense of the strange cocoon in which foreigners lived in Beijing, as well as the pleasant but guarded existence of intellectuals in the most prestigious university in the capital. The Sino-Soviet rupture in 1960, not surprisingly, created a much stricter and more suspicious attitude toward foreigners. The inner workings of the leadership were as mysterious to Wills as they were to other observers, both native and foreign. He had great difficulty arranging to marry his wife, which soured him on Mao's China and the prospects for his children there.

Adams (also an African American) had spent the last several years translating children's books from Chinese into English. He had reportedly made broadcasts for Radio Hanoi in 1965. Clearly a hustler, Adams described widespread demand in Beijing for foreign black market items. He took pleasure in pricing watches in Hong Kong and lamenting the profit he would have made.

With the exception of Wills, who wrote an article for *Look Magazine* and spent a year at Harvard on a fellowship, these men returned home without fanfare and blended quietly back into Middle America.

## "These Are The Good Old Days"

As a family, we loved living in Hong Kong in the mid-sixties. The work was compelling and the surroundings exotic. Sheila and I took an ample apartment at 2 Old Peak Road overlooking the botanical gardens and the harbor and located across the street from Canossa

Hospital. Adam and Oliver, Tiger Number One (Dahu) and Tiger Number Two (Erhu), were soon to be joined by Nicholas Jr., Tiger Number Three (Sanhu), and we wanted good medical facilities close by. (As it turned out, I found myself assisting at the delivery of Sanhu, when the anesthetist was unavailable for his midnight arrival).

The children settled in at British schools nearby. Oliver was the fastest infant at Victoria Barracks Infant School, down the hill. Adam went to Glenealy, a Hong Kong government school up Old Peak Road. The Wang family of Anhui Province, immigrants from Shanghai who fled the Mainland in the 1950s, moved in to work for us, providing expert household service and the lively company of three young children roughly the age of ours, who gave them a feel for Chinese friendship, the language, and local life. The Wang family had suffered every horror early twentieth-century China could inflict: famine, war, dislocation, even a tiger eating an older daughter alive. They taught us that hardship could produce sympathetic, accessible human beings. Years later, the Wangs immigrated to the United States and prospered in the employment of Joe Alsop's sister, Corinne Chubb.

Social life for transient foreigners in Hong Kong was organized around occupations and activities. The more different things one did, the more circles of people gave you access. In addition to watching China, we played guitar and sang folksongs and choral music, went to church at the Cathedral, and rowed and played squash competitively for the Royal Hong Kong Yacht Club. Sheila began her social work career as a volunteer, doing house calls in her fluent Chinese for a nonprofit agency that cared for refugees from Mandarin-speaking parts of China. Our continued language study with the painter Tang Hung gave us a look at Hong Kong's artistic community.

Tang was a student of the world famous painter (some say forger) Zhang Daqian. He took us one day to meet Zhang at his "studio" in a rundown apartment building in Kowloon. The place was jammed. Students, concubines, clients, and critics all milled about, watching Zhang paint. There was not an easel in sight. The Master had a painting of a different style or period under way in each room, on whatever surface was handy. A trademark horse scroll was working on the bed, a lotus and bamboo in the Chan (Zen) Buddhist style on the top of a dresser, a Ming landscape taking shape on the dining room table, a delicate circular Qing bird forming on the sofa in the living room. Zhang went from room to room, surrounded by a cloud of observers, adding brush strokes and colors, a bird beak here, a flower there, a flying horse's hoof on another. The audience marveled at the rapid, flawless work, the seamless transitions from one style and century to another.

Hong Kong was less crowded and polluted in the sixties than it is now. The population was under four million, as against seven million plus today. But it was a confining place, particularly since the Mainland was closed tight. To get away, we bought a sailing junk and hired a boatman. The boat was a converted fishing smack, painted blue, with bulging eyes set into the bow, almost thirty feet long and ten feet wide, carrying three sails and a one-lung diesel engine. It cost US$900. We named it *Star Elephant*, and shared it with Inger McCabe (now Elliott), whose then husband Bob was the *Newsweek* correspondent.

The boatman was from a fishing family in Aberdeen. He and his colleagues used a big tree beside the road on Middle Bay as their office, with awnings stretched between branches and a telephone nailed to the trunk. On an hour's notice, he would be ready after work when the family and a picnic arrived to set sail into a sunset on the South China Sea. Regulations required that boat owners pass elementary navigation and engineering exams. The reward was a certificate describing the bearer as a "licensed junk master."

Sheila and I told each other from the first day of our years in Hong Kong that "these are the good old days." That said, the history of the territory from 1964 to 1968 was dotted with crises of different kinds. We arrived in the midst of the massive drought of 1964, when water supplies to apartment houses were limited to three hours every four days. CEOs and Taipans would leave board meetings abruptly when the water came on in their zone. A frequent topic of analysis at gatherings of China experts during the dry days was the best way to flush a toilet.

The year 1965 saw the drought broken by nine consecutive typhoons, which frightened us all with torrents of water dashed against the picture windows by ferocious, quirky winds that played strange tricks. One tore open the closet doors of a friend and hurled his entire wardrobe out into the night.

In 1966, Hong Kong's financial bubble burst. The boom/bust cycle in the years before the territory's economy became the vestibule for Mainland growth in the 1980s was between three and five years. Stocks tumbled, real estate prices plummeted. Our landlord called on us and begged that we accept a 30 percent decrease in rent. The entire period, climaxed by torrential rains that triggered unprecedented mudslides and deaths in collapsed buildings, has been immortalized in James Clavell's novel *Noble House*.

In 1967, we had to deal with the Cultural Revolution in Hong Kong itself. But, as I wrote my family then, "We are actually thriving on our diet of disturbance. The boys are well, and Sheila, whose political sense is as sharp as her others, has been fascinated. As for myself, I can only admit to having a ball. Political trouble is what we are trained for and wait for."

# 5

# The Cultural Revolution

## Earthquake Warning

The first tremor of the political earthquake that almost destroyed the People's Republic hit Shanghai in late 1965. Publication in the local press of a review fiercely criticizing the revival of an opera, *Hai Jui Resigns His Office*, set off alarms throughout China and among the Watchers in Hong Kong. Hai Jui was an official revered in history for having the courage to criticize a misguided, overbearing emperor and to retire in protest. The opera was seen as an allegorical attack on Mao. The stinging review, experienced hands in the Mainland Section agreed, was aimed at Mao's enemies. It was the kind of sensitive signal that sends snakes and roaches scurrying before a seismic event. Something huge was in the offing.

My placid apprenticeship as a China analyst came to an abrupt end as we struggled during the following months to track the torrent of media attacks, first on the leadership of the Beijing Party Committee, and then during the summer of 1966 on the top leaders of the national party apparatus. The Red Guards made their debut then at a series of gigantic, hysterical rallies in Tiananmen Square worshipping Chairman Mao that launched their rampage throughout the country and the society. They first attacked their teachers and parents and all remnants of traditional culture and then, directly, the party apparatus throughout China.

The early vehicles of attack were "Big Character Posters," handwritten broadsheets, pasted by the thousands to the walls of buildings throughout China's cities. Historically used by students to voice their protests, these sprang up everywhere, excoriating Beijing Party boss Peng Zhen, President Liu Shaoqi, Party Secretary

Deng Xiaoping, and others down the line. Red Guard groups began publishing their own newspapers expanding the attacks. On the ground, mass public criticism sessions ended with target officials paraded through the streets in dunce caps, their arms stretched out wide behind them in a derisive and painful position known as the "jet plane." Red Guard student groups ravaged historic sites, destroyed valuable old books and paintings, and ratted on their parents and teachers.

## The Origins of Upheaval

Most simply, as we pieced it together over time, leftists in the party, led by Chairman Mao, his wife Jiang Qing, and Army Chief Lin Biao, had organized and launched the movement in an effort to restore the primacy they had lost when the Great Leap Forward collapsed in 1959. Ever since the victory of the Communists ten years earlier, the party had been divided between those who believed that you could use the same techniques to run a nation state that you used when you seized power—mass campaigns of struggle and attack—and those who felt you needed more practical approaches. Tension between the "red" and the "expert" factions were the Yin and the Yang of Chinese politics.

The failure of the Great Leap—a huge mass political effort to force the Chinese economy to new heights, mobilizing the people to build blast furnaces in their backyards, and reorganizing the Chinese peasantry into agricultural communes—had discredited Mao and the "red" approach. Millions starved as agricultural production fell. The alliance between the Chinese and the Soviets fell apart, and the industrial economy suffered as Russian experts abruptly left the factories they had designed. Pragmatic elements in the party, led by Liu Shaoqi and Deng Xiaoping, gained steadily in power and prestige throughout the first half of the sixties. Brooding, Mao came to the conclusion that his revolution was dying because two key elements of society were rotten through with bourgeois influence—the party and the youth. He decided to turn one against the other in one climactic purifying event—the Cultural Revolution.

## A Different Job

The tools and techniques of China watching changed radically. Gone was the careful listening for sour notes in the daily symphony. The orchestra dissolved into bedlam, and musicians threw their instruments at each other and fought on stage. We paid attention to the central media, because the leftists still controlled it. But wall posters and Red Guard newspapers became the most sought after sources of information, always juicy and often wrong. Our demands for these were insatiable. Friends from foreign embassies in Beijing obliged, ripping posters from the walls and stuffing them, flakes of concrete still attached, into diplomatic pouches bound for Hong Kong.

The staid weekly dispatch I had produced became a daily telegram, approved in person by Consul General Edward Rice, in a vain effort to satisfy Washington's voracious appetite for news and analysis. I was in the hottest of seats, and enjoying the temperature, but wondering whether I could maintain the pace.

Happily, help arrived in the form of Charles Hill, a fresh graduate of the language school in Taichung. He shared my fascination with China's domestic politics, love of rowing, and unwillingness to take too seriously either himself or the momentous events we witnessed. Perhaps the highpoint of our collaboration occurred when the turmoil of the Cultural Revolution arrived in Hong Kong during the summer of 1967. We stood together on the roof of the Consulate General, transfixed by the absurd sight of local fat-cat communist officials leaping from their Mercedes cars to wave Mao's *Little Red Book* at the Governor's Residence. Together we followed the tortuous course of the Cultural Revolution and formed a lasting partnership that took new shape decades later when we both served as special assistants to Secretary of State George Shultz.

## The Violence Grows

In the summer and fall of 1966, the Red Guards were encouraged to travel throughout the entire country spreading the chaos originally focused on the capital. The results were often deadly, as the targets of mass criticism and humiliation cracked under pressure, killed themselves, or were beaten to death. The Red Guard generation, liberated from school, free as never before to rebel against their elders and to travel anywhere they wanted, were willing instruments of the Leftists during the early months of the movement. But by the turn of 1966, the party structure was still standing. Officials, driven from their office buildings, were performing their duties from garages and other makeshift headquarters.

Realizing that the youth were not capable of toppling the party structure by themselves, the Leftists pulled out the last stop in Shanghai, declaring the "January Revolution" of 1967, which empowered anyone, of any age or walk of life, to rebel against established authority. That blew the lid off. In city after city throughout China during the next nine months, party structures were swept away by the waves of warfare waged between rival factional organizations.

These factional entities formed very quickly after the lid came off. They were marvels of Chinese organizational skill, with their own propaganda arms, dance troupes, street combat units, and work and welfare brigades. As the weeks passed, they united into mass coalitions along "have" and "have not" lines. Those with something to lose—the children of party and government cadres, the established workforces of state-owned enterprises, the peasants from rich suburban communes—combined to defend themselves against the attacks of the dirt poor and the disenfranchised. Anyone with a grudge or a score to settle piled on. The factions outdid each other in adopting revolutionary nomenclature—East Is Red, Red Flag Fighting Corps—making it very difficult for observers to understand the underlying motivation of the struggle. And they killed each other in large numbers. Sailing our pleasure junks in Hong Kong waters, we would encounter bodies floating out from the Pearl River Estuary, casualties in the battle for Guangzhou (formerly known as Canton).

I learned about the "have–have not" cleavage from a young man who had served as a telephone operator for the big "have not" faction in Guangzhou. He had fled for his life when his side began to lose, swam to Hong Kong, evaded border patrols, and turned himself in to the central police. Under the Colony's hide-and-seek immigration rules, he was accepted as a refugee and put through the intelligence screen. I hardly ever had the time to interview refugees, but dropped everything to spend eight hours with him, going over the table of organization of his faction and his opponents. He knew the whole structure and helped us understand why the fighting was so intense. His attitudes were also instructive. He had not the slightest interest in the freedom offered by Hong Kong. His escape was simply an act of survival. He despised Madame Mao, whom he described as shallow and uneducated, and adored Chairman Mao, to whom he felt he owed his life. It was the Chairman's teaching to fear no enemies and overcome all obstacles that inspired him during his swim.[5]

This, in broad outline, was the stuff of my analytical work during our last years in Hong Kong. There was little certainty in our judgments and a lot of debate and argument at each stage of the process. The knowledge that the Chinese were just as confused as we were lent scant comfort.

## Turmoil in Hong Kong

The Cultural Revolution finally spread to Hong Kong during the summer of 1967, bringing with it labor unrest, serious riots, and mass demonstrations. Leftist agents sought to sow terror by putting lethal explosives into ordinary items, even toys. Our upscale neighborhood was not spared. One morning we awoke to find a bomb squad outside our window, in full armor, gingerly inspecting a suspicious object in the middle of Old Peak Road. It was Sheila's handbag, left there by a cat burglar, who had shinnied up the pipes outside our bathroom and taken the purse without disturbing our sleep.

In a June 1967 letter home, I described what was going on, as follows:

> The situation now is quite favorable to our side. The communists are essentially weak, and have been forced to try to save face by showing what strength they have through a series of token strikes, each of which affects the ordinary citizen whose support they seek much more than the "imperialists" they are trying to protest against. They have threatened food, water, electricity, and gas supplies, and stopped

ferry and transport services, not in any case long enough to cause lasting disruption, but just long enough to make everyone cross. It's a stupid performance, which reflects clearly the lack of direction across the border. I was taught to respect the organizational ability of the communists (and still do as a sensible hedge to all bets), but thus far it's the other tiger that turns out to be paper.

The local government, for its part, despite a few tactical blunders, has performed far better than any longtime observers of its pukka bumblings in the past would ever have dared hope. The younger officials, many of whom are in responsible jobs because their bosses are on leave, have risen to the occasion and delighted everyone by fighting the communists with their own weapons, propaganda campaigns, poster wars, etc., all with good effect. The governor turns out under his sun helmet and ostrich feathers to be a sound and unflappable man. At bottom, it has been the cops who held the key, managing through good training and self-control to deny to the communists the martyr and the emotional issue they were looking for. . . .

Across the border the Cultural Revolution has ground to a halt with the basic issue becoming not whether Mao can impress his antediluvian ideology on the Chinese people, but whether the government in Peking can extend its influence in the provinces sufficiently to restore order and maintain economic production. I think they probably can, but at a cost of almost everything the old man has sought to achieve. When they finish up—God knows when that will be—they will probably be back roughly where they started, with much of the old Party apparatus intact and society galloping towards Russian-style revisionism even faster than before.

In the meantime, the Chinese appear to have lost the respect they had for what once was a pretty effective government. Some of the legendary discipline is gone—streets are dirty, people are beginning to steal things in a minor way, mass calisthenics are skipped, and once automatic response to mass appeals to rush out and do things like kill sparrows is no longer taken for granted. Organizations are fighting in the streets and in the communes for political power in battles so confused that even local residents don't know which side is which. The only answer is tough army sanctions, which I suspect are soon to be imposed. The net result of such sanctions, however, to judge by the happenings of February and March when the army cracked down briefly, will be "Fascist atrocities" that make Hong Kong look like a teddy bear's picnic. And where will it leave the "great Red Sun in our Hearts," Chairman Mao? In charge of a garrison state as far removed from communist Nirvana as any you can find.

## A Difference of Opinion

Throughout the chaotic months of 1967, the People's Liberation Army, led by Mao's chief lieutenant Lin Biao, stayed on the sidelines making half-hearted, localized attempts to referee the violence but avoiding decisive action in most cities. By August, public order in the cities, and with it the fate of the People's Republic, seemed to be sliding away. Consul General Rice asked me to do a detailed analysis and make a judgment about the survival of the regime. The result became notorious in the analytical community in Hong Kong and Washington as the "bifurcated airgram."

After a week of writing and rewriting, I sent Ed Rice a detailed draft arguing that the situation had deteriorated alarmingly, but that the point of no return had yet to be reached. Mao still had the option of calling in the PLA to quell the violence and form the basis for a new structure. The consul general disagreed, believing that the deterioration of order was irrevocable. He asked me to go back, review my data, and come up with a new draft. I did, but with the same conclusion.

Famous for his fairness, Rice decided to send in my analysis without edit and append his own dissent as a cover page. I was relieved and delighted. This approach would guarantee a wide readership. Rice's comment argued, on the basis of his long experience in China, that the regime had entered a "descending spiral," a tailspin from which it could not pull out. The deputy consul general, Allen Whiting, a noted China academic on loan to the government, agreed with Rice and added a short statement to this effect at the bottom of the cover page.

## Order Restored

After the message was sent off, I departed with the whole family on two months of home leave, our first since 1965. Having always flown to Asia, transiting from one almost identical airport to another, we were determined to return home on the surface of the earth and get a sense of the real size of our planet. It took five weeks just to reach New York, via boat from Japan to the Soviet Union, trans-Siberian Railway across Russia (with Soviet expert and Hong Kong colleague Kurt Kamman as our guide), and the final leg from Europe aboard the SS *United States* from England.

While we were in America acquainting our three tigers with their grandparents, Chairman Mao called on the People's Liberation Army to restore order throughout China. The violent stage of the Cultural Revolution came to an end that summer of 1967. Military men, all party members to begin with, took over the key positions in the provincial governments and party committees and ran the country for more than a decade. The Red Guards and their contemporaries were sent down to factories and farms, most of them far from home, where they were to spend the next ten years. The political tensions of the Cultural Revolution would last until Mao's death in 1976 and his wife's arrest immediately thereafter, but the killing and chaos were over.

We returned to Hong Kong months after the PLA crackdown, time enough to spare superiors the sheepish discomfort of "I told you so" encounters. We spent our final months in Garden Road reporting the militarization of the Chinese government, the rustication of the Red Guards, the suppression of the fighting factions, and the return to a nervous, inconclusive calm.

## Heading Home

We prepared to leave the Crown Colony after almost five years, assigned to an additional year of language training in Taiwan to prepare me to be the U.S. interpreter at the Warsaw talks, our sole formal point of contact with the Beijing regime. On the eve of our departure these long-standing orders were changed in favor of a job on the Mainland China desk at the State Department in Washington. I was relieved. The Cultural Revolution had dried up the talks. Sheila and I were delighted at the prospect of returning to the United States.

The changes in our own country were in many ways as deep and disruptive as those we had observed in China. Since we had been away, President Kennedy had been killed, President Johnson had turned the Civil Rights Movement into law, feelings against the Vietnam War had exploded, forcing Johnson's decision to leave the presidency, Martin Luther King had been shot and Washington burned, the feminists were transforming women's rights, Robert Kennedy was dead, and the campaign to choose the next president was in full and turbulent swing. The country was going through a revolution of its own, less violent but in many ways as profound as the one that we had covered in China. It was time to go home and relearn the country we represented.

# 6

# Signs and Signals

## Signs of Change

My first chore as junior man on the Mainland China desk at State was to chronicle the achievements of Lyndon Johnson's China policy. Every bureau in the executive branch was given an equivalent task during the waning months of LBJ's presidency. The result, a slim volume at best, was revealing. Digging into the files since 1964, I found that every initiative to improve relations with Beijing—proposals for exchanges in journalism, sports, education, and culture, as well as ideas to resume trade and new approaches to the talks in Warsaw—had only gotten as far as Secretary of State Dean Rusk's inbox before being returned without action. The Chinese, embroiled in the Cultural Revolution and dominated by radicals, would not have been interested. Neither, apparently, was Secretary Rusk.

After President Nixon took office in early 1969, the office of the new Secretary of State, William P. Rogers, called for new China initiatives. We dusted off the previous proposals and sent them forward. This time they were not returned but disappeared, apparently sent to the White House for consideration. The change was striking. Something was up. We had all noted the 1967 Nixon article in *Foreign Affairs* calling for a new approach to China, but had no inside knowledge of the new President's thinking.

The "bifurcated airgram" from Hong Kong had made my reputation as a China analyst. In March 1969, I was asked to head the division in the Bureau of Intelligence and Research (INR) that covered the People's Republic of China (PRC), and, later, other countries in Northeast Asia. My new boss, once again John Holdridge, left shortly after I arrived to join Dr. Henry Kissinger's staff at the

National Security Council, another sign of White House interest in China. Happily, I was able to persuade another old mentor from Hong Kong, Bill Gleysteen, to replace Holdridge in INR.

Our "watching" in Hong Kong had focused purely on what was happening in China. In Washington, our analyses' main purpose was to help decision makers deal with policy issues. The most important among these were

—developments in the heated Sino–Soviet dispute and their significance for U.S.-China relations;
—the evolution of China's leadership after the violent phase of the Cultural Revolution;
—China's attitudes toward Taiwan; and
—the growing momentum of the campaign by the People's Republic to replace Chiang Kai-shek's Republic of China at the United Nations.

My office also prepared background material for sessions of the Warsaw talks, which resumed quietly in early 1970, another sign of changing attitudes in both Washington and Beijing.

I was now a boss, supervising the work of five analysts and two secretaries. The analysts ranged from crusty, learned senior civil servants like Edward Jones to young Foreign Service officers just starting to specialize in Asian affairs. Lynn Pascoe, later ambassador to Indonesia and UN undersecretary general, was a feisty new star. We were a tiny publishing company, producing papers on demand from senior officials, including Secretary Rogers and Assistant Secretary Marshall Green, participating in preparing larger policy papers like National Security Study Memoranda (NSSM), and representing the State Department on the interagency intelligence community committees that produced National Intelligence Estimates. I was a combination writer, editor, briefer, and salesman for our products around the bureaucracy. In addition, I was expected to maintain my academic contacts in the China-Watching community, and project State Department thinking in public speaking appearances around the country.

Putting a human face on intelligence analysis struck me as a good idea. I enjoyed not being hidden. More important, I found that I could make a more cogent analysis to the policy makers once I had explained our thinking in terms understandable to public audiences. Regional Councils on Foreign Relations, specialist audiences at universities, and the different War Colleges were eager for speakers, and I welcomed the chance to travel the country after six years away. I also taught a seminar at my old graduate school, the Johns Hopkins School of Advanced International Studies, called "Communist China: The Aftermath of the Cultural Revolution" during the fall semester in 1969.

I also had secret duties. The first of these was to interview the highest-ranking Chinese defector to the United States, the number two man from the PRC embassy in The Hague, who had changed sides in late January 1969. The intelligence community was intensely curious about what he knew. The State Department wanted its own access and sent me to have a talk.

Five minutes of conversation in the suburban Virginia safe house where the diplomat was hidden confirmed that the answer was zero. He was too far removed from Beijing to hear even gossip about Chinese leadership attitudes and moves or anything else of priority interest. So we spent the rest of our time together comparing notes on how Chinese and Westerners got their information about China and its leaders. I was fascinated and even comforted to learn that a Middle Kingdom bureaucrat read the *People's Daily* the same way I did, focusing on the first and last pages (in villages and city streets, these are the ones posted on the public walls), searching editorials for unfamiliar formulations, analyzing who stood where in photographs, and other tricks of the trade.

### Sino-Soviet Hostility Changes the Game

During my years in INR, 1969–71, the Nixon White House laid the groundwork for its opening to China. My office covered the growing alarm in Beijing over Soviet actions and attitudes, which forced a major shift in PRC strategic policy and which the president and Dr. Kissinger were quick to note and secretly exploit.

March 1969 saw the beginning of violent armed clashes between the Chinese and the Soviets along the Ussuri River that formed the boundary between the two countries. Tank battles and artillery exchanges across the frozen river marked a new stage in an ideological rivalry that had become national and personal. Bizarre photographs, like the one showing a horde of Chinese swarming over a Soviet armored personnel carrier and beating at it with sticks, demonstrated the depth of Chinese fear and, we concluded, sent a calculated message to Moscow: If you attack us, we will drown you in the sea of people's war. The incidents spread, occurring as far west as the border between Xinjiang and Kazakhstan. The Soviet buildup in Mongolia and other areas along the frontier grew from twelve poorly equipped divisions in 1964 to forty divisions in full readiness.

The result was "an atmosphere of war panic in China," Assistant Secretary of State for East Asian Affairs Marshall Green wrote later. "Air raid shelters were built on a massive scale. A CIA estimate of October 1969 placed the chances of a Soviet effort to knock out China's nascent nuclear weapons factories at about 1 in 3."[6]

As the State Department representative on the interagency committee that produced the intelligence estimate, I remember a lengthy debate on whether the Soviets could really perform a "nuclear castration" of China. The conclusion was no. China, as one analyst put it, had at least "eight balls," and these were not clustered in one place.

Four broad options were under discussion within the administration as to how the United States should position itself in response to Sino-Soviet hostilities, I told a Council on Foreign Relations audience in Chicago at the end of September 1969. I spoke off the record. Stewart E. Hoyt of the *Milwaukee Journal* reported my talk without attribution:

> 1. Make it clear to the Soviet Union that Washington would do nothing to impede its confrontation with China. Proponents of this approach did not want to sabotage agreements that the United States was working on with Moscow (notably arms limitation). Opponents worried about preventing improvement of American relations with China.
>
> 2. Do the opposite—make it clear that the United States will oppose any effort to bring China to heel. Proponents said that this would speed an improvement in relations

with China. Opponents said it would jeopardize relations with Russia—and the United States had more in common with Russia than with China.

3. Do nothing. This had already been ruled out.

4. Adopt a positive attitude toward both sides, while making it clear that they could not take American support or lack of support for granted.

Option 4 was chosen. Intentionally vague, it gave Washington the freest hand to influence events without being committed to one side or the other. It left both China and Russia guessing, worrying that Washington would help the other.

Many judgments went into the making of such a subtle policy, I told the Chicago audience. For one thing, American expert opinion judged that China and Russia would not go all the way to war, despite the military buildup and the whipping up of animosity for the other in each country. Yet allowance had to be made for miscalculation. Each side had made big mistakes already in handling the other, so escalation to a war that neither side wanted was conceivable.

U.S. policy makers sensitive to the balance of power believed that U.S. interests were best served when Russia and China were more evenly matched. Russia was stronger than China. Therefore the United States should consider ways of bolstering the Chinese side,

China, to be sure, might not want overt American help, because it might provoke a Russian attack. Moreover, there remained issues between the United States and China (especially Vietnam and the future of Taiwan) on which Beijing and Washington appeared irreconcilable. So help that Washington gave to strengthen Beijing's hand had to be subtle, more to be thought of as "signals" than as a genuine relaxation of the long feud between China and the United States.[7]

## The Mating Dance Begins

None of us were privy to the operational details of White House secret diplomacy, but public signals were indeed sent and received.

In late 1969, the United States announced limited relaxation of travel and trade restrictions with China. In January of 1970, the Warsaw talks started again after years on hold. In previous years the venue had been an old palace in downtown Warsaw so compromised electronically, wags said, that taxis passing in the street could tune in the talks. The new arrangements, alternate sessions in each other's embassies, were serious and secure. In his Foreign Policy Message to Congress in February 1970, President Nixon called for "a more normal and constructive relationship with Communist China."

## China and UN Representation

These years also marked China's worldwide campaign to replace Taiwan as China's representative in the United Nations. We reported extensively on Beijing's progress, as country after country recognized the People's Republic and broke formal ties with the Republic of China on Taiwan. As early as December 1969, we were asked for our views on what kind of UN member the PRC would make.

We replied in a memorandum that UN membership would not tame the PRC but would force its representatives to exercise discipline. As a Security Council member, we guessed that Beijing would not be a helpful influence on peacekeeping but would be less negative than many observers now thought. Beijing would champion the underdog against the superpowers and generate a larger number of Security Council meetings, but it would be careful in exercising its veto, assessing net impacts as other countries did.

We thought the PRC would be a baleful influence in the General Assembly for the former colonial powers and those like the United States that had bases overseas. It would oppose waste, slipshod procedures, and high-cost measures, and lobby for larger representation on the Secretariat. We estimated that China would observe our security and espionage rules sufficiently to avoid being thrown out of New York. The PRC presence at the UN would provide a convenient point of contact for the U.S. government. Perhaps most significant for U.S. diplomats who devoted months each year to lobbying in capitals worldwide on the issue, the Chinese representation question would be over, although Beijing would maintain pressure to prevent Taiwan's participation throughout the UN system.

The vote that seated the PRC in the UN occurred in October 1971 and helped set the stage for Nixon's visit in February 1972.

## Comparing Notes Abroad

In addition to managing the preparation of reports and analyses, an important part of my job involved travel to Asia and Europe to compare our findings with other governments and our own Foreign Service analysts. During a "parish visit" to Hong Kong at the end of 1969, I found the Mainland section downright boring after years at the center of attention. The long slow process of picking up the pieces after the Cultural Revolution was vitally important to track. But what had been a daily diet of juicy wall posters and hot Red Guard news was now, once again, dry rusks from the Communist press and radio. Divisions within the leadership, still very much there, had gone back underground.

The most exciting thing about Hong Kong was the change in climate for Sino-American contact. The Communists in Hong Kong were extremely interested in recent American moves and clearly under instructions to adopt a more relaxed attitude toward contact with Americans. Local officials from the New China News Agency, the Chinese Chamber of Commerce, and other go-betweens were striking up conversations with consulate general officers and expressing their own views in surprisingly cool and objective ways. All this was absolutely new and reflected the changes we had noted elsewhere.

The rest of Asia remained intensely interested in PRC developments. Japanese and Korean government officials as well as U.S. ambassadors and their staffs pumped me hard during stops on my way back from Hong Kong. Europe was also intrigued. In March 1970, the Allied Planning Advisory Group in Brussels met to discuss the implications for NATO of Sino-Soviet tension. I attended as the resource person on China in a delegation led by William Cargo, director of the department's Policy Planning and Coordination staff.

A newcomer to multilateral diplomacy, I was unprepared for the pace of the deliberations. We spent three days discussing the Sino-Soviet dispute, what course it was likely to take, what adjustments in its own posture NATO should make, if any. During the next two days we drafted a seven-page document summarizing our conclusions and recommendations. Discussion rambled painfully. Counting alliance members and NATO staff, there must have been sixty people in the great conference room. I thought of a large dairy barn with dignified cows locked in stanchions around the table, chewing the same cud, mooing at different intervals.

The substance of our discussions and conclusions was simple. We examined three contingencies: (a) continued Sino-Soviet antagonism short of war, (b) major hostilities, and (c) a major reconciliation. All agreed that continued Sino-Soviet antagonism short of war was the most likely, and the most advantageous to the Western alliance, although there was little that we could or should do to exploit the situation. All agreed that major hostilities would be dangerous because of the possibility that other countries could be dragged in or nuclear weapons used, and a host of other imponderables. There were some kinds of hostilities that would be of more advantage to the West than others, such as a protracted conventional land war limited to Asia that would exhaust both the Soviets and the Chinese. All agreed that the Soviets would work to avoid this kind of conflict.

In any case, all agreed that we had no control over the situation. An outbreak of major hostilities was undesirable. Genuine reconciliation, putting the Sino-Soviet relationship back on the same basis of close ideological and national cooperation that prevailed during the 1950s would be disadvantageous to NATO; but this was so unlikely, even after Mao's death, as to warrant little real consideration. Under the circumstances, the NATO allies concluded that they should sit tight, behave in an impartial manner towards both the Chinese and the Soviets, watch the situation, and keep each other informed.

This summary of the proceedings took me twenty minutes to write, and I could have done it before going to Brussels. Was it worth five whole days? There were times when I wondered. At one critical point during the proceeding, I had a flash of revelation: all the disjointed utterances and clarifications arising around this enormous table represented an alliance thinking aloud, something quite marvelous. Getting countries to do anything together is hard enough under any circumstances. Here were fifteen governments focusing on one problem, and making sense.

In November of 1970, I traveled to Paris and London with Marshall Green and Alfred L. Jenkins, then head of Mainland China Affairs at State (and later a close colleague in Beijing), to exchange assessments with the French and the British. Our talks, conducted in genteel, ornate chambers of the Quai D'Orsay and Whitehall, covered the Sino-Soviet stalemate, the impact of Vietnamization on our Asian relationships, and the growing strength of China's position vis-à-vis Taiwan in the UN. French President De Gaulle died just before we left Paris, bringing to my mind our secret toast to him seven years before in Taiwan when he recognized the PRC.

The French remained irate about the U.S. military intervention in Cambodia, which had occurred in May 1970. Green's opposite number, Henri Froment-Meurice, repeatedly called our action "deplorable," helpful to China's position in Indochina, and harmful to the prospects for the peace talks with North Vietnam underway in Paris. Less visible to the French, the incursion into Cambodia had also stopped our private mating dance with the Chinese in its tracks. Promising action at the Warsaw talks had been canceled, and the Chinese remained, so we thought, uninterested.

Our shared assessments found Sino-Soviet relations congealed in a state of *guerre demi-froide* (half–cold war), and the situation inside China remained a stalemate between pragmatists picking up the pieces in the provinces and radicals in Beijing huddled around an aging Chairman Mao. Japan continued to grow in economic strength but seemed unwilling, our London colleagues agreed, to exercise political influence in Southeast Asia.

This trip was my last major duty in the Bureau of Intelligence and Research. My two-year assignment was coming to an end, and I was ripe for a change. I had done nothing but China for ten years. The fascination of the country and its growing importance to U.S. policy notwithstanding, I was stale and burned out. The mere mention of Mao made me feel ill. I needed to learn more about the practice of diplomacy in general and requested a job that would provide the broadest possible overview of the Department of State and its operations.

Personnel obliged by assigning me to the Secretariat Staff (S/S-S), the office that manages the daily affairs and travels of the secretary of state, where I would serve during the next two years. The move, by pure serendipity, would lead to my participation in President Nixon's historic China trip and, later, to assignment at the U.S. Liaison Office in Beijing, developments of which I had then not the faintest inkling.

# 7

# Office Manager for the Secretary of State

## Birth of a Bureaucrat

I had to switch gears in a hurry. My new job was to move paper and manage people, rather than to think, write, and explain. Putting words on paper was less important than telling other people by phone to perform specific tasks, and fast. I was office manager of the Secretariat staff, or "the Line" in State Department slang, after its original layout along the hallway next to the secretary's own rooms. Our goal, simply put, was to get the secretary through his day. We determined the briefing documents and talking papers he needed for his meetings, set deadlines and standards for the bureaus writing them, then tracked any decisions that emerged. Each "Line officer" rode herd on a cluster of bureaus, imposed discipline, urged promptness, rejected sloppy work, and insured that all interested parties had cleared every paper sent up. The Secretariat sits astride all official lines of communication between the State Department, the White House, and the other government agencies. Its staff is central, respected, feared, and, at times, loathed by those working under its lash in the bureaus.

The young Line officers, as spirited as they were competent, had to be tracked and guided. I was the bareback rider in this circus, standing precariously on top of my staff horses, guiding them in the same direction with toes and fingertips. If papers the secretary needed did not arrive on time, or were sloppy, I was the one who took the heat from our front office. The executive secretary, Theodore Eliot, was himself directly answerable to Secretary William P. Rogers. Smart and good-humored, Ted did not have the time to stay mad for long.

The pace of the secretary's life in Washington was intense and the pressure high; the heat came from below as well as above, as action officers and assistant secretaries complained about the demands of the Secretariat. Our work covered all the issues of interest to the secretary, from disputes over Ecuador's fishing rights and the importation of Polish golf carts to the Strategic Arms Limitation Talks. Having once been responsible for knowing everything about China, I now needed to know just a little about everything else, enough to judge whether a paper about a given topic was intelligible to a decision maker pressed for time.

Managing the secretary's travels was another important function of the Secretariat. The challenge while on the move was to replicate an office that would perform our services at home, making sure at each stop that the boss was ready for all his meetings, had received his telegrams from other parts of the world, and was in touch with Washington. Once the plane arrived at our destination, our job was to get an office running immediately, usually in the hotel where the party was staying. Normally, we sent officers on ahead to be ready when we arrived. We learned a lot about the tricks of working without much sleep. One ploy, when everything was quiet for a while was to slip into your hotel room, get into your pajamas, sleep an hour or two, get up, take a shower, and brush your teeth as if you were waking to a new day. The idea was to fake your body into thinking it had had a full night's sleep. Your body could be fooled, but not all the time.

All this was new to me, but I found I liked being a bureaucrat and was good at it. My immediate boss, James Carson, a dedicated and experienced tutor, showed me that a touch of irreverence and wicked humor actually improved the rate of speed and the quality of performance required to get things done. When asked a question he could not answer, a Secretariat officer always looked up, not down, Jim taught.

Carson also hammered home the most important lesson anyone trying to influence policy makers needed to know: No matter how sound and elegantly argued your recommendations might be, they were worthless if they did not get to the decision makers on time and in a concise form that could be absorbed quickly. Knowledge of the pace and complexity of policy makers' lives was crucial to making an impact. Understanding the machinery that moves decisions was as important as the actual substance itself. At the same time, those who operated the machinery could not function without a grasp of the substance.

I developed and used an entirely different set of muscles in the Secretariat. As an analyst, I knew my subject and what should be reported, but I had no idea how wide the readership was or what I might do to make my work hit home. Now I understood the mechanics, how to make things happen, and how important my earlier work had been in relation to the other issues facing the secretary of state.

I also learned that the most effective Foreign Service officers were both diplomats and bureaucrats. As diplomats abroad, we learned difficult languages and lived in different cultures, interpreting these to our own government and ours to theirs. We are supposed to lubricate relationships, smoothing the sharp edges between presidents, chairmen, premiers, and kings. As bureaucrats in Washington, we are tasked to herd a gangling, often obtuse, foreign affairs community, pounding our shoes on countless staff-meeting room tables in an effort to get our way with representatives from the State Department, Pentagon, Treasury, Commerce Department, and intelligence community. This, I later found out, is what ambassadors do, too.

Philippine Foreign Minister Carlos P. Romulo, a legendary raconteur, described the difference this way in one of his famous stories. "When confronted with an ugly woman, the bureaucrat will say, 'You have a face that would stop a clock!' The diplomat will say, 'When I look into your eyes, time stands still.'" The Secretariat taught us both approaches, and when to use them.

### Kissinger's Secret Trip

The early months of my work in the Secretariat involved practically no China content. Generally speaking, State Department relations with the White House were terrible. Both President Nixon and National Security Advisor Henry Kissinger distrusted the ability of our institution to keep secrets and kept from it the information needed to do its work. They regularly undercut Secretary Rogers, making life difficult with directives that were frequently impossible to follow. Fortunately, Brigadier General Alexander Haig, Kissinger's deputy, was a brilliant Pentagon-trained bureaucrat and knew how to translate these often peremptory orders into language with which we could work.

Ironically, White House mistrust did not apply to individual Foreign Service professionals like my old boss, John Holdridge, and INR colleague Richard Smyser, who were brought to the NSC and relied upon for expert advice. We continued to meet with them, although, like all good pros, they guarded their principals' secrets tightly.

As a result, President Nixon's announcement on July 15, 1971, of Henry Kissinger's secret trip to Beijing and his own intention to visit the PRC the following year came as a total surprise. I remember lounging with Sheila on the lawn behind our house at 3734 Oliver Street with our colleagues from language training in Taichung, Stan and Claire Brooks, listening to the president's announcement from California on a small radio. If we had not been lying down, we would have fallen to the ground. We reworded our private 1963 toast in Taiwan to De Gaulle, this time to Richard M. Nixon.

I was beside myself with curiosity about what had happened in Beijing. John Holdridge had accompanied Kissinger. After a decent interval, I invited him to lunch at the Metropolitan Club and pumped him on his experiences. Here, at last, was someone who knew the Chinese at first hand, from the Mainland, Taiwan, and Hong Kong. For Americans, Beijing was the other side of the moon. I was all ears and wrote careful notes right after our meal. Many of the details of the mission became legend later on—the deceptive departure for Pakistan, complex conversations with Zhou Enlai, the tour of the Forbidden City. Holdridge's observations to me were more what one China watcher would make to another.

For example, he told me that there were no differences in style between the Communist Chinese officials he met and their counterparts across the Taiwan straits. Foreign Minister Huang Hua, for example, came across as an old, honorable Chinese gentleman, not a Marxist ideologue. The food was the best Chinese palace cooking, but all the dishes were ones that Holdridge had seen before. The accommodations, however, reflected Soviet influence. The Kissinger group had stayed at a Middle European–style villa in the western part of the capital. Beijing seemed very subdued—people quietly going about their business on a Sunday, no crowds jamming the parks, no gongs, hubbub, or street vending cries, as in the city Holdridge remembered. He used his Chinese, especially at meals.

Marshall Ye Jianying, Deputy Foreign Minister Zhang Wenjin, and Ambassador Huang Hua met them at the plane. The Chinese made a point of identifying Ye as a military man, and pains were taken, Holdridge said, to show that the People's Liberation Army was firmly behind the opening to the United States. Marshall Ye sat in on all the talks. I noted that of all the PLA men in the top leadership Ye was the one with the closest ties to Premier Zhou Enlai. The premier, John commented, looked old and drawn, as if "he had been through hell." His approach was low key, but forceful, humorous, and intelligent.

The hell he had been through, I surmised, was the Cultural Revolution.

"Have you heard of our Cultural Revolution?" Zhou had asked Holdridge.

"Yes," he had replied politely, "but we would not want to deal with something that we believed to be an internal matter of the PRC."

"Oh no," said Zhou, "I want to tell you," and he went on at length and with apparent sincerity to describe this time of "great turmoil, great upheaval, and great reorganization." Holdridge was convinced that Zhou's use of this familiar Maoist formulation now applied to the world outside China. The Chinese were ready to change the power equation with the Soviet Union and the United States.

During the first day of talks, Zhou presented Chinese positions in familiar set-piece form, as if to get them on the record. Later, after the U.S. side had responded, he relaxed and became more candid. The United States made no deals and no promises, Holdridge insisted. There were no conditions set for President Nixon's visit. The Chinese appeared very anxious for Kissinger's trip to be successful and for an announcement of the president's visit to be made public. In fact, it was the Chinese who stayed up all night drafting the announcement. The Americans went to bed around 3 A.M. The main discussion centered on the announcement's second sentence, "Knowing of President Nixon's expressed desire to visit the PRC, Premier Zhou, on behalf of the Government of the PRC, has extended an invitation etc, etc." The problem was how the sentence would be cast to satisfy the Chinese that the Americans had made the initiative and the Americans that they not appear to be coming hat in hand. There were some tense moments over the interpretation of the word for "knowing," *liao jie,* which has the broader meaning of "understanding."

The entire Forbidden City was closed off for the Kissinger party. The tour of the palaces included viewing a spectacular, recently discovered imperial body stocking made of small squares of jade sewn together with gold thread. There was also a look at the Empress Dowager's bedroom. The dust on the floor—the group left tracks—suggested that very few visitors were taken here. (Kissinger told Joe Alsop about the jade body stocking and was furious that the way he wrote it up suggested inside knowledge to support Alsop's pure speculations on the substance of the conversations with the Chinese.)

Kissinger had been skillful, irrepressible, and humorous throughout the visit, Holdridge said, and was the only person who could have brought it off. He and Zhou enjoyed their meetings. John relished the supreme irony that the Chinese were sitting down at the same table with the representative of the man they had only months before labeled "the God of War."

I probed Holdridge about onward preparations for the president's visit. No one had focused yet on the question, he replied. His impression was that the entourage would be small by normal presidential visit standards—no larger than a planeload.

After lunch I returned to my office on the seventh floor of the State Department, hoping against hope that there might be a way for me to tag along when President Nixon, accompanied by Secretary Rogers, visited China the following February. As I plied my bureaucratic trade during the rest of the year, I was aware that additional Kissinger trips were in the works to prepare for the Nixon visit, but the secretary of state's office continued to be cut out. Instead, State Department officers like Al Jenkins, William Brown, and Roger Sullivan worked directly with John Holdridge to create briefing papers and draft communiqué language for the national security advisor's use.

# 8

# Preparing for China

## Getting Picked

As 1972 began, I was down in the dumps. The dates of the president's trip to China had been set for February 21–28. State Department representatives, most notably Mainland China Desk Director Al Jenkins, had been involved in Dr. Kissinger's second, much more public, visit to Beijing in October, but the secretary of state's office had no role. Kissinger's Deputy, Brigadier General Alexander Haig, was leading a technical team to China in January.

I reasoned that the secretary of state simply had to accompany the president on this trip, which would require his Secretariat to brief and accompany him, as normal. Jim Carson had ordered tabs, binders, and fact books from my old office in INR, normal precursors for preparing traditional briefing books, but nothing real was happening and time was getting short. Both Carson and Ted Eliot assured me that they had my background and abilities at heart, and no interest in going to China themselves.

Dr. Kissinger had made plain to the Chinese that the usual entourage for a presidential trip would be cut to the minimum. The White House had informed Secretary Rogers that instead of his usual planeload he could take one secretary, one staff assistant, one administrative manager (who would handle logistics for the entire presidential delegation), one interpreter and one policy adviser. My chances of becoming involved seemed dim at best.

On the morning of Friday, January 21, Carson returned from the Front Office and said, "Shine your shoes. Your chances have improved. The secretary is thinking of interviewing you. He may call anytime today or Monday." I waited.

At 6 P.M. the phone rang. "Go immediately to the secretary's office." I hurried through the hall, hopping furtively as I buffed my shoes on the back of my pants leg. Maggie Runkle, Rogers's secretary (she was definitely going) showed me into the cavernous office, in those days furnished in a somber Frank E. Campbell funereal style. Secretary Rogers was alone.

A Washington lawyer from central casting, Rogers was tall and fine-tailored, with gray-white hair surrounding soft, pleasant features. He formed his words at the back of his throat and swallowed them from time to time. He greeted me affably, sat me down on a sofa and asked about my Chinese language background. In several carefully rehearsed, self-serving paragraphs, I sketched out my training in Washington and Taiwan and my jobs in Hong Kong, the China Desk, the Bureau of Intelligence and Research and the Secretariat.

"Is there anything in your background that could embarrass me? Do the Chinese know you?" Rogers asked.

I explained that the Chinese must know about me from Hong Kong days, but as an analyst; I had made no statements for attribution. Articles I had published about Chinese politics in academic and government journals had been under the pseudonym Adam Oliver (my elder sons' first names) or credited to the editor.

"I am looking for an aide for my trip to China," the secretary responded. "Normally, I would take Peter Johnson or Rush Taylor from my own office. For this trip, I need someone who knows something about China."

I cited the ten years I had devoted to China before assignment to the broadening experience in the Secretariat.

"This job is more important." Rogers interjected.

"I can help," I said.

"Don't count on anything," Rogers replied, ending the interview. "I'll let you know in a couple of days." Total elapsed time: four minutes. I left, passing the glass cubicle at Rogers's office door in which sat a frowning Peter Johnson, whose background in Latin America had not helped him that day.

During the weekend, I bit my nails and pretended nothing was going on. Monday afternoon Ted Eliot called Carson and me into his office and told us, "It looks like you are going to do some traveling!"

Much excitement, cheers, handshakes. I called immediately on Al Jenkins at the China Desk and Marshall Green in his office, who both expressed delight that I would be part of this adventure.

Green told me that Rogers had called Friday evening for a reference. "I gave him an earful," he laughed. I thanked him, and floated home to tell Sheila. I was to see some history, after all.

## The Care and Feeding of a Briefing Book

The next morning, I was escorted to a locked door at Task Force Area One, another part of the Executive Secretariat's Seventh Floor complex. Inside, I found my colleagues from the East Asia Bureau and INR, sitting at desks and waiting for guidance on the shape of the papers to be prepared for the secretary. Had I not moved to the Secretariat, I would have been in their place, working on papers, but with no chance to be one of the first FSOs in China. Who could have known?

The immediate task was to organize the briefing books for Rogers, and, in theory, the president. Every time the secretary and the president travel, papers are commissioned outlining the scope and objectives of the mission, as well as the issues he or she will confront, how they arose, and how they should be handled. These are then put in ring binders and hand-carried everywhere the boss goes. The form, quality, and production of the briefing books are carefully guarded responsibilities of the Secretariat and managed with a strict punctilio that often rankles contributors.

The production of a concise informative book required a mix of art, science, and coercion. The secretary traveled constantly, and his ability to function demanded that everything he needed to know for the particular stop and meetings be at hand when he needed it. He relied on the books to know where he was, why he was there, whom he would see, and what he should say. The Secretariat commissioned the papers from the bureaus of the State Department. The experts who did the writing had strong and often voluminous views about what the secretary should know and say. Their products often tended toward the obese and the obscure. Our job was to sweat them down and sharpen them up, saving time for the principal. Secretariat officers then went back to the assistant secretaries to make sure that the changes were acceptable, a process that stretched bureaucratic and diplomatic skills. The creation of a good set of books, on time, was the measure of a Secretariat staff officer.

How the books were used depended on the consumer. The secretary not only relied on but also helped shape what we gave him. The president would normally get his own set from the NSC staff, which provided unique guidance but often appropriated whole chunks of material from the State Department books and presented them as their own. This was expected. Policy influence in the bureaucracy depends, I had found, on the extent to which you can get others to take your ideas and call them their own. Constructive plagiarism is the name of the game. As soon as I heard of my role, I telephoned Kissinger's key aide Winston Lord, an old friend and former FSO, pledging to work closely. He said that was what he wanted, too.

My immediate task was to merge the considerable substantive work that had been done so far, particularly in connection with the Kissinger trips, into the format that Rogers was used to and could send to the president. To my good fortune, the East Asia Bureau writers were among the best in Washington. I knew them and Marshall Green, their boss, very well. Issues papers on bilateral questions—trade, travel, cultural exchanges, American citizens in China, Chinese assets frozen in America, and so forth—were already done. But the secretary had yet to address crucial questions that had emerged in Kissinger's negotiations with the Chinese so far on the final communiqué. These included: (1) how to treat the status of Taiwan, (2) how to acknowledge the People's Republic as the government of China, and (3) how to handle reduction of the U.S. military presence in Taiwan.

We were flying blind in two major respects. First, we did not know how Rogers really felt about the opening to China. What role, if any, had he played so far? What role would he play during the trip? Second, the White House had not shared with the State Department the records of Kissinger's talks with Zhou Enlai in which the substantive issues had been raised. We had very little time. Air Force One would be taking off on February 17, little more than three weeks away. I set to work immediately with the

Task Group editing and producing papers on the issues on which Rogers's reaction was urgently required. The materials had to be ready for a meeting with the secretary two days hence. His reactions would provide the answers we needed. We made the deadline, but only just.

## Rogers Reacts

That first session with Rogers was disappointing. The entire hierarchy of the department that dealt with Asia was assembled; Undersecretary U. Alexis Johnson, Assistant Secretary Marshall Green, his deputy Winthrop Brown, and my boss Ted Eliot were there with others from the Task Group, anxious to sink their teeth into the meat of the issues. Instead, we drank Cokes while Rogers, who clearly had not read the materials, asked shallow questions about tourism in China, business opportunities including possible aircraft sales, cultural exchange, and trip arrangements.

In the following days, the secretary began reading his brief. Word of his deep concern over the central issues filtered down to Al Jenkins. Accordingly, we reworked and fussed over the papers, in preparation for a climactic meeting on January 31.

In the meantime I had lunch with Richard Solomon, an academic China researcher from Hong Kong days, at a sandwich deli near the White House called Kay's. Dick had moved from academe to Kissinger's NSC staff. He told me, my notes relate, that he was writing a paper for Henry on the PRC strategy toward Taiwan.

"How would you describe that?" I asked.

"Isolate the die-hards, split the supporters, and make it impossible for Taiwan to do anything but unite with the Mainland," he replied.

Munching on a gigantic roast beef sandwich, I asked what policy we should adopt to deal with this strategy.

"Help them," he responded, referring to the PRC. I agreed, but thought the process should be gradual.

On the afternoon of January 31, the same cast of characters met with Secretary Rogers for an intense substantive discussion that lasted more than two hours. My notes tell the story:

Rogers has really read all the papers. He asks penetrating questions:

1. Why recognize the PRC explicitly as the government of China? Do we have to? Isn't this an unnecessary red flag in front to the ROC? Doesn't it suggest that we have been thoroughly out-negotiated by the PRC if we do?

Answer (from Green and Jenkins): We don't have to, but why not make explicit what is implicit in the president's visit, especially if it will guarantee a better relationship with the PRC?

Rogers counters: We are doing plenty going there in the first place. The president is meeting with Zhou, who is lower in rank. We want to move, but we can't look like we've given too much. How do I explain? How does the American public understand?

2. Why say we want to withdraw troops from Taiwan in two years? Jesus Christ! The American right will charge sellout. Why not say we'll lower our presence as tensions are reduced.

Decision: Leave recognition moot, go for a PRC declaration of intent to use peaceful means in search of a Taiwan solution while we pledge to reduce our military presence. Note Beijing's position as the government of all China. State we have no fixed idea of a future solution for Taiwan.

Comment: The secretary… has wit, good humor, and a good mind when he wants to use it. His whole approach is political. I get the impression that he sees himself as the president's major advisor on the domestic political effects of foreign policy moves. He is the man to tell Nixon how what he plans will look to Congress and the public. He looks at issues from the role of a spokesman and explainer in a domestic political context. A grand designer he is not. A competent advisor he is, and plays with gusto the only foreign affairs role with which Henry Kissinger cannot compete.

During the next few days, we worked all hours to put the briefing books into finished form and sent them in draft to the White House on February 2. Ted Eliot was pleased, describing the results

as "spectacular" in such a short time. John Thomas, assistant secretary for administrative affairs, who had been picked to manage
the logistics of the entire trip, heard this accolade and brought me
quickly back to reality.

"Today's eagle is tomorrow's turkey," he commented dryly,
adding that the reverse was seldom true.

A brilliant administrator and budget manager, Thomas deeply
resented the downstairs/upstairs class distinctions in the department between administrative specialists, the "adcats," he called
them, and the substantive political and economic officers, or "subcats." I had discovered these festering attitudes during earlier travels together. It took me hours to convince him that subcats like me
knew we could not accomplish anything without adcats like him. It
was as important for adcats to know the substance as it was for subcats to understand administrative procedures. Thomas had asked
me to prove it. I made a point of keeping him up to speed on the
issues whenever he asked and made an important career ally.

## The White House Reacts

The State Department and NSC tracks merged at a meeting in
Henry Kissinger's West Wing office on February 4. Green, Jenkins,
Haig, Holdridge, and Lord were there.

"Oh, yes. I know you," Kissinger remarked when we were introduced. "You are one of Joe Alsop's sources." I bit back the temp-
tation to retort that at least we had one thing in common, along
with everyone else in the room, and made a self-deprecating reply
appropriate to my lowly station.

Sitting us down, Kissinger made it clear that he had no great
problem with the books or with the general tack Rogers wanted to
take. He, too, was worried about appearing too soft to the American Right and suggested some revision to the talking points on Taiwan. He asked for more detailed specific proposals on trade and
cultural and scientific exchange, in apparent search for concrete results, given the unwillingness of either China or the United States
to move on the basic issue between them. This was the wording of a
U.S. statement to reduce forces progressively in Taiwan juxtaposed
with a Chinese statement to seek a peaceful solution to the Taiwan

question. Kissinger asked for additional papers on the renunciation of force and on intelligence operations, among others.

Henry went on to explain the futility of quid-pro-quo bargaining with the Chinese. The negotiations over the number of Americans connected with the Nixon visit were illustrative. After promising the Chinese to keep numbers to a minimum, Kissinger had been appalled to learn on returning from his first visit to Beijing that the normal number associated with past presidential trips was rarely less than 900. After making many enemies, particularly within the Secret Service, he scaled the number down to 350, took that to the Chinese explaining exactly what he needed and why. They bought it. If he had started at 700, then fallen back in the customary Western way, it probably would not have worked.

In closing, Kissinger made it clear that he wanted a unified delegation, with everyone working from the same set of briefing books prepared by State (which would have been unprecedented). As he mentioned to Green later in a private aside, the damage to relations between State and the White House was, to some extent irreparable. But on this trip at least we must move as a unit.

My notes of the meeting (which lasted an hour and a half, interrupted by a fifteen-minute call from President Nixon in Key Biscayne) comment that Kissinger seemed to be feeling exposed and wanted to reduce the criticism he was under for operating alone. This represented no problem to the China people at State. We agreed with the policy. His idea of one big happy family as long as he was in charge seemed less grating under the circumstances. It was clear he trusted Al Jenkins, who represented no threat. (In the event, Kissinger admitted later in his memoirs that the president worked from his own set of briefing materials.)

### Final Tuning

I returned immediately to the State Department for a discussion of travel arrangements with Secretary Rogers. He was engaging and funny. A condescending memo sent by White House Advance Chief Dwight Chapin advising all travelers in the party how to dress, what shots to take, and how many bottles of liquor they could bring back to the United States drew his ire. Commenting,

Rogers refused to wear any hat with earlaps on the Great Wall. As for liquor, he continued, Americans will do almost anything to get something for nothing, and he described little old ladies staggering around airports loaded with whiskey bargains they would never have bothered with at home. He then got up and staggered around his huge office, hands weighed down past his knees, mimicking an old lady in an airport with her liquor purchases.

Rogers added some dry comments about the schedule. "Admiral McCain sure as hell will be there to meet the president in Honolulu. Two bits he'll bound halfway up the ramp before the plane door is even open," Rogers laughed.

The days leading up to liftoff on February 17 were marked by more meetings designed to fine-tune substance and arrangements and unify the delegation, including a lunch hosted by Rogers on February 10 and another White House gathering with Kissinger the next day. Henry waxed effusively about the briefing books, terming them "the best he had ever seen from State for any trip or visit." He embarrassed me by poking Jenkins and saying with a big laugh, "Since I have worked with you before and know what kind of book you produced, the quality of the current set must be Platt's fault." He continued. "Substantively we are in very good shape. State's books are our basic position." If the trip was a disaster, he would make that known. And if it was a success? Marshall asked. In that case, as usual, the White House would take the credit, Kissinger twinkled.

The talk turned to gifts. I knew that there were a number of clocks in the gift list, and explained that in Chinese culture the gift of a clock was the equivalent of inquiring when the recipient was going to die. "Clocks are out!" Henry said, horrified. I commented on the planned presentation of two musk oxen to the Chinese, pointing out the parallels with past barbarian tributary missions to the emperors of China bearing strange animals—rhinos, giraffes, and the like. "The musk oxen are out!" came the refrain. (Actually they were not, but the gift was rearranged as a present to the Chinese people, rather than a personal present to Premier Zhou.) Kissinger cracked that State would put the oxen on his plane and arrange for him to follow them off.

Kissinger inquired about the commemorative George Washington medallions being reminted in large quantities to be given as mementos to Chinese banquet guests during the visit. This was an idea cooked up, he said, between Treasury Secretary John Connally and the president. I was the only person in the room who had seen the medals and described to the others the reverse side, which showed one hand with a naked, presumably savage, forearm clasping another, clothed and civilized, beneath a crossed peace pipe and tomahawk. I wondered about the suitability, but opined that the Chinese might interpret the savage extremity as ours, and the civilized one as theirs. "The medallions are dead," was the deep-voiced judgment.

After the meeting, Kissinger's staff, somewhat embarrassed at not having paid attention to such matters, found out that the medallions were originally struck during George Washington's administration and handed out to Indian chiefs who behaved themselves and signed treaties.

The gifts that were finally picked, handsome Boehm porcelain birds, were both suitable and spectacular. Attention to detail was not the strong suit of White House Protocol, however. Later in Beijing, the gifts were put on display in the Nixon guesthouse before presentation to the Chinese. I took a quick preview look and noticed that the gift for Mao was labeled "President of the People's Republic of China," a title of which he had been ignominiously stripped more than ten years before. This was corrected to "Chairman of the Chinese Communist Party" before any damage could occur.

In the last days before departure, as orientation, Secretary Rogers and I got a chance to watch home movies of the first two Kissinger trips, featuring long pans of John Holdridge and Kissinger grinning. "That's just the cat-swallowed-the-canary type of smile we want to avoid," Rogers commented. Other features of the film were shots of Henry's toothsome secretary, Julie Pineau, and a gruesome, graphic sequence of a lady under acupuncture anesthesia slit open to remove an ovarian tumor, wide awake and chatting while needles were twiddled in her wrists.

On February 15, before our last delegation meeting, Rogers suggested that I focus on communications rather than taking care of him. I assured him that the flow of cables would be light. In Peking, the entire delegation would have available just one circuit, capable of carrying only 1670 words per minute. I would have plenty of time to help him. He agreed, and confirmed to the group that I would be the coordination point for all communications with him from the department. "See you in Hawaii," he said.

## En Route to China: Hawaii

We took off on February 17 aboard the president's backup plane, an old Boeing 707 from the presidential fleet that Secretary Rogers had used many times before. The president, Rogers, and Kissinger departed fifteen minutes later aboard a brand new 707 making its maiden voyage. At each stop throughout the trip, we would land fifteen minutes ahead of the president, ourselves preceded in turn by a separate press plane, and be perfectly placed to view and photograph the grand arrivals.

As we headed for Hawaii, the first stop of an itinerary designed to reduce the effects of jetlag on the president, Holdridge, Jenkins, Chas Freeman (the interpreter), and I had a stateroom to ourselves, a flying office with desks, typewriters, Xerox machines, and white phones. The presidential suite just in front was chock full of presents. At Travis Air Force Base in California, we stopped to refuel and pick up four redwood saplings, which were shoehorned, sweating in plastic bags, into the big office. This did not prevent me from wedging myself into its white Naugahyde throne, with a multibuttoned console at my imperial fingertips, and phoning Sheila and the boys.

We were all still pinching ourselves. My colleagues, professional diplomats trained to be taciturn, did not even try to hide their excitement at lifting off on this voyage into the history books. Holdridge regaled us with the cloak-and-dagger details of Henry's escape from Islamabad, disguised in dark glasses and a hat pulled way down, scooting through early morning streets in a battered Volkswagen to a deserted end of the Chaklala Airport, where a Pakistan International Airways Airliner waited, poised to take him on his first secret trip to Beijing.

Ten hours later, we emerged, groggy and stuffed with food, into the bright Hawaiian sunlight at Hickham Air Force Base, watched the president land, and then were whisked by presidential Marine turbojet helicopter to the golf course of the sumptuous Kahala Hilton. We set up operations at the Hilton and went to sleep in great comfort.

## A Reversal of Roles

The next morning, I took the overnight telegraphic traffic to the secretary, who, along with the president and the senior members of the delegation, was staying in more Spartan officers' housing at the military base. Rogers and Marshall Green appeared shortly, windblown and cheerful after an early golf game. After reviewing the cables, they invited me to stay for lunch. We were digging into our salad when Henry Kissinger, unannounced, padded in on Hush Puppy–style shoes, sporting a striped yellow terry cloth shirt and white pants. I had never seen Rogers and Kissinger together and was fascinated to watch the two adversaries interact, relaxed and genial as country club associates.

Kissinger had eaten, but sat with us and made to Rogers many of the same points he had emphasized in previous meetings. These Chinese will not bargain quid pro quo like the Soviets. They assert principles and stick to them, and expect us to as well. Kissinger expressed the strong hope, and Rogers agreed, that the president would stand up to the Chinese and give back as good as he got, right away. Both were worried that Nixon might not react this way. Tough as he was in public, in private confrontations the president customarily stepped back and tried to move around his opponent. This would not work with the Chinese, Kissinger said. Both agreed to urge the president to be firm, and not to worry about offending the Chinese by refuting their statements if the need arose. This would gain respect, not offense.

The conversation continued, covering familiar ground about how key issues should be handled to limit damage and gain the support of Congress, the media, and the American public. On issues of policy substance, Kissinger talked, Rogers listened. The roles reversed when management of domestic politics came up. I wondered as I listened whether Nixon's foreign policy might not function better if Rogers were the White House adviser and Kissinger secretary of state.

I also wondered why Kissinger showed up without warning and came on the way he did. Later, Marshall Green told me he had put Kissinger up to it, believing that Rogers would benefit from the exchange. Both Rogers and Nixon were steeped in standard Western legal bargaining processes and had engaged in quid-pro-quo bargaining with the Soviets. There was also a sense that Rogers, as an old friend of the president's, could reinforce the message with his boss more effectively than Dr. Kissinger.

Returning to the hotel, I treated myself to a massage administered vigorously by an enormous Russian lady, who turned out to have been born in Manchuria and lived in Shanghai until 1952.

"Saying 'hallo' to Shanghai for me!" were her parting words.

## Labor Is Divided

Later in the day, Green, Jenkins, Freeman, and I returned to Rogers's residence to discuss what tack to take in the counterpart talks in the PRC. We had learned that three separate sets of conversations had been proposed for our consultations with the Chinese: Nixon and Zhou on the world situation; Kissinger and Qiao Guanhua on the wording of the final communiqué; and Rogers with Foreign Minister Ji Pengfei on the mechanics of day-to-day relationships after the visit. Despite all the talk of a unified delegation, the State Department was, in fact, to be segregated from the strategic substance that drove the Nixon initiative and was to be relegated to deal with the nuts and bolts of exchanges, trade, and travel. This was not an illogical division of labor. The issues were ones that we knew cold; and they would turn out to be crucial in the decades to follow. Kissinger made plain in his memoirs that the president wanted it that way, and he did too. At this point in Hawaii, we were so excited about going to China, we would have been happy to negotiate about the weather.

Rogers asked smart questions about what we hoped to achieve, the tactics to follow, and the misconceptions the Chinese harbored about us that needed to be corrected. Green and Jenkins noted that we were dealing with people who believed the United States had betrayed them ever since the Marshall Mission in 1946. We were a different set of Americans, but the Chinese were the very same people, trained to regard Americans as untrustworthy.

Rogers believed that the most important goal of our talks was to create a sense of momentum—tangible evidence of movement in our relationship after the visit was over. We went over the kinds of exchanges the Chinese might approve: sports in general, particularly basketball, music, and ballet, many of which turned out to be prophetic. We also noted that the Chinese were using their new mission in New York much more broadly than UN representation required

Rogers's knowledge of history was spotty, I found. He had forgotten General MacArthur's threats to bomb across the Yalu River, words and gestures that preceded the Chinese entry into the Korean War. The meeting turned into a relaxed and rambling dinner, giving us a chance to get to know Rogers and bond as a group. We agreed to take further cues from whatever happened at the president's talks and at the plenary sessions. Tactically, we would begin the proceedings with our Chinese counterparts by thanking them for their hospitality and then put the ball in their court.

### Guam

On February 19, we flew to Guam, the second stop on our jet-lag-reduction itinerary. I worked on a paper for Rogers during the long flight. Arriving, as usual, in time to observe the big welcome prepared for the president, we got one of our own: soft kisses and leis made of shells and orchids from scantily clad Guamanian maidens at the foot of the ramp.

That night I sat bolt upright in my bed. "My God! They've gone without me!" Not so, I was relieved to find, but never did get back to sleep.

# 9

# China at Last: Nixon in Beijing

## A Quiet Arrival

The approach to Shanghai under overcast February skies took us over stretches of snow-dusted paddies and villages interlaced with canals, up which floated junks with tall flat sails. The airport was empty except for a smattering of officials, tiny against the vast expanses of concrete. At the foot of the ramp stood Zhang Wenjin, the courtly head of the American Department at the Ministry of Foreign Affairs, and Deputy Chief of Protocol Wang Hairong, an awkward young woman reputed to be Mao's niece. Both had been important figures in Kissinger's trips and were to prove key operatives during the early years of the new relationship between the United States and China. Holdridge and Jenkins knew both and made the introductions. From the cavernous terminal building, tea and pastries in hand, we watched Air Force One land, the history of the occasion marked by total silence.

After a brief interval, we returned to our plane across the wide tarmac with the PRC navigators, who were the real reason for the Shanghai stop. The distinctive Chinese field smell with the hint of night soil so familiar from our time in Taiwan wafted from the surrounding farms, conclusive evidence that I had arrived in China at last. Not a reason to fall and kiss the ground, perhaps, but a significant sensory jolt nonetheless.

The Beijing airport was sunny and cold. Again, the place was empty except for two long lines of exceptionally tall, disciplined, and magnificently dressed soldiers, forming the honor guard of the People's Liberation Army, and a small knot of civilian officials. The people on our plane were not permitted to join them and mar the photo opportunity. Instead, we were herded into an area just be-hind the left wing of President Nixon's aircraft after it rolled to a stop. From a worm's-eye vantage point framed by the engines of the Boeing 707, I took my own films of Nixon's historic, and some felt endless, handshake with Premier Zhou Enlai.

The president knew what he was doing. John Foster Dulles had refused Zhou's hand in a famous slight at a Geneva conference years before, and Nixon wanted the world, as well as the Chinese, to know that that he was determined to put this right. He even kept everyone except his wife, Pat, penned up on his plane until he got the job done, coming down the ramp alone in the dead quiet, a dra-matic entrance he felt the occasion demanded.

After a brief ceremony, we raced for the motorcade, a long line of small, green Shanghai-brand cars behind several big black Red Flag limousines, the Chinese handmade equivalents of stretch Ca-dillacs or Mercedes. I rode into the capital with John Thomas across flat, brown-white farmland, with occasional small factories and rows of young trees planted along the roadside. Driving through the city and into Tiananmen Square, where Chairman Mao's huge portrait stared stolidly above the gate to the Forbidden City, I won-dered where all the Chinese were. Not one was to be seen, unless one peeked quickly down the side streets whipping by, where Pub-lic Security Police had cordoned off crowds of curious onlookers half a block away.

We arrived at the Diaoyutai (the word means "fishing platform"), the official guesthouse compound, a large complex of Russian-style villas with high ceilings and rooms full of stuffed chairs, with antimacassar doilies draped over the backs. I unpacked and got my bearings. Our State Department contingent, including the secretary of state, was segregated in a separate villa of our own. The White House and the NSC were in other buildings close by. So much for the "unified delegation." I checked for messages at the communications room and ate lunch with our group. It was the best food and service of any Chinese restaurant anywhere in the world. This visit was going to be fattening.

**Not Meeting Mao**

After lunch we were scheduled to gather for a plenary session to kick off the proposed counterpart discussions. It was abruptly postponed, and we waited—and waited—and waited. What had intervened was the crucial meeting between Mao and Nixon, called without warning during a bright period in the uncertain daily forecast of the chairman's health. Henry Kissinger and Winston Lord (as note taker) accompanied Nixon. The secretary of state was not included and, to my knowledge, not even aware of the meeting.

The press made much of this deliberate omission, yet another humiliation in the long rivalry between Kissinger and Rogers, and none of us could explain it. Kissinger's memoirs insisted that the Chinese wanted the meeting small and that Nixon never intended for Rogers to participate anyway, but he apologized in his book *The White House Years* for not insisting that the secretary be included. Rogers, always the grownup, did not complain or even raise the issue around us. Later, he admitted it had bothered him.

Participant list aside, the Nixon-Mao meeting was the key to the success of the entire visit. In contrast to past presidential visits to other countries, there had been no specific time slotted for a meeting with the leader of the country. Nixon went to China without knowing exactly when he might meet with Mao. That the chairman's blessing came so soon and so emphatically relaxed the Chinese and assured a smooth path in the days ahead.

The long-delayed plenary took place at the end of the afternoon, a pro forma ceremony at which the decisions already made about who would talk about what and where were endorsed. We then left for Tiananmen Square and the opening banquet at the Great Hall of the People.

**Dinner with the Elders**

No one who attended that opening dinner will ever forget it. The sheer size of the Great Hall of the People made one feel like an ant in a movie set. Everyone in the president's party was invited, including aircrews and baggage handlers, flowing in an excited crowd up the wide staircase. As the official party was photographed on a grandstand at the top of the stairs, we could hear music wafting from the giant banquet hall. Just inside the hall's entrance on a raised platform sat the People's Liberation Army band in baggy, rankless uniforms, playing a sublime and authentic rendition of "Turkey in the Straw." The hall was lit dramatically, the focus on the Chinese and American flags hanging side by side.

I moved in something of a trance through a receiving line of Chinese leaders I had read and written about for years, headed by Premier Zhou Enlai, Marshall Ye Jianying, and Vice Premier Li Xiannian. Gathering my wits, I noted from a swift scan of the tables in the cavernous room that many of the Chinese guests were extremely old, some in wheelchairs with oxygen tubes attached to their noses. Two of these were at my table—a famous historian named Tang and an old politician from Sichuan Province named Liu. They were museum pieces produced periodically to maintain an image of democratic unity. Mr. Liu could not eat, drink, hear, or speak more than a few words and had to be lifted bodily by attendants for the historic friendly toasts by Zhou and Nixon.

Others at the table were younger and better able to communicate—a pair of revolutionary opera stars, she very stiff, he a heavy drinker with jowls; the director of consular affairs at the Foreign Ministry; and, on my right, Qian Dayong, deputy director of the American and Australasian Section at the ministry. Qian was the closest thing to a direct counterpart for me (and became an important colleague when I returned to live in Beijing fourteen months later). We chatted amiably, basking in the incongruity of the situation.

The Chinese returned to the question of age, commenting on how young the American delegation was. They were not talking about me, but about Nixon and our top leaders. They were right. The Chinese leaders were the same people who had taken power in 1949, twenty-three years before. To be a match, our delegation would have had to be led by Harry Truman and George Marshall. China, I now understood, was caught in a generational logjam. It would be six more years before Deng Xiaoping—under house arrest and nowhere in sight that evening—would break it.

Geriatric observations aside, nothing could take away from the excitement and magic of the event. In the stampede for the doors that traditionally marks the end of Chinese banquets, I ran into several journalist friends from China-watching days in Hong Kong. Bob Keatley of the Wall Street Journal sidled up. "History, I'm here," he muttered, smiling. Stanley Karnow of the Washington Post, preceded by his paunch, was also on the prowl, the circles under his eyes making him look like a joyful, inquisitive Panda.

The next morning (February 22), I was itching to get out of our guesthouse cocoon. So, after delivering the overnight telegrams to Secretary Rogers, I took advantage of a free moment and headed for Wangfujing, then as now Beijing's top shopping street. Huge, subdued, curious crowds were gathered around the sidewalk bulletin boards displaying the morning's *People's Daily*. Front-page pictures of Chairman Mao meeting with President Nixon and Premier Zhou at the banquet drew top attention. The function of Chinese media is less to report news than to tell the masses what to think. Today it did both, a resounding plus for U.S.-China relations.

Feeling strange, I went up the street to the biggest department store, the Bai Huo Da Lou, to check out what was for sale. The sturdy, drab, limited output of the Cultural Revolution economy was all that was on offer: padded coats, Mao suits, PLA hats, cloth shoes, leather boots, and the like. I bought Ping-Pong paddles for my boys and covered teacups for Sheila.

## Phoning Washington from the Great Hall of the People

The first session of the counterpart talks between Secretary Rogers and Foreign Minister Ji Pengfei took place that afternoon in the Xinjiang Room of the Great Hall of the People, with me at the end of the table taking notes for the United States. On the Chinese side others included Xiong Xianghui, Premier Zhou's foreign policy adviser; Qian Dayong, the deputy director of the American Department who had sat next to me at the welcome banquet; and underlings from his office. Others on the U.S. side were Marshall Green, Al Jenkins, interpreter Chas Freeman, John Scali and Ron Ziegler from the White House Press Office, and Commander Jonathan Howe from the NSC staff. I noted that everyone had observers at our talks, but that State was not represented at the discussions involving the president and Dr. Kissinger.

The major topics covered during the three-hour session were:

1. The U.S. desire for better contacts between the governments, including channels of communication and some kind of presence in each other's country. The Chinese promised to get back to us on these issues, but took pains to point out the obstacles presented by the presence in America of representatives from the Nationalist government on Taiwan that we continued to recognize.

2. The Chinese desire for more people-to-people programs and exchanges to be facilitated by both governments.

3. U.S.-China trade. The Chinese believed that we were under considerable pressure from the business community to start trade relations. Rogers responded that we were not being pressed but wanted trade, particularly as evidence of an improved political relationship. Foreign Minister Ji undertook to invite American businessmen to the annual Canton Trade Fair.

During the course of the conversation, the Chinese asked why the United States continued to require fingerprints of Chinese visitors. Members of our delegation believed that this regulation was no longer valid, but no one was sure. Rogers asked me to check. I left the room in search of the Secret Service Command Post in the Great Hall. Wherever the president goes, a White House phone can never be far away. Sure enough, discreetly placed behind a huge pillar was a telephone with a picture of the White House on the dial. I picked it up.

Click. "White House switch" (clear as a bell).

Me. "State Department Operations Center, please."

Click. "State Department Operations Watch Officer. How can I help?"

"This is Nick Platt in Beijing. We are in talks with the Chinese and need to know right away whether we still require fingerprints for Chinese visitors. Please wake up whoever knows the answer. I'll hold." (This was fun.)

The Watch Officer rousted the head of the Visa Office (it was around 4 AM there), who sleepily confirmed that no fingerprints were required for PRC visitors. I was back in the meeting within fifteen minutes. Rogers, on my prompting, told the Chinese that our swift response showed how instant communications could quickly clear up misunderstandings.

## Madame Mao Entertains

That evening, the president and most of his party attended a performance of *The Red Detachment of Women*, a revolutionary ballet developed under the patronage of Madame Mao and one of the few cultural works authorized for public consumption. Imagine a mix of modern ballet choreography and stereotypical Chinese opera movements, supported by a traditional Chinese orchestra and shrill voices, presenting a heavy propaganda libretto. Uniformed ballerinas in puttees pirouetted, vigorously pointing their Mauser automatic pistols, uttering piercing denunciations of the Japanese invaders and paeans of praise for Communist heroes, all to the loud accompaniment of gongs, drum, and cymbals.

The political event of the evening was the appearance of Madame Mao herself, looking sharp, dignified, and self-contained in a well-tailored blue Mao suit. She shook hands at the end, with a firm, polite, schoolmarm grip. I had now met the top leadership of China with the exception of Mao himself; but, strangely, I had not met Richard Nixon.

## Media Makes the Message

The visit took on a carefully choreographed rhythm with a telegenic event each morning and evening and substantive talks, interrupted by superb meals, taking up the time between. The White House advance men had taken smart advantage of the twelve-hour time difference between China and the east coast of the United States, assuring live TV coverage of the visit in American homes at the breakfast and prime evening hours. The Chinese cooperated in every way, seizing the opportunity to present their country in the most favorable light to a huge and growing audience, not just in America but worldwide.

Thus on the morning of February the 23, Mrs. Nixon visited a People's Commune while the president closeted himself with Washington work. I wrote up the meetings of the day before. In the afternoon, Secretary Rogers's talks centered on Taiwan, a standard exchange of positions. The evening event was a spectacular display of gymnastics, Ping-Pong, badminton, and other similar activities, set against a crowd of 18,000, all dressed in new sweaters of different colors. I sat a few rows behind Premier Zhou, watching with fascination how he operated. The leadership dais where he sat featured a long table for teacups and snacks. In addition to keeping several conversations going with President Nixon and others, he was approached by an aide, who placed in front of him the layout for the next day's *People's Daily*. He proceeded to move pictures and text around until they met his approval, then dismissed the assistant. Zhou's attention to detail was legendary, but this struck me as a vivid testimony of the new height and importance he attached to the media impact of the Nixon visit.

The Great Wall was the happening of the next morning, February 24. We left early, soon after breakfast. A beautiful day was in the making. The Western Hills were shrouded in a delicate mist, which had frozen in the trees. An incredible scene awaited us as we approached the old barrier, begun thousands of years before to keep the barbarians out. Poking out of the first battlement we saw not a cannon but an NBC color TV camera. No soldiers were in sight, but the turrets were fully manned by American correspondents and anchormen: Walter Cronkite, Eric Sevareid, Bob Keatley, and Jerrold Schecter, to name a few, wearing bushy fur hats. Parked right up against the Great Wall was a long mobile TV satellite trailer, cables sprouting in all directions.

For me, the vision of the Great Wall wired for worldwide communications was *the* symbol of the visit, dwarfing even the appearance of the President of the United States on China's most famous landmark. Everyone was drunk with the excitement of the moment, resulting in some famous inanities. When asked to comment on the scene, all that President Nixon could manage was, "It's a great wall!"

We also toured the Ming Tombs, a mob scene resembling Sunday afternoon at the Metropolitan Museum of Art. Returning to

Beijing, our session of the counterpart talks featured a strong ex-change between Secretary Rogers and Ji Pengfei on the world situation and America's place in it. The Chinese foreign minister led off with a diatribe against U.S. foreign policy since World War II, which sounded like an old *People's Daily* editorial. Rogers presented our position vigorously in his own words, straight from the shoulder, following to the letter the advice Kissinger had given him in Hawaii. Once both sides had placed on the record their positions on "matters of principle," we moved directly to the room where President Nixon and Premier Zhou had been conducting their talks. They had finished, and members of the three teams who had engaged in substantive discussions stood around chatting, drinking tea, and waiting for an informal, unscheduled Peking duck dinner that Zhou had arranged in Nixon's honor.

## Chatting with Zhou Enlai

I was introduced to Premier Zhou as a speaker of Chinese. We stood face-to-face, and the premier began to talk, quoting in his thick Zhejiang accent a famous Mao poem with the line that one could not be considered a real man until he had been to the Great Wall. Did I think the quote would be appropriate in a toast to President Nixon on the day he had visited the Wall? I was having some difficulty understanding but nodded sagely and uttered a few grunts of comprehension.

"Of course it would be appropriate, Premier Zhou," I blurted, stunned that he had thought it worthwhile to seek out and address the most junior person in the room. As we talked, who should come barging rapidly between us but Henry Kissinger, on his way to the side of President Nixon, who stood about five yards away. That broke up the conversation.

Standing nearby, Ron Ziegler laughed and asked Kissinger if he knew he had just interrupted the premier talking with a member of the U.S. delegation.

Henry muttered in reply that when the president called, he came. "And anyway," he added, looking at me, "who cares?" Kissinger was famously uncomfortable when Americans on his delegations spoke to foreign leaders in languages he did not understand, so I shrugged off his clumsy intervention. In subsequent years he helped me in many ways and showed a kindness that more than made up for this flash of insecurity. The dinner was a small, cozy affair, with everyone seated next to his counterpart. I drew Qian Dayong again, who seemed to have become mine.

Our final day in Beijing, February 25, began with a tour of the Forbidden City, magnificent in the snow, with the grand scale of the public spaces in striking contrast to the intimate dimensions of the Imperial living quarters. There was more shopping, desultory consultations, and an American return banquet at the Great Hall, which was subdued in comparison to the unearthly euphoria of the welcoming affair. Clearly, we had just about run out of things to say and do in the capital of China.

# 10

# Trouble in the U.S. Delegation

## Haggling in Hangzhou

Meanwhile, trouble was brewing for the U.S. delegation. Throughout the visit so far, Henry Kissinger and Deputy Foreign Minister Qiao Guanhua had worked steadily on the wording of the final communiqué. After long and difficult negotiations they agreed on the final form of the artful document that enabled both nations to begin a relationship despite the deep differences that divided them. The device was simple and ingenious; both sides stated their own positions clearly and without agreement, while acknowledging or at least not challenging, broad principles that both could accept. The language of the commonly accepted principles was finally hammered out the night before the president's party left for Hangzhou, submitted to the Standing Committee of the Chinese Communist Party Politburo, and accepted.

The problem was that Secretary Rogers and State Department members of our "united" delegation had not been privy to the negotiations and did not even get a look at the communiqué until we got on the planes for Hangzhou on Saturday, February 26. There were two Russian IL-18s set aside for the American delegation, *PRC One* and *PRC Two*. A freezing wind from the northwest was blowing out of Mongolia as we boarded the small turboprop planes. President Nixon, Rogers, and Green were in *PRC One*. Oblivious to the unfolding drama, along with the rest of the staffers, I struggled onto *PRC Two*, wrestling two large cases of classified documents into postage stamp–sized seats configured for Chinese passengers. The flight from snowy Beijing across the brown North China plain to green Hangzhou took about two hours.

The photo op of the day was a stroll through the lovely park next to legendary West Lake, planted meticulously to provide casual little vistas, through bamboos across lotus floating on ponds at graceful pavilions. Walking with the presidential party and the TV crews, I watched Nixon and Zhou feed the fishes and exchange banter. Little children danced and sang winsome, preplanned, Communist kiddy songs. In a nearby pavilion, I found Rogers, Marshall Green, and Al Jenkins sitting in a grim row, clearly having just had an argument with a furious Henry Kissinger. I was not meant to be part of the discussion, which was clearly over, but the secretary of state handed me a draft of the communiqué marked up with his handwriting and told me to destroy it.

Marshall Green had major problems with the document Rogers was given on *PRC One*, and Rogers agreed he was right. I knew nothing of this and rely here on the memoirs of John Holdridge to tell the story: "Two elements above all caught Marshall Green's eye, and Secretary Rogers relayed them to the president through a reluctant Henry Kissinger. The first, in the section dealing with Taiwan, spoke of 'all people' on either side of the Taiwan Strait regarding Taiwan as part of China."

Green felt this language would erroneously include inhabitants of the island who considered themselves Taiwanese. It was proposed to substitute "Chinese" for the phrase "all people," a fix that the Chinese accepted quickly.

"The other point was more difficult," Holdridge continued. "In the original draft, . . . the United States reaffirmed continued support for the security obligations it maintained with Japan, South Korea," the Philippines, SEATO, and ANZUS, "but no mention was made of U.S. obligations under its security treaty with the Republic of China on Taiwan." Green felt that those in the Republican Party opposed to the president's China trip, particularly Vice President Agnew and Treasury Secretary Connally, would accuse the president of "[selling] Taiwan down the river."[8]

All accounts report that the president blew up when he heard of Rogers's objections, concerned that State Department "nitpicking" after the Chinese had approved the text would endanger the outcome of the visit. But the issues were important, and the president worried about the possibility of returning home with a divided delegation that might argue with each other and ruin the outcome. Kissinger worked late that night with Qiao to deal with the issues before we took off the next morning for Shanghai, the last stop of the trip. Minor adjustments in the text were approved. The Chinese would not allow any reference to our mutual security arrangements with Taiwan to appear in the communiqué. Kissinger made sure to reaffirm those arrangements in response to a planted question at the press conference presenting the communiqué the next day.

## Premier Zhou Calls on Rogers

We flew to Shanghai the morning of February 27. Unaware of the drama the night before, I accompanied Secretary Rogers to his suite on the twelfth floor of the government guesthouse in the Jin Jiang Hotel (a separate Art Deco tower, the now beautifully renovated Grosvenor House). From there we had an overview of the great gray expanse of the city, which had been run down over the years but remained physically the same as photos I had seen taken at the time of the Communist victory in 1949. As we were unpacking, the elevator doors opened without warning and Zhou Enlai stepped out, accompanied by Mao's influential Brooklyn-born interpreter Nancy Tang, Foreign Minister Ji Pengfei, and two vice chairmen of the Shanghai Revolutionary Committee, Wang Hongwen and Zhang Chunqiao, who later gained notoriety along with Madame Mao as members of the "Gang of Four."

"Is Secretary Rogers in?" Zhou asked.

"Of course. Let me tell him you are here, Premier Zhou."

"Be right out." Rogers said when I knocked on his door and told him who had come to call.

For a prime minister to call unannounced on a cabinet officer of a visiting head of state in his hotel suite was unheard of. We were in the land where protocol was invented. Rogers, who was as surprised as I, emerged to greet Zhou in the most natural and affable manner, and the two men moved in to the sitting room, where tea awaited on tables beside the stuffed chairs. The staff certainly had known someone was coming.

The sun was streaming in the windows as we sat down. I peeked at the others from the Shanghai Revolutionary Committee of whom I had read much but never seen. Wang Hongwen, in his mid-thirties, had risen fast through the Party ranks, earning the nickname "helicopter" in the Red Guard press. He was nattily attired in a tailored Mao suit and shiny calf-length black leather boots. In stark, proletarian contrast, Foreign Minister Ji was a classic, gnarled, Long Marcher, whose long underwear curled out below his baggy trouser cuffs. Zhang Chunqiao had a long intelligent face that betrayed no trace of emotion. Nancy Tang, with her cute bobbed hair, chirped away in idiomatic English. Zhou Enlai was all smiles.

Secretary Rogers began by asking Zhou how he thought the visit had gone. Zhou replied it had been beneficial and asked if there had been any reaction from people opposed the visit. He was aware from his channels that there were still some in America who did not understand it. "We have our Goldwaters, too," Zhou continued. "We are explaining the visit carefully to them, and did so before you came." Rogers asked about television and radio news of the visit.

Zhou replied that coverage had been extensive worldwide. The Chinese government, he continued, read the world press carefully. He described the layered system of publications, *Reference News, Reference Materials,* and the even more detailed daily publication for the top leaders, which kept the Party informed (exactly as defector William White had told us in 1966, as recounted in chapter 4). Mao was the most careful reader, Zhou said, and spotted the Nixon *Foreign Affairs* article in 1967. He underlined it in red and told us, "This is important." (Emperors invariably used vermilion pencils in notes to their ministers, I recalled.) "Mao voted for Nixon in spirit," Zhou added, smiling, "although, of course he did not approve of all his policies."

Rogers said he anticipated criticism of the trip. The president had made a statement that there could be no news without controversy, and he expected attacks. But these would neither reflect nor affect U.S. policy. Zhou said he understood. Marshal Green would be visiting several countries in Asia to explain our policy, Rogers continued, and he himself would be briefing ambassadors and appearing before Congress. We must be able to tell everyone that we stood up for our principles. Zhou indicated his understanding of the point and assured Rogers of China's interest in gradually normalizing its relationship with the United States.

Rogers said he was deeply impressed by the premier's command of details and his ability to relate them to the big picture. He reiterated his interest, as earlier expressed to the foreign minister, in establishing direct telephone links. Zhou replied that the foreign minister had been late in telling him about this request. An answer would be forthcoming.

And so the extraordinary meeting ended—and remained a secret for decades. When the premier and his party had left, Rogers asked me, "What was that all about?"

I told him I thought Zhou was trying to make up for the exclusion of Rogers from the meeting with Mao. With hindsight, we now know that the Chinese were deeply concerned about potential splits in the American delegation. Zhou paid the call, in part, to see for himself how deep they might be. In the event, he had little to worry about.

## End Game—The Shanghai Communiqué

The visit was winding down. I called home from Shanghai, taking advantage of the extraordinary free White House communications service to stay in touch with Sheila and the boys, and to try out the new RCA satellite station that had been specially installed in Shanghai for the visit. The connection was so clear that I could hear our dog barking outside the kitchen door and startled my wife by suggesting that she go and let him in. The Chinese asked that we leave the station behind and later bought it. The other station erected in Beijing was already being taken down for shipment home.

On the morning of February 28, Secretary Rogers held a final round of counterpart talks with Foreign Minister Ji, which revisited earlier proposals on exchanges and channels of communication. The two men broke no new ground but laid the institutional foundation for future contact, specifically designating umbrella organizations like the National Committee on U.S.-China Relations, which had handled the Ping-Pong exchanges the previous year, as coordinating agents. The Chinese did not want to commit themselves at this point to communicating through their new mission at the United Nations or through special phone links. They agreed that we could announce that a selected group of firms would be invited to the next Canton Trade Fair but thought it premature to establish trade offices on the Japan model.

Exchange of language materials was agreed. The Chinese had remarked lightly that our interpreter, Charles Freeman, had used "feudal" terminology. We noted that both languages had changed in the decades since we had had relations and discussed ways of updating our usage.

Rogers designated Marshall Green as the person responsible for follow-up, in consultation with the White House. He closed with a vote of thanks to the Chinese for the flawless planning and execution of an historic trip and pledged to do everything in his power to avoid misunderstandings as the governments moved forward. He stressed the importance of maintaining momentum with gradual but concrete actions, lest the visit end up being judged only a "euphoric event."

The Shanghai Communiqué was issued the afternoon of February 28 at the theater on the grounds of the Jin Jiang Hotel, where Henry Kissinger and Marshall Green conducted the briefing. The national security adviser took pains to reassert the existing mutual security arrangements between the United States and the government on Taiwan in response to the carefully planted question. Neither the president nor the secretary of state attended the press briefing. I spent this historic moment where I was supposed to be, assisting William P. Rogers, who needed my advice on which of several available models of panda bear souvenir figures would make the greatest hit with his grandchildren.

## Meeting Richard Nixon

At the banquet that night that formally ended the visit, Nixon toasted the "week that changed the world." A meeting later that evening gave me an inkling of how it would change my life.

I had remarked to Secretary Rogers earlier that I felt strange having met most of the Chinese leadership but not my own president. He invited me to attend a meeting in President Nixon's suite at 10:30 that evening. The agenda concerned the positions Marshall

Green and John Holdridge would take with the different Asian leaders they would be briefing on the results of the visit, as they flew throughout Asia while the rest of the party returned to Washington.

As related in this book's Prologue, I arrived early, along with Secretary Rogers, to find the president sitting in a flowered silk dressing gown over an open-collar shirt and trousers, a long, fat cigar in one hand and a tall scotch and soda in the other. He looked drained but satisfied with what he had accomplished. What an extraordinary-looking man he was up close! Huge head, small body, duck feet, puffy cheeks, "about three walnuts apiece," my notes indicated, and pendant jowls hanging down, the entire combination exuding authority. The president's chief of staff, the close-cropped H. R. Haldemann, was there, with yellow legal pad and a fistful of sharp pencils. Green and Holdridge arrived a bit later, and the discussion began.

The president, I was impressed to note, did most of the talking. He shaped the approach to be taken with each leader, whether from Japan, Taiwan, or the Philippines, based on his own knowledge and relationship with each. "Tell them the president says . . . ," adding a personal message for each. He predicted a generally favorable reaction from Asia's leaders. Only Taiwan had reason for disappointment. However, Chiang Kai-shek could be confident that we would maintain our security commitment. Our 9,000-man force stationed in Taiwan was not important in the grand scheme of things, especially when compared with the 450,000 we had in Vietnam. Anyway, Nixon concluded, where else could he turn? The president implied from his remarks that he was well aware of the difficulties his China visit would cause for the Soviets.

His performance was a tour de force, and confirmed for me Nixon's reputation as the great foreign policy president of his time. As the meeting came to an end, he made a point of thanking each of us for our work. Secretary Rogers introduced me to the president as one of the new China specialists in the State Department. I told Nixon that I had spent ten years preparing for this trip and was grateful to him for making it happen.

He accompanied me to the door of his suite, placing an avuncular flowered arm on my shoulder as we went. "Well," he said, "you China boys are going to have a lot more to do from now on."

The departure scene at the airport next morning could not have been more different from our somber arrival. There was no protocol at all. Everyone milled about, Chinese and Americans, saying cheerful good-byes, without a clue as to when we might meet and see each other again. We flew home to a noisy and enthusiastic welcome at Andrews Air Force Base, confirmation that Nixon's bold gamble and his staff's careful media planning had paid off. My own family was included in the welcome, which gave the event a special excitement and joy.

## Dealing with the Disgruntled

We arrived in Washington at night on Tuesday, February 29, and were at work early the next morning. Rogers's first priority was to brief senior State Department officers on the results of the visit. He was angry about media reports of grumping at State about the trip. The president of the United States, he began, had just returned from a great historic visit to China, the results of which he believed to be in the best interests of the country. He felt the Department of State played a significant role in the success of the trip. What does he read? Our morale is bad. We were cut out. We are depressed. What would he like to read? The department is happy with the results of the trip and providing strong support for the president.

President Nixon, Rogers went on, also got depressed from time to time, but did not wear it on his sleeve. Drawing on his old friendship with the president, Rogers recounted several occasions in a long career, particularly after Nixon's loss in California, when the press buried him alive and upset his family. Nixon did not let those occasions get him down. Rogers had trouble with the concept that morale is like temperature. Supporting Nixon was what would help morale the most.

"What troubles me, from our standpoint," Rogers said, "is the Mao meeting." He explained his absence in the context of Mao's fragile health. Mao was supposed to go to Hangzhou, presumably for wider meetings, but had caught cold and could not go. So the quick initial meeting was arranged instead. From that point on, Rogers spent more time with the head of government on this visit than on any other past summit. Premier Zhou was with him for more than an hour and a half on the plane to Hangzhou and came to see him in Shanghai.

Rogers said he was happy with the outcome of the visit and felt the State Department deserved a lot of credit. It was the best of the five summit meetings he had attended. He had spent a lot of time with the president on the way out to China. Obviously, Henry Kissinger was going to do the negotiating, but we worked with him on the communiqué and gave our views.

Rogers concluded with a rundown on the counterpart meetings, his desire to develop practical momentum for the new relationship through exchanges, and some random impressions of the visit. *The Red Detachment of Women* was "inexcusable." Zhou Enlai was a "bundle of nerves," in command of every detail. Mainland society struck him as "spiritless." The system on Taiwan worked better.

I doubt that the Rogers briefing had much impact one way or another on attitudes in the department. Certainly, "China boys" like myself were excited and upbeat about the visit, as were many people throughout America. Invitations for speaking engagements poured in to everyone connected with the trip, from baggage handlers on up. My bosses wanted me back at work and let me accept only one. I chose Brigham Young University, in part for its strong missionary connections and Asian language programs, but most of all for its proximity to the legendary powder snow at Alta, Utah. I gave a speech to a large audience of students and faculty, presented the university with copies of the *People's Daily* covering the historic week, did radio and television interviews in Salt Lake City, and then met Sheila at the Alta Lodge in Little Cottonwood Canyon, the first of many visits. It was our first time off together since Secretary Rogers called me to his office six intense, unforgettable weeks before.

# 11

# Birth of the Bruce Mission

Back at work in the Secretariat, there was an immediate flurry of follow-up action to work out interagency guidelines for trade, travel, and exchanges with the People's Republic of China. These were set forth in National Security Study Memoranda 148 and 149, which listed approaches to the Chinese in the order of attractiveness to them. Arguments with the Pentagon over trade were, as always, emotional. The Department of Defense was against selling anything to the Chinese that might make them stronger, and that included practically everything. Secretary Rogers, remembering the fingerprinting dispute during his talks in Beijing, was particularly intent on developing visa procedures that would accommodate Chinese sensitivities. There was also talk of beefing up our China expertise at the U.S. Embassy in Paris, with the possibility of establishing a U.S. Interests Section in Paris in a friendly country's embassy, a form of diplomatic halfway house, which would provide a cockpit of contact with the PRC

I had no inkling that fourteen months later, I would be on my way with a handful of other Foreign Service "China Boys" to open the U.S. Liaison Office in Beijing, our first diplomatic presence in China in over two decades. My plan, after finishing in the Secretariat a few months later, was to take a year of Japanese language training in Yokohama, followed by assignment to Embassy Tokyo as deputy to the political counselor. The concept of using expertise on China as a base for a broader Asian capability had taken shape for me. I had visited Tokyo a number of times as a China analyst and found fascinating the way Japanese had taken Chinese cultural influences to form their own distinctive style. The old family ties with the Doshisha in Kyoto also exerted a pull for me. Secretariat officers usually got what they wanted, and these requests struck my bosses as sound, even modest. All this would eventually happen, but hardly as planned.

## Explaining the Paris Peace Accords

One of Richard Nixon's reasons for moving toward China had been to facilitate an end to the war in Vietnam and the U.S. role in the conflict. Chinese support for his strategic objectives never amounted to more than a tacit understanding to stay out of the way. In fact, Beijing had objected strongly to his tactics, including the bombing of Hanoi and the invasion of Cambodia. Finally, after a long and tortured process, which straddled Nixon's reelection in November 1972, U.S. and Vietnamese negotiators reached agreement on the Paris Peace Accords to end the war and signed them on January 23, 1973, three days after the inauguration ceremonies for Nixon's second term. The president decided to send Vice President Agnew on a lightning trip to brief the leaders of Southeast Asia on the agreement. I was assigned to provide Secretariat support.

The trip began in haste and ended in frenzy. On Wednesday afternoon, January 24, at 5 P.M., I was told we were leaving for eight countries (Vietnam, Laos, Cambodia, Thailand, Malaysia, Singapore, Indonesia, and the Philippines) the following Sunday morning and to start getting the papers ready the next day, a federal holiday marking the funeral of President Harry S. Truman. The holiday turned out to be a blessing, providing the concerned desks of the State Department some quiet time to do a quick job. By Saturday noon, the briefing papers were ready, and I delivered them to the Executive Office Building, where General Mike Dunn, the vice president's national security advisor, and John Negroponte, the NSC staff member assigned to the trip, were waiting. Dunn said he was anxious to project the image of a working trip. "Substantively, it's a hand-holder," he said. I rushed home to pack. *Air Force Two* left Andrews AFB early the next morning.

## The NSC and State—Finally Working Together

Once the plane door had closed, Negroponte and I did something unheard of: we handed each other the State and NSC briefing books we had each assembled. John was a longtime friend and Foreign Service colleague from the East Asia Bureau (later deputy secretary of state, director of national intelligence, U.S. ambassador to Iraq, and U.S. permanent representative to the United Nations). The NSC had, as expected, prepared a separate set of papers for each stop. Normally, NSC staff members, trembling at the thought of White House wrath, would tightly protect any materials they produced.

I suggested to John that we pool our efforts and prepare one coordinated book for Agnew, saving him (and General Dunn) the chore of wading through two sets of material and sorting out the differences. He readily agreed. Not a fearful type in any case, John was on his last assignment for Kissinger and would leave the NSC staff after this trip. We spent the next hours in the flight, reading each other's papers, deciding which were better and which the vice president should use.

The NSC papers for the Indochina stops were models of clarity and authority. I sat goggle-eyed, reading the memoranda of conversations General Alexander Haig had conducted just the week before on the impending Paris agreements with the heads of government in Vietnam (Nguyen Van Thieu), Laos (Souvanna Phouma), Cambodia (Lon Nol), and Thailand (Thanom Kittikachorn). These were extraordinary documents—free flowing, almost verbatim, laced with Haig's toughness and humor. Two main points emerged, as my notes record:

> 1. Hanoi *was* bombed back to the conference table. As Haig put it, when you are dealing with a mule (Hanoi), you have to hit him between the eyes with a baseball bat (the Christmas B-52 bombings of Hanoi/Haiphong) to make him more flexible.
> 2. If South Vietnam would not come along, we would sign alone, and no further aid would be forthcoming from the US. The argument was that the Congress and the American people would not stand for new aid appropriations for

Saigon without a peace agreement. The message was clear: no signature, no help.

In turn, the State Department papers for the Southeast Asian countries (Singapore, Malaysia, Indonesia, and the Philippines) were fuller and more up-to-date. In some cases, NSC staffers had simply taken the State papers, superimposed their own NSC letterhead, and imported them into their books. For the first time in my experience, the State Department and the NSC were cooperating at a level of trust that made for maximum effectiveness. Dunn, a bureaucrat of great sophistication, saw what was happening and approved. What we were doing would strengthen the performance of his boss. From then on, I was shown the back-channel traffic from the White House direct to the vice president's party and given an opportunity to play a role close in.

This was heady stuff and great fun. Negroponte and I rewrote all of Agnew's public statements en route at 30,000 feet. The Saigon arrival statement, which raised press eyebrows for its toughness, was based in part on a blunt letter from Nixon to Thieu that Negroponte was hand-carrying. During the flight, John shared some of his views on the Paris negotiations, in which he had been intimately involved from the outset. He was also thoroughly familiar both with Kissinger's discussions with the Chinese on Indochina and with the results of General Haig's recent swings through Southeast Asia.

As an experienced Vietnam hand who had served in Saigon for years, Negroponte worried that we were letting the countries of the area down. He remembered Henry Kissinger's getting onto the Embassy elevator during his last trip to Saigon and saying, with his characteristic owlish leer, "I've screwed so many people, I ought to open a whorehouse." John also said that there had been real arguments within the small inner circle of advisors around Kissinger—Peter Rodman, John Holdridge, Alexander Haig, Jonathan Howe, and Winston Lord—as to whether to go for a comprehensive agreement or a simpler bilateral agreement with Hanoi.

### Breakthrough for Liaison Offices

After we had finished holding hands in Southeast Asia that February, Henry Kissinger returned from another visit to Beijing, to our surprise and delight, with an agreement to establish Liaison Offices in Beijing and Washington on an urgent basis. These were just the kind of diplomatic halfway houses, somewhere between embassies and private offices, we had speculated about. The move was at China's initiative, way ahead of any American timetable. John Holdridge's best guess was that Zhou Enlai, pressured by domestic political infighting that was growing as Mao's health and that of Zhou himself deteriorated, sought to give more permanence to the opening with the United States.[9]

For me, and other eligible China Boys, the following weeks were agony as we waited to find out who would staff the new office. State Department recommendations had gone to the White House through the Secretariat. I knew I was on the list. My bosses were asking me how I planned to train my successor and how quickly I could do so. Then the president announced that Ambassador David Bruce would lead the mission. We also learned that Al Jenkins and John Holdridge would both be his deputies. Two deputy chiefs of mission? That was a new one. Originally, Jenkins and Holdridge were supposed to lead the Liaison Office as numbers one and two. But the Chinese had raised the stakes by naming their most senior diplomat, Huang Zhen, former ambassador to France and the only member of the Chinese Foreign Service to survive the Cultural Revolution unscathed. Kissinger needed an American of equivalent stature, and Bruce, a close friend, was clearly the right person. Former U.S. ambassador in Paris, Bonn, and London under three presidents, he had headed the delegation to the Paris Peace Talks just concluded.

Where did all this leave me? The mission was top heavy with political officers. Kissinger's early reaction was to "drop Platt." But Jenkins, Holdridge, and David Bruce himself lobbied for my inclusion. On March 26, Roger Sullivan, then in charge of the Mainland China Desk, called to say I would be going to Beijing as chief of the Political Section. Joy.

## Meeting David Bruce

I planned to leave for Beijing in a month and spent more and more time at the Mainland Desk. David Bruce arrived to start reading in.

Two weeks helping him answer his mail and setting up his appointments showed me what a bright and happy choice he was. There had been some question about Bruce's age, whether he was still up to par. In fact, he was just the right age, a little older than Zhou, a little younger than Mao.

My notes recall,

> Bruce was entirely whole upstairs, his famous sense of humor intact, wit pouring softly and clearly out of his marvelous, lined, lived-in face. I came into his office one morning while he was reading a CIA report on the health of the Chinese leadership. He was laughing aloud at the long list of conditions and complaints, from Chiang Kai-shek's pneumonia to Mao's emphysema and arterial sclerosis, to Zhou's stretched capacities. Reading a sentence that said Zhou had reached the stage where the addition of any more duties left him confused and exhausted, Bruce commented 'I know just how he feels.' David Bruce is the most comfortable of creatures. He will do very well.

**The Chinese Come to Town**

Shortly before I left for China that April, the Chinese Liaison Office advance party arrived in Washington. It included Deputy Chief Han Xu, who had managed the Nixon visit as Chief of Protocol; Qian Dayong, formerly deputy head of the American Desk in the Foreign Ministry and my counterpart during the Nixon Visit; Ji Chaoju, Zhou Enlai's interpreter, and others.

Bruce welcomed the Chinese with a dinner at his house. The guest list included Henry Kissinger, General Brent Scowcroft, Win Lord, John Holdridge, Richard Solomon, and Commander Jonathan Howe from the White House and, from the State Department, Deputy Assistant Secretary Arthur Hummel (later ambassador to China), Roger Sullivan, and me. Bruce had been worried about the food and asked my advice. I said stuff them with a good American dinner. Pay them back for what they did to us in China, where we had been wined and dined to within an inch of our lives and waistlines. Bruce let them have it with both barrels; crabmeat imperial, Chicken Kiev, endive, a super-rich chocolate pudding, red and white wine and champagne.

I was at Dr. Kissinger's table with Holdridge, Qian, Ji, Dick Solomon, Art Hummel, and a bun-faced bagman named Wang, who knew no English. Henry was unaccustomed, he joked as he sat down, to dining with so many State Department people. My notes reflect that he spent most of his time reminiscing about earlier contacts with the Chinese to Ji Chaoju, who had participated in all the talks. I got Henry's usual sweet and sour treatment. Greeting me most pleasantly, he asked when I was leaving for Beijing. He hoped that when I had gone "Alsop would get off [his] back." Joe had written him a letter about me, I was horrified to learn, early on in the process of choosing the USLO staff. When Alsop did his homework, Kissinger added, he was the finest reporter in town and had a tough, first-class mind. Again, Henry displayed his irritation with Americans talking Chinese in his presence and asked point-edly whether moon-faced Wang, with whom I was chatting, spoke any English. Later, rising to depart, he announced "I am leaving early, so everyone has a chance to say bad things about me."

Bruce enjoyed himself enormously. He liked the idea of having the Chinese to his house; they were at their most charming, and he found them "cozy," a word I had not heard applied to Chinese before. He told a bemused Han Xu an incomprehensible story about an American who wore a flower in his buttonhole while foxhunt-ing. Bruce gave a graceful toast welcoming the Chinese to his coun-try and his house. If we could not develop a relationship, given the good will and inclination of the peoples and governments on both sides, he said, we would have ourselves to blame. Han replied with a natural speech of thanks for the friendly "family party." At the end, the ambassador saw them off, standing on the Georgetown brick sidewalk, and, with only minimal prompting from me, waved (in best Chinese fashion) until their limousine was out of sight. We were all suffering from end-stage euphoria.

**The Longest Day**

The trip from Hong Kong to Beijing took up all of a long, long May 2. In 1973, the only way Americans in Asia could enter China was to cross the wooden railroad bridge separating the border village of Lo Wu from sleepy Shenzhen (now a city of more than three million). Then a train took us to Guangzhou, where we caught a plane for Shanghai and Beijing. My secretary, Lucille Zaelit, and four Marine Security Guards accompanied me.

The day was steaming hot and we were all sweating and excited. Friendly China Travel Service officials helped us cope with twenty-nine pieces of baggage and freight and ushered us into a private waiting room, where I gave the Marines their first Chinese lesson, an uproarious session that focused on, "Hello, how are you? Where is the bathroom?" They were a handpicked group of enthusiastic and earnest young men, the first U.S. Marines to return to China in twenty-three years.

The two-hour train ride to Guangzhou was straight out of a Pearl Buck novel, past brilliant green fields of young rice, water buffaloes, burial bone pots like those on the other side of border, and farm women in wide straw hats. The six of us crossed muggy, seedy Guangzhou to the airport in taxis groaning with luggage. At the airport I ran into Pakistan ambassador Agha Shahi (later foreign minister), who wanted to know all about the U.S. Liaison Office and how David Bruce would be greeted when he arrived in ten days time. He wanted me to apologize to Bruce for not being in Beijing at that time.

We flew to Shanghai in a four-engine Russian Ilyushin 62 jet. I sat next to two friendly foreign department cadres from Anhui province, who assured me that the Cultural Revolution was purely ideological and had had no effect on their daily lives. Straining not to laugh out loud, I focused on their carry-on luggage, which consisted almost entirely of green bananas. Newspaper columnist Marquis Childs and his wife were also on the plane but out of touch with the latest news. They were appalled to hear of the Watergate scandal now dominating the United States.

Our layover in Shanghai reminded me of an old-fashioned Greyhound bus stop. The plane landed, parked, everyone got out, including flight crew and the cabin attendants, who turned out the lights. We repaired to the terminal restaurant, where dinner was served. After the pilot finished eating, the airplane lights were turned on, passengers boarded, and off we flew to Beijing. Arriving after dark, we were met by Chas Freeman (our interpreter during the Nixon visit, now helping for a few days with the opening of the post) and Bob Blackburn, the administrative officer, who had preceded us by about a week. They drove us past the building site for USLO (near the present St. Regis Hotel), where workmen were swarming under lights, and around Tiananmen Square to our new home at the Beijing Hotel.

## Gritty Realities

Ordinary life in Beijing contrasted starkly with the carefully programmed glitter of the Nixon visit. Our first office was in two rooms on the ninth floor of the Russian wing of the Beijing Hotel, with windows looking west over the golden roofs of the Forbidden City. Our living quarters were along the same hallway, which was lit and ventilated by transoms above the doorways, from which every sound escaped. Family arguments, body noises, policy discussions—we heard them all. With only a few of us in residence, this was manageable, but when the rest of the staff arrived, the din would become unbearable, and a major morale issue.

The staff of the hotel, infused with Socialist work ethic, moved at a lethargic pace. The local saying "work or not, you get 36 *yuan*" (the frozen minimum wage) infected the entire nonfarm economy. In the countryside, where 80 percent of Chinese lived, you worked hard or starved. The front entrance of the hotel was grand enough to stage a performance of *Aida*, but the elephants would soon have been covered with the fine layer of Gobi Desert dust that permeated everything in the Chinese capital.

In the days that followed, I called on Chinese officials at the Foreign Ministry and their Diplomatic Service Bureau, the government organ that managed every aspect of our lives, and made friends with members of the local diplomatic corps, particularly the Brits, who greeted us with open arms and went out of their way to show us the ropes. Richard Samuel, Michael Richardson, and Elizabeth Wright, China hands who later rose to high rank in the Foreign Office, shared their rich stores of local lore, including knowledge of the best restaurants and picnic spots at the Ming Tombs. Canadians and Australians, led by their new ambassador, Steve Fitzgerald, a contemporary who studied Chinese in Hong Kong when I was there, made me feel at home.

My most important immediate task was to negotiate with hard-nosed cadres at the Number One Flag Factory the shape, material, price, and delivery dates of drapes for David Bruce's temporary residence at the Nine Story Building in the Sanlitun diplomatic area. I also bought some furniture for USLO at local stores. After years of arcane, long-distance China analysis and policy formulation, these gritty, hands-on tasks gave me a satisfying sense of dealing with reality. I also spent time at the USLO permanent building site, where 250 workmen, spurred by a poster on the wall that said "Grasp Revolution—Promote Production," were charging around under the watchful eyes of construction experts from the U.S. Navy Seabees. The Seabees told me they were amazed at the quality of Chinese joiner work and plastering. Arranging treatment for a case of the clap contracted, in record time, by one of our Marines also occupied my attention.

As chief of the political section, my responsibilities included liaison with the U.S. press. What became a flood of interviews had already begun, along with pressure for permanent media representation. During these first days, I spent time with Keyes Beech of the Chicago Daily News, Jack Reynolds and a camera crew from NBC TV, and, of course, Stan Karnow, to name just a few.

# 12

# The Liaison Office Starts Work

## Beijing by Bike

Official calls excepted, I went everywhere on the bicycle I bought the day after I arrived, a heavy, old-fashioned, Shanghai Phoenix, British racing green with a sonorous and commanding bell. The Liaison Office had a small motor pool, but the drivers' hours were limited and rides had to be arranged well in advance. On one early errand, I biked out to the Capital Zoo to make inquiries on behalf of the Steinhart Aquarium in California about an obscure freshwater species called the Yangzi River Dolphin. There were no dolphins at all (the species is nearly extinct), but I got a good first look at the west city. It struck me as poorer than the east and less interesting.

The Chinese capital in 1973 was dusty and down-at-the-heels, for all its ancient and well-kept splendors. The bleak and cramped way of life had food as its only obvious pleasure for the people and, less obviously, sex, although no one went out of their way to be very attractive. To the contrary, drab, patched, baggy clothing was the fashion in the waning days of the Mao era.

But I found myself bowled over by the beauty of local speech. Having been educated that the Beijing dialect is the purest of all Chinese, I was still surprised to find every urchin in the street sounding like a grand concubine. Even insults were elegant. One kid I almost ran into in a lane shouted after me, "*Cao nin ma!*" His use of the honorific possessive *nin* transformed the gross expletive into "Fuck thine honorable mother!"

One of my earliest messages to Washington summarized the local scene that spring, as quoted in David Bruce's *Beijing Diaries*:

Peking is a cyclist's town. The best way for a foreigner to move around and see things is on two wheels, which carry him fast enough to avoid collecting a crowd, and slow enough to observe life and chat with other bikers, all of whom wobble along at roughly the same pace....

*The Pace of Life.* This is a busy city during the hours that the Chinese use it. Society operates from dawn to dusk, not much before and precious little after. The restaurants are empty by seven, when most of us are prepared to eat. But at six they are full and doing a roaring trade in all the good things the city is famous for. There are traffic jams and rush hours at opening and close of business, with flocks of ringing bicycles flowing around horse-drawn carts. Double-length buses edge not so gingerly out from the right into the blue flow of bikes, while speeding cars, honking to announce their whereabouts, form a hazard to the left. Stray pedestrians add more imponderables to an already complicated scene. Shoppers throng the stores and the shopping streets. This is all over by suppertime. There follows a short period of life in the streets, where teenagers play cards in the shallow pools of light under street lamps, and lovers nestle on Rectitude Road and other dark spots. Then the night belongs to the water trucks hosing down the dusty streets and the long lines of limousines pulling away in silence from banquets at the Great Hall of the People.

*The Attitude of the People.* The Chinese in Peking are quite nice to each other these days. One girl who had just fallen flat on her chest in the street off her bicycle after being sideswiped by two adolescent boys stood up, dusted herself off, and though blushing with rage, told them sweetly, "You know, I thought that was your fault." Others are polite, leave room for each other, and swear only rarely at cars. Policemen, however, back on their stands for some time after years in limbo during the Cultural Revolution, seem as rude as if the great upheaval had never happened. They bellow through bullhorns at all intersections and wave their arms. No one seems to pay much attention, which may explain their behavior.

The Chinese are also quite nice to foreigners on bicycles. Somehow it is less threatening to talk moving along at nine miles an hour than on foot. One young secretary at an embassy here reported that a man rode up level with her as she was pedaling home one evening, turned to her, opened his mouth, sang an unintelligible but pretty song, and then dropped back not to appear again. The reporting officer, cycling near Peking University, asked directions from a round gray cadre in sandals and was answered in slow but flawless English. When asked where he had learned it, the cadre, who turned out to be an electrical engineer at the university, said, "From Hollywood movies." "That must have been a long time ago." "Yes," came the fading reply as he pedaled off into a side road.

The image of Chinese Communist discipline remains intact, though marred at times by very human touches. The children march singing to events at the People's Stadium, behind fluttering red flags. But once when an empty bus pulled up to a stop near one militant group wearing Red Guard armbands, all ranks broke and scrambled aboard. The People's Liberation Army appears to have the respect of the populace. But one little boy dressed in shorts and a blue and white striped shirt could not help but dance up and down and shout derisive cadences when a company swung past near the Peking Hotel last week.

*The Shape of the City.* Many of the street signs removed during the Cultural Revolution are still down, making it hard sometimes for the newcomer to find his way. The signs are gradually being replaced, and none of the radical names are coming back. Many of the public buildings have placards which identify them, however. The lanes (*hutongs*) that lace the city are readily accessible and are as quaint and interesting to the newly arrived American as they were to the old hands. Life there appears to go on much as it always has. The city is almost as clean as everyone says, despite the fact that children relieve themselves with impunity through customary split pants, and spitting definitely remains a practice in People's China. The public monuments and treasures are carefully kept and vigorously enjoyed by a population that seriously takes its Sundays off. The only problem at this time of year is dust—especially from the great shelter-subway excavations that dot the city. It blows everywhere and sometimes rises to hide the sun. Everyone is covered with it, especially the cyclist.

*Supplies.* The shops are full of goods, and people appear to be buying, particularly the simple things. Vegetables are everywhere, even dumped down on corners and hawked loudly to people going home in the evenings. The corner markets appear to be free, but several bikers pedaling along, back-wheel racks festooned with radishes and leeks, have assured the reporting officer that the impromptu trade is totally government run.[10]

Cycling broke the membrane of isolation surrounding foreign diplomats. During USLO's early months, we scheduled regular biking hours every Wednesday afternoon, the first and probably the last U.S. diplomatic establishment to do such a thing. Though we worked Saturday mornings to make up for our midweek excursions, the practice came to an end when we moved into permanent quarters and conventional bureaucratic practices resumed their grip.

**The Policy Context**

During my first week, I had a long talk with Australian ambassador Steve Fitzgerald about the future of China and the current status of relations. We both agreed that this was a particularly key time to be here. I told him I thought the recent Chinese decision to accept long-term credits to finance foreign trade was particularly significant. The Chinese could not have made the decision without deciding to change the way they managed their economy. The old conservative methods—pay as you go, no foreign debt, no domestic debt—are finished. Fundamental principles must have been debated. Do we want ideological purity or economic development, or both? How much of each? The latest decision would surely benefit development, but purity must suffer as foreign influences borne on the winds of foreign purchases blow once again into the Central Kingdom. I told Steve that what we were seeing could be as significant for China as the Meiji Restoration had been for Japan in 1868.

Steve felt that Zhou Enlai was moving more and more toward the past in developing his policies toward the rest of the world. I disagreed, arguing that he was looking to the future, trying to set China onto irreversible paths, building, like the traditional Chinese gentleman that he was, the historic coffin in which he would like to lie.

Clearly, the core issues that had divided the Chinese leadership since they took power in 1949 and that had led to the Cultural Revolution in 1966 remained unresolved. The competition between realist "experts" and revolutionary "reds" had, if anything, intensified as Mao's health continued to fade. Madame Mao and her Shanghai cohorts led the radicals and still controlled the media. Party Secretary Deng Xiaoping, just rehabilitated, Vice Premier Li Xiannian, and the military men who ran the provinces were on the side of pragmatism. So was Zhou, whose role, as always, was to be the balance wheel that kept the Chinese body politic from flying apart. The tension that infused the leadership, which was prevalent throughout the early life of USLO, would remain a feature of life in the capital until Mao died in 1976.

## An Odd Table of Organization

In addition to Ambassador Bruce, his deputies Al Jenkins and John Holdridge, and me, the roster of the Liaison Office would comprise only seven officers: my deputy in the political section, Don Anderson (later consul general in Shanghai and Hong Kong); Herb Horowitz, chief of the Economic Section (later ambassador to the Gambia); and his assistant Bill Rope (who became a deputy assistant secretary of state). Other key figures included CIA Station Chief James Lilley, ostensibly a member of the Political Section but actually the manager of the special communication channel between Bruce and the White House (later ambassador to China and to Korea); Brunson McKinley, Bruce's aide; Robert Blackburn, who was responsible for consular and administrative affairs; and Virginia Schaeffer, the budget and fiscal officer (later ambassador to

Papua New Guinea). Each section had a secretary. Lucille Zaelit, a smart, friendly, funny, and flexible member of State's elite staff, was mine. The five-man Marine Guard detachment rounded out the initial table of organization.

The Liaison Office in Beijing would be unique in U.S. diplomatic annals, a small embassy in everything but name, staffed by Foreign Service professionals, most of whom knew the language. We would be denied the formal responsibilities of attending functions at the Great Hall of the People for visiting foreign leaders; but otherwise we could participate in the diplomatic life of the Chinese capital, complete with diplomatic license plates, ready access to the Foreign Ministry, and the right to fly our flag.

USLO would also be unique for having two deputy chiefs of mission, an arrangement without precedent or since repeated in the Foreign Service. The double deputy arrangement would present the mission with a variety of peculiar problems until Al Jenkins retired in 1974. While I was in Beijing, the deputies focused their attention on Ambassador Bruce and each other, leaving de facto management of the post to the section chiefs—Herb Horowitz, Bob Blackburn, and me. There was little overt friction, only an awkward sense of discomfort in the ranks, and one additional hazard to bear in mind as we navigated daily life and work. Bruce admired both DCMs, and they him. Henry Kissinger liked the arrangement, too. He had invented it because he needed his own trusted representative, John Holdridge, as DCM to manage the direct channel from the White House to USLO and Bruce. Jenkins was the senior FSO in protocol terms and had expected to lead the mission before Bruce was appointed. He had Kissinger's trust but was in Beijing more as a symbol of State Department participation in the opening to China than as an operator in the tight White House loop.

Housing our odd couple was an issue of special delicacy for the Chinese. Each mission was allotted one seven-room apartment for its deputy chief in the Nine-Story Building at the Sanlitun Diplomatic Compound. Both of our deputies felt entitled to one. The Chinese agreed at first, postponing the issue. But as more and more foreign embassies arrived in China, the pressure would grow until it affected the housing and, indeed, the morale of our entire staff.

Jenkins arrived May 10. Already a grizzled veteran after a week in Beijing, I gave him a tour of the temporary offices and residence the next day, and took him to meet the acting director of protocol, Zhu Quanxian, a charming young man who had served as Han Xu's deputy. We discussed the arrangements for the Bruce arrival. In contrast to the United States and most countries other than France, China assigned its most capable officers to protocol work. When I asked why, the answer was crisp and clear. A substantive mistake can always be fixed with words, but protocol errors are most often irrevocable.

That evening at dinner, Al voiced concern over the division of labor between himself and John Holdridge. I replied that we would have to develop a mechanism that would keep both of them aware of everything that was going on and of each other's views. Al said, "Well, we're both adults. It will work out." He then went on to worry about office procedures and precedents being decided while he was absent. He would be going home soon to make a speech and receive an honorary degree from his alma mater, Emory University. I told him simply to make his worries plain.

David and Evangeline Bruce arrived in Peking the evening of May 14, following much the same tortuous route that I had from Hong Kong. They were accompanied by John Holdridge and the Brunson McKinleys and met by Zhang Wenjin and a gaggle of lesser Foreign Ministry people, as well as a group of ambassadors from friendly countries. After Bruce's brief arrival statement expressing delight to be in China, we whisked them to the Nine-Story Building. En route, the flag almost fell off the car. We stopped and removed it. All in all, it was an appropriate halfway diplomatic welcome. The Liaison Office was in business.

## Making the Rounds

The next day, after more flag trouble involving a pole that was much too small, Ambassador Bruce began an arduous, monthlong round of calls on Chinese officials and diplomats, including the ministers responsible for all aspects of our new relationship—foreign affairs, trade, sports, culture, science, and technology.

Qiao Guanhua, the vice minister of foreign affairs who had negotiated the Shanghai Communiqué, was the official whose company Bruce enjoyed the most. Qiao was a tall, intense, and witty man, master of our own and other foreign languages, a heavy smoker and eager drinker. He and Bruce were two peas in a pod. During Bruce's first call, they shared Kissinger jokes and pledged to cooperate and continue the normalization process. I accompanied Bruce on most of these calls and benefited from the additional access they gave me to leading figures.[11]

A cozy welcome banquet hosted by Qiao for the entire USLO staff gave us a chance to meet the new PRC Liaison Office chief ambassador, Huang Zhen, Mao's alleged niece Wang Hairong, and the new head of the Foreign Ministry's American and Oceanic Bureau Lin Ping. Huang, we were told, would arrive in Washington in June. Making family small talk, I told Qiao and Lin Ping about my sons, the Three Tigers, and of the decision of Tiger Number Three, Sanhu, to use his Chinese name in America. All conversation stopped.

"You mean that's what they call him at school?" Qiao asked, astonished. When I confirmed this, the entire table toasted Sanhu (his family name to this day) and his arrival in the capital later in June.

I sat next to Madame Huang, whose appearance—a round, jolly, Chinese version of Mrs. Tiggywinkle—masked a strong reputation as an effective diplomat in her own right. She told me she had seven children and loved gardening. Her husband, China's answer to David Bruce, who had a heavy cold, hawked loudly but managed to refrain from spitting. Lin Ping, a tall, thin cadre of dour mien who had served as ambassador to Chile, was pleasant during this honeymoon event. He later turned out to be the principal messenger when there was bad news to pass on. Bruce was in top form, commenting that the mao-tai liquor had a "kick like a mule," an expression that stumped the interpreters.

Bruce moved quickly to define the Liaison Office as a small, low-key mission empowered to negotiate on substantive matters of mutual interest. During his call on the dean of the Diplomatic Corps, the Nepali ambassador, it was agreed that USLO staff should not attend formal functions involving the diplomatic corps as a whole, including national days and Chinese events related to visiting foreign leaders. This was a relief to Bruce and, in fact, to all of us. It meant that we could choose whom we wanted to see and when. Ambassador Bruce briefed the visiting U.S. press on these guidelines, as well as the staff. He was anxious that Washington also get the message. Every agency in town wanted to have representatives on the ground in China, and he wanted to keep his mission lean and nimble. After all, the United States had yet to grant full recognition to the People's Republic and still maintained a full-scale diplomatic establishment in Taiwan. He would remain adamant in fending off pressures for additional staff.

**Premier Zhou Welcomes Bruce — Kissinger Is Cross**

"When are they going to give us something to do?" Bruce asked, fidgeting in his office on May 18. The answer came fifteen minutes later in a call from the protocol department announcing that Premier Zhou would like Ambassador Bruce to call between 6:30 and 7:00 P.M. Jenkins, Holdridge, and I accompanied Bruce to the same room in the Great Hall of the People where Nixon and Zhou had talked fifteen months before. Qiao Guanhua and Huang Zhen were the top officials at the premier's side.

After the obligatory photo and tea, Zhou got down to cases, my notes indicate. He named Qiao as Bruce's opposite number in Beijing and announced that Huang Zhen would be leaving Beijing May 25 and arriving in Washington on June 1. Having established the lines of communication and made it clear that he wanted substantive exchanges to start right away, Zhou urged speedy implementation of the Shanghai Communiqué and asked Bruce to assure President Nixon that his government and the North Vietnamese "ardently" wished to comply with all the clauses of the Paris Agreements. He wished Dr. Kissinger success in his talks with Le Duc Tho, Hanoi's top negotiator, and expressed the hope that a peaceful solution could be found in Cambodia. Zhou praised Cambodia's Prince Sihanouk (a close friend of the Chinese who spent months each year in Beijing), and hinted that perhaps Bruce would be willing to meet with him. Bruce did not reply.

Bruce left the meeting elated and deeply impressed with Zhou, who struck him as "one of the most remarkable statesmen of our time." Zhou and Bruce clearly hit it off, establishing a rapid rapport that enabled the serious substance of the meeting to be transacted gracefully and without strain. I was flattered when Zhou, ever the well-briefed politician, remembered that we had met and discussed poetry during the Nixon visit.

After the meeting, we four Americans dined at the Beijing Hotel on vodka, caviar, and simple Chinese dishes. When the total bill came to about US$6.00, Bruce almost fell off his chair. Jenkins, Holdridge and I then worked up a report of the conversation. I did the writing, based on their comments and ideas. The entire process took about two hours and went much more quickly than I expected. It was difficult to sleep that night given the excitement of the evening and the shouts of hilarity coming over the transoms of our hotel hallway from the Seabees, who repeated every joke they had ever heard until 3 A.M.

The next morning, we went over the draft with Ambassador Bruce, who carefully reviewed every word and made his own elegant edits in spidery handwriting with the finest of fountain pen points. By the time we had finished, he had made it his own message.[12]

Dr. Kissinger reacted to Bruce's report with a back-channel blast of anger objecting to my inclusion in the meeting. My presence had violated the secure channel he had created for exchanges between the Chinese leadership and the White House. I was not to take part in future meetings. Jenkins and Holdridge were used to working with me and knew the team approach would save them time. But, they explained apologetically, Henry had laid down the law.

From then on, I remained outside the mechanics of high-policy communication with Washington, focused tightly on Chinese domestic politics and developing day-to-day relationships with the Chinese. The stream of visitors that would preoccupy much of US-LO's work and attention—businessmen, athletes, musicians, scholars, and scientists—had already begun. Politics were my responsibility, and the Chinese treated sports and culture as important tools of diplomacy. We would find ourselves thoroughly occupied with "nuts and bolts"—initiating key links for trade, investment, travel and study, academic, and cultural exchanges. Over time these would grow huge, outweighing and outlasting major changes in the international balance of power and constituting the thick sinews of current U.S.-China relations.

## Huang Zhen Leaves for America

On May 23, I went with Bruce to call on Huang Zhen, whose cold was better. He was genial and funny. He carried a fan, which he fluttered from time to time, oddly incongruous and at variance with his crew-cut, military, tough-guy appearance. He told Bruce he was changing his travel plans to arrive in Washington earlier, no doubt to keep track of the Nixon Summit in Moscow, which had begun on May 22. We all turned out at the airport two days later to see off Huang and his wife amid a most impressive entourage, including the foreign minister, two vice foreign ministers, and a host of minions. I interpreted small talk between Mrs. Bruce and Madame Huang, an easy and pleasant task. I was struck by the contrast between the tall, urbane beauty of Evangeline Bruce and the ordinary round jollity of Madame Huang, who was also known as Zhu Lin. Both were equals, however, when it came to position and brainpower.

## Building the Red Ass Bar

Meanwhile, construction of our permanent office, which would also house the Bruce residence, was in full swing. I visited the site on a Sunday at the end of May and spent some time translating for the Seabees, adding some new vocabulary in the process— shellac, varnish, sealer, amperes, and such. While not trained as an interpreter, I found myself pressed into service on more and more occasions. The Seabees were friendly and totally professional, but rough-hewn and foul-mouthed. Their frustrations were magnified by the social success of the clean-cut Marines, who within three weeks were squiring pretty secretaries from other diplomatic missions, attending parties, and having a ball. The Seabees occupied their time building a beautiful bar for the Marine House, in an apartment on the Avenue of Lasting Peace (*Changandajie*) in the Jianguomenwai area near the new USLO office. (I had already spoken for an apartment on the top floor of the same building.) The bar, meticulously crafted of laminated strips of packing crates, would be the centerpiece of what the Marines named "The Red Ass Saloon," their traditional term of endearment for Seabees the world over. The bar would last longer than the Marine detachment at USLO, but that is a later story.

During the rest of May, we continued to connect with Chinese officials who would become important contacts later on. One of these was a talented young diplomat named Ma Yuzhen, who had managed the foreign press during the Nixon visit and now was in charge of the Press Division of the Foreign Ministry. Ma would later become ambassador to London and the first Chinese High Commissioner in Hong Kong. For now, he was the key official responsible for fending off our efforts to secure permission for permanent American media representation in Beijing.

In the coming months, our relationship would evolve considerably, from wonderment at simply being in China, to a period of groping about amiably while learning the ropes of daily dealings with the Chinese, to a clear and hard-eyed recognition that the process was exacting, tough, and often petty. We would learn that below the lofty, affable plane on which Kissinger and Zhou operated, there lurked a breed of Middle Kingdom bureaucrat, narrow, orthodox, unable to shake completely their thorough schooling in antipathy towards the foremost capitalist power in the world.

# 13

# Shepherd of Sports

The U.S. swim team would be arriving soon, and the two top American basketball teams, one men's and one women's, would be playing in Beijing at the end of June. The Philadelphia Orchestra was scheduled to come in the fall. These would be major milestones in the development of our relationship that would need careful handling. I lobbied hard with both Bruce and the Chinese for permission to attach U.S. Liaison Office personnel to major visiting American delegations. I argued that our expertise and experience would help the visitors deal with their Chinese hosts and give our officers a chance to travel and get a feel for China. After expressing some worries about stripping his staff in Beijing, Ambassador Bruce agreed, naming me, in the privacy of his diary, "our shepherd of sports."

## The Politics of Swimming

Anxious to confirm a precedent for USLO participation, I called on Guo Lei, the ranking official of the All China Sports Federation responsible for the swim team visit, at his office at the Beijing Gymnasium. We drank tea, smoked cigarettes, and talked about the swimmers' schedule. The call was an important warm-up.

Guo expressed disappointment that the U.S. swimmers would not be permitted to compete directly with their Chinese hosts. In 1958, the PRC had withdrawn from FINA, the international swimming body, because Taiwan remained a recognized member. FINA forbids competition with nonmembers upon pain of disqualification, not only of the actual competitors, but of all competitors from the violating country. One of the leaders of the U.S. delegation, Al

Schoenfield, was a high-ranking member of the American Athletic Union and highly sensitive about this threat. The other U.S. team members were retiring from competition and had little to lose, but they worried about younger American colleagues losing their status.

The next day I flew to Guangzhou, the first stop on the swim team's tour. Guo Lei, sweating profusely in the muggy air, met me at the airport with other responsible sports officials including Lu Dapeng, a slight former sprinter, and Zhao Jixin, a wizened high jumper, both of whom spoke good English. China's Sports Federation operates a fully developed bureaucracy with functional bureaus (water sports, field sports, etc.), country desks, and regional branches, all staffed by retired athletes. Over a lunch punctuated with toasts and expressions of enduring friendship, I began to realize that these people were as much in the dark about the U.S. team as I was. All we had to work with were the names of the swimmers, a vague agreement for them to come to China, and a rough itinerary. I asked Guo for as much information as he had on the itinerary and those questions he wanted me to discuss when I met the team at the border the next day. After he finished, it was clear I would have plenty of work to do.

In the afternoon, we went for a swim at the pool where the exhibition would take place and inspected the facilities. Chinese girls in swimsuits, rid of their shapeless proletarian uniforms, were knockouts. Mr. Lu, the sprinter, and I swam up and down, while Guo floated his potbelly back and forth, aided by occasional pulls on the lane ropes. Our bonds grew stronger in the water.

On June 2, exactly a month since my arrival, I took the train to the border at Shenzhen with sprinter Lu and high jumper Zhao. The group of young Americans that crossed the bridge into China could not have been handsomer or more wholesome. All of them were world-class Olympic athletes. Most had competed at Mexico in 1968 and Munich in 1972, the year that Mark Spitz won seven medals. Spitz was not among them, an absence for which no one expressed regrets. The women's roster included swimmers Jane Barkman, Ellie Daniel, Karen Moe, Lynn Vidali, and gold medal diver Micki King. The men included swimmers Frank Heckl, Mitch Ivey, Brian Job, Steve Power, and another champion diver, Bernie Wrightson.

The next weeks would bring us close, particularly the divers, who were a few years older and natural leaders. They were a disciplined but relaxed lot. All were deeply interested in China and the job at hand.

I immediately engaged in a discussion with Men's Coach Jim Gaughran and Team Leader Al Schoenfield, describing the Chinese desire to compete or at least exhibit together. I outlined a schedule that would include Guangzhou, Changsha, Shanghai, and Beijing. They were happy with the schedule but remained adamantly opposed to competition. I worked out a compromise whereby divers would exhibit together and swimmers would go off in heats, first the U.S. swimmers, then the Chinese. Technically, it was important that swimmers from the United States and the PRC not be racing in the water at same time.

In the train on the way to Guangzhou, I told high jumper Zhao and sprinter Lu what we had discussed. A plenary planning session at the Dong Fang hotel ratified the compromise arrangement. The Americans knew what to expect and handled themselves well. Guo Lei, briefed by his own people, expressed understanding of U.S. problems with competition, though he worried privately that spectators would find the exhibitions boring.

### How to Make Olympic Champions

The next day, swimmers, divers, and coaches from both countries mingled poolside in an informal joint training/teaching session, a scene to be repeated several times at each stop on the tour. The Chinese were consistently interested in the answers to two broad questions: (1) what is the training formula that produces Olympic champions? and (2) how do you increase speed by the one second that separates Olympic gold from sixth place. The American answers were forthright and, in those days, difficult for the Chinese to manage.

Coaches and swimmers alike acknowledged that there was a certain length and quality of training required to make a swimmer world-class competitive. But there was no set formula. Every swimmer was an individual and rounded into shape at different times in the season. Some needed to be in fine condition before competition began, while others competed best starting the racing season with more training remaining to be done. Still others started finely honed, slacked off, then sharpened up again. The Chinese seemed to be looking for a simple sausage machine into which you could insert a swimmer, turn it on, and in due course a champ would pop out. There was no such thing. But individualized programs ran afoul of the regimentation that marked the communist system.

Replying to the question of how to shave that second off the clock, the American swimmers began by asking their Chinese hosts how far they swam each day. Five thousand meters, came the answer. The Americans replied, we swim 5000 meters in the morning, then do two hours of calisthenics, then swim another 5000 meters in the afternoon. If you want that second, you have to work at least twice as hard. But how, the Chinese swimmers asked, can you maintain that schedule and be a soldier, worker, or peasant at the same time? Answer: You can't. Competing for the Olympics is a full-time job.

The PRC rise to competitiveness in Olympic swimming and diving over the last several decades suggests that they mastered these lessons. The teaching began with this trip. It gave me sharp pleasure to hear laid-back American youths tell Chinese they needed to work harder.

### The Interpreter's Nightmare

Among other notable conversations at poolside in Guangzhou was a dialogue between Ingrid Daland, the American women's coach, and her Chinese counterpart, Ms. Chen. By default, I found myself the interpreter. It was a hot South China morning, the sun beating down hard. We were standing under umbrellas, wearing bathing suits and big straw hats. About fifteen curious male coaches joined us to listen in. The specialized vocabulary flew thick and fast—interval training, endurance laps, frog kicks, butterfly strokes, and so forth—but I was managing reasonably well, having boned up on swimming terms before leaving Beijing.

Then the trouble began.

Ms. Chen asked sweetly, "What is the impact of the menstrual period on training and competition for your swimmers?"

Ingrid replied, "It's nothing, really, a minor discomfort. We swim and compete as usual."

I had no problem whatsoever translating these words. A look of complete incomprehension set itself upon Ms. Chen's face. She asked the question again, verbatim, and got the same reply.

I began to sweat hard, realizing that I faced the deepest dilemma that can confront an interpreter. When you are missing a specific term, you can always work out a parallel expression, but when the concept you are trying to describe does not exist in the other culture, you are in the hottest possible water. In Chinese tradition, I remembered, objects are never placed in the orifices of the body, except at death. When one dies, body plugs made of a material that accords with your rank—jade for the emperor, on down to wood for the peasant—are inserted. A tampon, in short, was not only unknown, but unthinkable.

The sun beat down, the male coaches, riveted, drew closer. I tried hard to describe a tampon, but failed miserably. My best effort, "a small, quilted tent pole," was clearly the wrong scale and puzzled my listeners totally. Finally, I gave up, turned to Ingrid and explained the quandary. Did she have one of these objects anywhere nearby?

"Why yes, as a matter of fact, there's one in my handbag over on that bench," she replied. So, the entire group moved over to the bench, where Ingrid reached into her purse and showed the Chinese their first tampon. Flashbulbs of understanding went off all around and the crisis was over.

I expected to learn shortly through clandestine sources of a massive Tampax order to Johnson & Johnson. The Chinese solution was simpler. Thirty years later I shared this story with the mother of a swimming daughter who had lived in Hong Kong in June of 1973. She reported a mysterious telegram arriving from the Guangzhou Swimming Association at that time requesting a box of Tampax and specific instructions in Chinese.

I was becoming, perforce, a fairly competent escort interpreter, the lowest form of life on the translator food chain. The higher levels are occupied by consecutive interpreters (like Chas Freeman), who work on formal conferences or conversations with speakers pausing to let them translate. Top of the line are simultaneous interpreters who operate in real time as the words come out of the speakers' mouths. Interpreters are never noticed unless they screw up.

Well, almost never. One of my heroes is a Korean interpreter who, when faced with a nightmare like mine, quite literally saved his country's bacon. The occasion was a speech by President Lyndon Johnson in Seoul during 1966, the climax of the highest-level visit by an American official to Korea since the Korean War. The grandest hall in the city was filled with the top leaders of the country, all paying close attention, intent on making their guest feel important. The U.S. embassy had some Korean language officers, but no one trained to interpret. The government interpreter was working smoothly from a text provided in advance. Then Johnson, enthused by the hold he had on his audience, left his text and winged a Texas joke involving hound dogs hunting for coons. The embassy language officers froze, sensing disaster. But the Korean interpreter did not break stride, and when he had finished, the audience broke up, slapping their thighs, some even weeping with mirth. Johnson beamed. The event, and with it the entire visit, was a success. What the interpreter actually said, never to be made public, was, "The President of the United States has just told a very funny Texas story that is impossible for me to translate. When I give the signal, please laugh uproariously!"

## Exhibitions and Tours

There were two exhibitions in Guangzhou. The first drew 10,000 people despite a torrential downpour. At the opening ceremonies, the Chinese marched in wearing smart matching warm-up suits on one side of the pool, while on the other, individual Americans sauntered along under plastic ponchos. Once in the pool, however, the Americans showed the Chinese the speed and performance they had come to see. The final exhibition drew 15,000 onlookers, with a spectacular finale worked out by Micki King and Bernie Wrightson involving two Americans and five Chinese diving simultaneously into the water from three separate heights. This was a political masterstroke and alleviated Chinese disappointment over the restrictions FINA rules placed on competition. During the children's event, which became part of every exhibition, the American athletes developed an endearing routine for helping the kids out of the pool at the end of the race—friendly giants pulling tiny creatures aloft, usually with one hand.

In between exhibitions and training, the American team toured the sights of Guangzhou and the surrounding area, along with their escorts. Among the escorts were Richard Williams, a Foreign Service Chinese language officer from Washington, and Tom Bernstein, the representative of the National Committee on U.S.-China Relations, which had organized the visit. Our itinerary included the famous Foshan porcelain factory; a school for deaf and dumb children; the Peasant Institute, where history has been rewritten to state that Mao started the entire movement; Ban Xi, a beautiful and renowned old Cantonese restaurant; an 880-year old temple; the arts institute; performances of revolutionary opera; acrobatic shows; and banquets and more banquets. Luckily the athletes' superb physical condition enabled them to endure the rigors of both the sports and the marathon cultural schedule. Although carefully scripted, we were all transfixed by these first looks at a part of China we had never seen. Even the bus rides around the seedy, beat-up city were fascinating.

We traveled by boat down the Pearl River to visit an island with a model production brigade, famous for growing fruit and clearly often visited by foreigners. Everything was spic and span, the fields well tended, the children washed and chanting "Welcome, Friends!" when we arrived, and "Goodbye, Friends!" when we left. I questioned an approachable official about the impact of the Cultural Revolution on the production brigade. He said the fighting had not reached them, although I privately suspected that plenty of bodies had floated by. The leadership of the commune had not changed, although wall posters criticizing the attitudes of the leading cadres made them all more careful of their relations with the people under them. Sharp-eyed Dick Williams, who later became our first consul general in Guangzhou, found a poster in the brigade store that exhorted members to "Sell your hair! Sell your jewels! Promote foreign trade!"

**Mao Country**

The next stop was Changsha, in Hunan Province. The team was welcomed with open arms and great curiosity—Hunan had never before received any sports team from the United States. As I had expected, these trips would provide fine raw material for reporting on China during the early days of our presence there. David Bruce thought so, too. Here's a cable I wrote, which he signed and sent to Washington on June 22:

Subject: Changsha by Bus

*The Look of the Town.* Changsha is a cement-gray provincial city of about 700,000, surrounded by lush green gently rolling countryside and split by a broad brown river, the Xiang. The older part of town to the south, burned by the Japanese in the late '30s, has been rebuilt in standard fashion, with wide streets flanked by undistinguished concrete office buildings, factories, and stores. Many of the small houses that line the residential side streets, however, are of wood with tile roofs. Unlike Beijing, where most life goes on behind walls, strollers and bus riders can peer directly into living and bedrooms and observe people eating, sleeping, working, and at night trying to read by the dim light of weak bulbs. A long island, from which Changsha—'Long Sand'—gets its name, sits in the middle of the river, dotted by clumps of attractive old wooden houses and small fields, and tipped by Orange Point Park, the scene of yet another famous Mao swim many years ago. The river, with its long, graceful, flat-sailed cargo boats, dominates everything. The northeast portion of the city, once countryside, has been built up since 1949 with showcase factories, workers' apartments, the usual Martyrs' Park, and a cavernous installation called the Hunan Guest House. The latter is where important visiting cadres, foreign officials, and itinerant American swimmers stay in rooms with 14-foot ceilings and hard box beds surrounded with mosquito netting, bathing infrequently in the rusty water that issues from groaning pipes.

*The Feel of the People.* The Hunanese we met seemed warmer, franker, and more open than the big city people we left behind in Guangzhou and were later to meet in Shanghai. Any foreigner takes some getting used to this far into China, but giant golden American youths strolling around the town in shorts and T-shirts advertising a California animal farm called "Frazier the Sensuous Lion" caused sensations everywhere they went. The reporting officer breakfasted one early morning with three team members at a tiny restaurant in an old residential district. As we ordered our steamed buns, rice noodles, and tea from the proprietress, a tough, authoritative, street committee type who hid her surprise behind a wrinkled smile, the restaurant and the street outside filled with people who crowded around and strained to hear who we were and applauded when they found out. Left in momentary peace by an outburst from the proprietress, which quickly cleared the restaurant, we worked at our heaping breakfast (total cost per person 11 US cents) until a middle-aged man approached us and politely asked if we were through. We were, and, thinking he was the waiter, said he could clear the dishes. He piled the leftover noodles furtively into a bowl and then slipped over to a corner table and started to wolf them down. Not for long. The breakfasters in that part of the room quickly formed a ring around him, criticized him severely, took away the bowl, and then removed him bodily from the premises. He had embarrassed them all in front of us. Sensing a thickening of the atmosphere, we made a brief speech about how delicious and plentiful the food was and left amid smiles and more applause.

*The Sights of Changsha.* Chairman Mao not only slept here, he ate, taught, organized, agitated, swam, discussed politics, and took cold showers from a well here. Every such spot is lovingly documented, and we saw them all. We moved dutifully from the peaceful Ai Wan Ting (The Pavilion Which Loves the Evening) on the western slopes opposite the town, where Mao held deep political discussions, to the comfortable little house where he established the first Hunan District Party headquarters, to the Number One Normal School where he studied and taught, to Orange Point Park where he swam. The advantage of such a pilgrimage, for the benefit of future visitors, is that it gets one into most parts of the city. The finale, of course, is the visit to the Chairman's birthplace, Shaoshan.

*The Chairman's Home.* It was not poverty that pushed Mao Tse-tung onto the revolutionary path. His house, set on three acres of prime land with a lovely pond in front and handsome green mountains on three sides, is comfortable by any standard. He and his sister and brothers each had their own cool high-ceilinged room with box beds (softer than those at the Hunan Guest House). At the back, around a courtyard pool into which the rain drains from the roofs, well-organized animal pens, storage bins, and grain-processing areas suggest that Mao's father was not only competent, but far more well-to-do than orthodox ex post facto hagiography will admit. Mao's primary school nearby is similarly comfortable. Small wonder he had to move further afield into the countryside to find out how the peasants really lived.

The countryside on the two-and-a-half-hour bus ride from Changsha to Shaoshan is practically identical to that in central Taiwan. The red soil, tea plantations up the hillsides, rice fields with water buffaloes, chaotic road conditions, sounds and smells are the same. Only here the slogans are red rather than blue and wish long life to a different leader. The farmhouses are larger, and the rivers have water all year round and are filled with sailing junks.[13]

## Tension in Shanghai

I expected trouble in Shanghai, our next and last stop before the finale in Beijing. My contact at Boeing, Ed Raymond, told me that he had found Shanghai politically far tenser than any other Chinese city he had visited. On Sunday, May 27, he had personally observed three incidents involving a group of people attacking a man with their fists and, with a large crowd looking on, beating him up and hustling him off, perhaps to a military or police installation. The last of these incidents was at the Peace Hotel downtown; the second, in the outskirts of the city on returning from a visit to a commune; and the first, in the early morning while taking a walk on the Bund, along the Whampoa River. Raymond, whom I ran into in Guangzhou, contemplated issuing instructions to Boeing people living in Shanghai to stay off the streets and keep to the hotel and their place of work at the airport.

The Boeing people were the most experienced and savvy of all U.S. business interests in China. Their operatives had been in the PRC for many months, and the "gee whiz" days we were now in were long gone for them. Their jaded acronym, AFWT, "Another Fucking Wall Trip," became a secret slogan for veteran resident foreigners over time.

For all the friendship at various pool sites and banquets, a sense of tension on the Chinese side underlay the visit. The struggle at our unauthorized breakfast in Changsha was an indication of what could go wrong in a fragile society, when foreigners departed from their hosts' careful scripts. One official in Guangzhou explained to me the painstaking way tickets for swimming exhibitions were systematically farmed out to various organizations, labor unions, government offices at all levels, and schools. The authorities in these "units" decided who could go and issued specific letters of introduction. No letter, no admittance. There were "bad elements," the cadre explained, who were dissatisfied with society for a variety of reasons, plus others who did not agree with the policy of rapprochement with the United States, hence the need for screening. The class struggle still continued, he concluded.

In the event, the city seemed calm enough as we were whisked from the airport to our plush accommodations at Shanghai Mansions, situated on the confluence of the Whampoa River and Soochow creek overlooking the Bund. The Mansions, a great yellow pile built during the 1920s, had been Japanese headquarters during their occupation of Shanghai during World War II. Pudong, across the way, now a showcase forest of skyscrapers, was then a farm village.

The difference in attitude from city to city was marked. In provincial Changsha, the divers, swimmers, and coaches were immediately responsive and grateful for any athletic tips the

Americans could pass on. Urbane, know-it-all Shanghai was different. The scene was a diving exhibition, billed as a master class starring Bernie Wrightson and Micki King, perhaps the two greatest divers in the world. The pool and stands were packed. Five thousand people sat quietly as our divers went off the board and then waited by the pool for Shanghainese divers to come forward and ask questions of the champions. Nothing happened.

"What is with these people?" King asked.

"We are in Shanghai," I replied. "They are supposed to know everything."

Together, we devised a special Shanghai exhibition/training ploy. King and Wrightson would stop trying to teach and each do their three most difficult and spectacular dives, then put on their towel wrappers and head for the lockers, as if to end the session. Each Olympic champion dive drew louder gasps from the onlookers. Then, when the divers made to leave, the cry went up, "Hey! Where are you going?" The Chinese divers crowded around, and the master class began.

I returned to Beijing on June 14 after two weeks on the road, glad to be "home." The hotel staff seemed glad to see me. The swimmers settled into their hotel, resting up for a final round of swimming and the great sights of the capital. David Bruce saw the exhibition on June 16 and loved it, particularly the diving. Zhang Wenjin accompanied us. I took great pleasure in teaching him, an avid swimmer, the technical terms for butterfly, breaststroke, and backstroke. Later, Bruce had the entire team to his residence for cocktails.

The USLO building was now finished, although not a stick of furniture yet stood in the reception area downstairs. While I was out of Beijing, a planeload of Drexel furniture had arrived from America for the official residence and other apartments. Bruce abhorred it and hid it upstairs. "The bastard style of our present furnishings would not be appropriate for an isolated motel at home," he was to write.[14]

Other events that occupied the interest of USLO in my absence included the visit of the North Vietnamese leader, Le Duan, and Richard Nixon's visit to Moscow, which sent frissons of anxiety through the Chinese leadership and required that Bruce pass along reassurances to them from the highest levels of the U.S.

government. John Holdridge supported Bruce in these exchanges with his customary competence, leaving me free to roam around the country with our swimmers, looking, talking, and learning.

## The Return Banquet

My final task for the swimmers was to arrange their "return banquet," a farewell custom that featured the visitors as hosts. The team had experienced the trip of a lifetime and charged me to do something really special in honor of their Chinese counterparts. My instructions were to order the kind of food Chinese really like, not foreigners' fare like fried noodles and sweet and sour pork. They asked me to pick a special venue that Chinese and Americans alike would always remember, rather than the usual faceless hotel. I succeeded, but in a way that could have ended my career then and there. This is what happened.

My principal advisor in these arrangements was Harry Liu, the chief interpreter/assistant assigned to the Liaison Office by the Diplomatic Services Bureau shortly after I arrived. Liu had worked for the British and been "sent down" after the Red Guards attacked their embassy in 1967. He appeared on our doorstep without fanfare, a somewhat infirm old man, with a spark in his eye and an invaluable inventory of lore about the Chinese Communist system and how one operated in it and survived.

So I approached Harry with my instructions from the swimmers. I told him I wanted to try a Sichuan restaurant called the Chengdu, notorious as a hangout for Sichuanese politicians like Party Secretary Deng Xiaoping that had closed when Deng and others became casualties of the Cultural Revolution. Deng had recently reemerged in public, evidence of the ceaseless competition among the top leaders, and the restaurant was now open. Did Harry think we could go? Sure, he said, without hesitation.

"What is the standard?" (Meaning, how much will you pay per person?), he then asked.

"Eight *yuan*," I replied, having dined sumptuously for that price.

"What is the rank of the most senior Chinese guest that you are inviting?" Liu asked.

"Wang Meng, head of the All China Sports Federation," I answered.

Liu sighed and said, "That's a cabinet rank. Eight yuan will never do."

"But Mr. Liu," I interjected, "I thought this was a classless society."

"Classless it is," he deadpanned, "but there are ranks!"

Startled by this pithy insight, I asked what standard would, in fact, do. We settled on eleven yuan, or US$5.50 a head.

Next we considered the food. I had especially enjoyed several Sichuanese dishes over the years. These included "Ants in the Trees" (tiny nodules of beef hidden among fine noodles in a spicy sauce), Smoked Camphor Duck, Eight Valuable Vegetables, and some others that I passed along for Harry's consideration. He would see what he could do. As he padded away on his cloth shoes, I urged him to focus on dishes that the officials would like and for which the restaurant was famous.

Two days later, June 18, I was sitting in my office in our dingy corridor of the Beijing Hotel, preparing to leave for the restaurant. Out the window, the sun was setting in the west, flooding the golden tiles that roofed the Forbidden City. Downstairs, the bus was loading the swim team. Harry Liu poked his head around the door and asked if I would like a quick look at the menu for our banquet. I went down the list, laid out neatly in Chinese characters, followed by translations. Sure enough, "Ants in the Trees," Smoked Camphor Duck, and Eight Valuable Vegetables were there. Then, a dish translated as "Ox's XXX à la Maison" caught my eye.

"What's this?" I asked, frowning.

"Well, read the characters," Liu suggested helpfully.

"*Jia Shang Niu Chong,*" I read, or literally "The Bull Lunges, Family Style."

"You mean it's his . . . ?"

"Yes."

"Mr. Liu, there are six American women on our delegation, from the states of California and Pennsylvania. If it ever gets into the U.S. press that they are serving bull's pizzles to their Chinese hosts, our careers are finished," I said.

"Mr. Pu," Liu replied. "I was only following your instructions.

This dish is a specialty of the Chengdu restaurant. The cadres will love it."

It was too late to make a change. I boarded the bus in a mood of deep apprehension, which contrasted sharply with the excited chatter of our athletes.

The Chengdu was located a few blocks west of Tiananmen Square behind the Great Hall of the People. It was in a grand, traditional Beijing courtyard house, famous in history for having belonged to Yuan Shikai, the warlord who failed to make himself emperor of China in 1916. Now beautifully restored, the house today is the Beijing site of the China Club. At the time, though, it was still a beat-up mansion, paint peeling from the walls, with only one of several courtyards in operation, where food was being served. The swimmers were thrilled with the venerable, exotic look and feel of the place and pleased to find all their Chinese counterparts at table. We had the place to ourselves.

The meal began. The athletes, relaxed after a grueling and successful tour, broke training and participated with gusto in the toasts. Mao-tai, the lethal liquor distilled 100 + proof from sorghum, was the drink the Chinese liked. The mood quickly turned convivial. My alarm grew when our swimmers started the American practice of toasting each dish when it first appeared. I could just imagine what would happen when the XXX was served. "Here's to the Smoked Camphor Duck!" "A Toast to Ants in the Trees!" "Bottoms up for Seven Valuable Vegetables!" The dreaded moment approached. The Mao-tai failed to drown my fears.

Waiters entered bearing large oblong platters. The meat was cut into long strips and covered with a marinade of vegetables, but unmistakably XXXs to those who knew. The cadres murmured in appreciation as the dishes were placed on the tables.

"Oh, this is delicious!" cried Karen Moe, a former breaststroke champion. "What is it?" My panic spiked in the silence that followed.

The Chinese officials looked at each other, and the interpreter sitting next to Karen leaned over and replied, in a serious manner, "It's a very special kind of tendon."

"Let's toast the tendon!" Karen exclaimed, and so we all did. I was saved. Once again, a smart, sensitive translator had come to the rescue. The evening was an unqualified success, lasting over three hours and leaving behind memories for a lifetime.

I waited until the moment just before the American team left for the airport to tell Coach Gaughran what we had actually eaten. When I identified the "tendon," we were standing in the parking lot of the Friendship Store, where the swimmers and divers were buying last-minute souvenirs. He started laughing and could not stop, practically rolling on the tarmac.

"It was your revenge," he said after he had recovered, "payback for three weeks of aggravation."

"Not at all," I replied. "The whole trip has been an unforgettable pleasure." I do not know what, if anything, he told the team.

## Basketball, High Diplomacy, and National Politics

The climax of my career as "Shepherd of Sports" came at the U.S.-China basketball games on June 19. Ambassador Bruce and I arrived at the VIP entrance of the Beijing Gymnasium, knowing that top leadership would be there but without a clue as to who it would be. At the door, we learned that Madame Mao would be the top leader attending.

When she made her entrance ninety seconds later, it was clear that the former Shanghai actress was playing a new role. Her costume had changed. She was wearing a dress, not a Mao suit. It was the kind of outfit Eleanor Roosevelt would have worn, a midlength grey gabardine, with a discreet collar and pockets. On her wrist, I was startled to note, was a Rolex watch—stainless steel but a Rolex, nonetheless. Her hair was gently but permanently waved, not the usual style for ultra leftist radicals. She wore white leather shoes with a handbag to match. Her first words of welcome were spoken slowly and in queenly tones, a tip-off to the new role she wanted to play. As we moved onto the dais in the gymnasium, I noted that the Chinese had not provided an interpreter for Bruce and Madame Mao and, emboldened by the clear and stately pace of her speech, slipped onto the stool behind them.

David Bruce was quite taken with her. As he told his diary:

I sat next to Madame Mao, with Nick Platt behind us as interpreter. On my other side was a jolly Vice Premier addicted to cigar smoke. From time to time, prominent functionaries came to present their respects to Chiang Ch'ing. In repose, her flat-featured face was impassive; when she laughed, as she often did, it became mobile and sympathetic. Her reputation for inspiring fear may be justified, but certainly last night she gave the impression of being thoroughly feminine, carefree, hospitable, and with a keen sense of the ridiculous. She has beautiful hands and feet, and challenging eyes.

Bruce reported the event to Washington the next day in a cable I helped him write:

1. High-ranking leaders of the PRC, most notably the top leftists, turned out in force for the first Sino-American basketball games in Peking June 19. . . . Madame Mao . . . was most welcoming to all the visiting team leaders at tea before the game. She asked the coaches and me to convey her best wishes to President and Mrs. Nixon, Dr. Kissinger and Secretary Rogers, adding that the American leaders had been brave enough to come and see for themselves that the Chinese were not "freaks and monsters." Praising sports as a vehicle for international friendship, she told the swimming coach that she had slipped out of a meeting two nights before to watch the swimmers train and then had returned to the meeting which "lasted until dawn."
2. [Shanghai radical] Yao Wen-yuan, who has always in the past been conspicuously absent when Americans were around, made a point of chiming in at this juncture to say how happy he was that the Sino-American relationship was developing, and how important sports were in the development process. He displayed some knowledge of English, having full command of the terms for basketball and table tennis, and appeared to understand some of what had been said in English before the interpretation. He was relaxed

and smiling throughout the evening. Wang Hung-wen made polite remarks during the half to USLO officers who accompanied me.

3. During the games, Madame Mao, who sat next to me, made quite spontaneous gestures of friendship to the visiting teams. Presented with souvenir emblem pins by the basketball and swimming team leaders, and having nothing similar with which to reciprocate, she fished in her pocket and brought out a handkerchief full of jasmine petals. She asked me to divide the petals into two equal piles and present one to the girls of each team, so that they could "flavor their porridge in the morning.". . .

4. Madame Mao watched the games with interest and good humor, taking delight in the victories of both the American men and the Chinese women. She worried good-naturedly to me about the unremitting dourness of the basketball delegation leader who sat on her right, hoping that the victory of the Chinese girls had not "made him tense."

5. COMMENT: I do not know whether the long meeting June 17 that Madame Mao mentioned had any link with developments tonight. Clearly, however, an important top-level discussion which in itself is a significant matter has been underway. In any case, the attendance of Madame Mao, Yao, and Wang transformed this international sports show into a major political event, with important domestic implications. Media coverage has been prominent (the games were televised live) and will demonstrate to the Chinese that all of the leftists, including Yao Wen-yuan, fully support the new relationship at its current stage of development. The leadership is at last united on what has long been a divisive subject. This, of course, is the message for us as well.[15]

In domestic political terms, Madame Mao's performance at this first U.S.-China basketball game turned out to be her public debut as a candidate to succeed Mao. Photographs of her in her dress appeared on newspaper front pages worldwide. Chinese viewers told me later that she seemed to be presenting herself as a modern-day Empress Wu, the legendary Tang Dynasty (600–900 AD.) female ruler. Her costume became famous, derisively likened to the dress found on the corpse of a 2000–year-old Han noblewoman at a recent archaeological find. The meeting she mentioned to David Bruce was one of a long series in the run-up to the Tenth Party Congress, a meeting long overdue, which kept being postponed. If the leadership were united on Mao's opening to the United States, they remained deeply divided on who should succeed him. Three years later, after Mao died in September 1976, Madame Mao, Yao Wenyuan, and Wang Hongwen were arrested by military authorities on the orders of Vice Premier Li Xiannan and Li Desheng, all of whom had been sitting in a row at that ball game. Qiao Guanhua, who was most attentive to Madame Mao that night, was also purged. They enjoyed the games, but not each other's company.

Basketball has since become the biggest people-to-people force in U.S.-China relations. When the giant (7'6") Shanghai star Yao Ming joined the Houston Rockets in 2002, 300 million Chinese watched his debut on television. More than 200 million Chinese regularly tune in TV broadcasts of National Basketball Association games.

# 14

# Family Liaison

## Apart Too Long

While I was living the sporting life, Chinese Communist style, Sheila and the Three Tigers were heading in my direction. I was to meet them in Hong Kong at the end of June and was beside myself with excitement at the prospect. Staying in touch had been difficult. Letters were slow and phone calls expensive. Nevertheless, I was well briefed on my mate's multiple triumphs: getting the boys through the school year; finishing her Master's Degree in Social Work at Catholic University and graduating; moving out and putting our house at 3734 Oliver Street up for rent; and packing for a new life in a place where American household supplies and food items were unavailable. She had also participated in some of the social events involving the PRC Liaison Office in Washington and made the acquaintance of Evangeline Bruce, the Georgetown "grande dame" described as possessing all the qualities of a diamond—brilliant, beautiful, and hard. Chilling reputation aside, we found Evangeline unfailingly friendly and supportive and fascinated by whatever we could tell her about China.

Back in Beijing, I spent the days before going to meet the family moving into my new office in the just finished USLO building. I had a nice bright corner room with a balcony that looked right at the apartment where we would be living, half a mile away. My early arrival in Beijing entitled me to pick a seventh floor flat in the new Jianguomenwai diplomatic compound on Changandajie, the main avenue leading west toward Tiananmen Square. This area, right by the Temple of the Sun, once an outskirt, is now part of the central city. We could move in as soon as the apartment was finished, cleaned, and furnished. In addition to arranging for housing, I had bought a small secondhand Toyota, as well as bicycles for everyone.

On June 25th, I participated in a discussion with Bruce, Holdridge, and Jenkins about a call they had just made on Zhou Enlai. The Chinese premier was clearly still worried about recent U.S. meetings with the Soviets. He expressed concern over the Nixon-Brezhnev communiqué, worrying that it would lull the rest of the world into a false sense of security, and render the Chinese more vulnerable to the Soviet threat. The triangle game would continue, my bosses believed. Dr. Kissinger was at that point scheduled to visit Beijing in August.

## "Fat Babies" in China

Our family had a jubilant reunion at Hong Kong's Kowloon Railroad Station. We spent the next four days shopping, visiting old family sites, and enjoying being together. I spent time at the Consulate General, smoothing ruffled feathers over the division of labor on substantive reporting and participation in escort duty, the main preoccupation of officers who had never been in China.

Sheila's diary of our time in China begins on Saturday, June 30, and records the now-familiar bridge crossing into China and the initial reactions of the children:

> [On the train,] the boys flexed their new cameras at paddy fields, and we all enjoyed lunch rather late (after the masses had eaten, so no mingling would occur). Sanhu did well with chopsticks and all hands could be seen deciding that if one could eat like this on trains in China, one could also live there.
>
> Canton (Guangzhou), where we missed our plane and spent twenty-six hours laying over at the Dong Fang Hotel, was steamy and oppressive. The children were discomfited by the large numbers of Chinese staring at them ("gawking," they called it) and making rude comments about "fat babies" [*pang wawa*]. Oliver was reluctant to go out, although he did finally. They turned crowd-gathering into a sport. "I like being gawked at," said Sanhu, bravely. [Oliver, today

an actor with more than fifty movies and numerous plays and TV series to his credit, no longer minds either.]

A family supper at the beautiful Ban Xi restaurant, which the swimmers had also visited, cheered everyone up. Sheila described the Ban Xi, still one of Guangzhou's landmarks, as "an island of gaiety and comfort in what seems to be a hard-working and rather joyless city." Our waiters told us the restaurant opened at 5:30 A.M. and could serve 10,000 people a day. We ate in the inevitable private room, reached by walking through a series of verandahs, over a bridge, and up stairs. Ours was made of black wood, carved and latticed, with colored windowpanes glowing in the evening light. One was rose-colored with etched flowers, and one pale green, shaped like a lettuce leaf with grasshoppers and bugs. The children were enchanted, and all hands went to bed cheerfully.

The next afternoon, after seeing the sights of the city, including the famous island "factories" from which foreigners had traded with China over the centuries, we went to the airport for the flight to Beijing. Arriving at our Beijing hotel, the family admired our three-room suite, which Sheila described as "Edwardian" and fell into bed. We were "home."

## Mission Headaches

The family fitted quickly into the life of the mission, which faced two major simultaneous challenges—our first July 4th celebration and our first congressional delegation, led by Senator Warren Magnuson.

We had invited eighty Chinese friends for the Fourth and many said they were coming.   Brunson McKinley and I spent hours developing choreography that would satisfy both our hosts and American traditions. The Chinese favored a set receiving line with ranking officials, then moving to sit stiffly in protocol order on a row of stuffed chairs. Americans were used to a free-form cocktail reception. The ingenious compromise was a self-destructing receiving line, which would dissolve into a formal, stuffed-furniture seating arrangement in one room and stand-up drinks in another. Thus do diplomats earn their livings.

Sheila described her first look at the Liaison Office during a July 3 briefing in preparation for our party:

> Mr. Bruce explained how things would go. … Whatever happened it would only last an hour! Mrs. B. was dressed in blue slacks and a shirt, her hair tied up in a silk kerchief. The downstairs of the Residence is a raw, high ceiling space shaped like a T, with windows giving onto the equally raw garden, which consists, at the moment, of a crazily paved terrace and several empty flowerbeds of gray Beijing soil. On one side there is a covered walk to the Liaison Office and the back offices from the other side of the Atrium. Brunson McKinley outlined the plans for handling the important guests and how the food would be served. The boys took it all in and behaved appropriately.
>
> Afterwards, NP showed us . . . our apartment on the 7th floor of the building next door. It's going to be nice and airy. Now it's stacked high with boxes of furniture and caked with mud on the floor. All hands claimed rooms and liked it.

July 4th began badly. Al Jenkins and John Holdridge were called into the Foreign Ministry and told by Acting Director of Protocol Zhu that Marine Guards could not wear uniforms at our celebration. This was contrary to Chinese diplomatic practice and would be totally unacceptable. No Chinese would attend the reception if Marines were in uniform. Jenkins defended our traditional practice, but Zhu insisted that Dr. Kissinger had agreed during an earlier trip to Beijing that military personnel would wear civilian clothes and not carry arms openly. Jenkins acquiesced and assured Zhu that our Marines would not be in uniform during the reception.

The presence in Beijing of uniformed Marine Security Guards with sidearms, a standard feature of all U.S. Embassies from early in our history, had rankled the Chinese from the beginning. They objected to foreign military units, no matter how small, being stationed on their soil. A Marine presence had been something we took for granted, but it had not been discussed in detail with the Chinese when making arrangements for the Liaison Office. We would hear much more about the Marine presence in the months to come.

Back to Sheila's diary:

July 4. Everyone rather keyed up all day about the party. The boys and I worked in the apartment, unpacking furniture with N's help. Sanhu has an excellent jumping technique for opening large cardboard boxes. He picks an edge and simply sits it down with his behind. Everyone applied themselves, and the apartment turned into a sea of cardboard and packing fluff.

The boys swam (at the International Club), and then we all rested and got into party clothes and were ferried in USLO Shanghais to the Liaison Office.

At 5:45 Protocol arrived with the list. Our biggest potato turned out to be Qiao Guanhua (not Zhou Enlai as Oliver had hoped.) At six, people started coming in absolute floods and were herded down the receiving line past Bruce, Jenkins, Holdridge, and Senator Magnuson. Qiao and other dignitaries went to the sofas in the end room and were plied with food and drink. I circulated until NP summoned me to sit in the sofa lineup between a Mr. Wang of the sports federation and another Mr. Wang of the Beijing Revolutionary Committee.

I talked to one, then the other, about where I had learned my Chinese and about pandas, Beijing vs. New York weather, my *pangzi* (roly poly) children (who were introduced to Qiao Guanhua). ... The boys were charmed by the party and had a wonderful time, especially Oliver, who was in his métier, hobnobbing with bigwigs.

By contrast, the visit of the congressional delegation was a debacle. Magnuson was headstrong and egotistical. Delegation escorts Dick Solomon of the NSC and Alan Romberg from State told us that the senator was miffed by the low rank of Chinese officials who met him at the airport, disappointed in the paltry press attention accorded his arrival, and angry that his group was quartered at the Beijing Hotel rather than the State Guest House. The Chinese clearly did not understand the importance of the Congress, Magnuson fumed. Consequently, he spent most of his time at the July 4th reception lobbying Vice Minister Qiao for a meeting with Premier Zhou.

Magnuson got his meeting, all right, but handled it badly. After a brief discourse on the importance of Congress's role in granting trade concessions, the conversation turned to Cambodia and stayed there endlessly. Zhou criticized the United States for the bombing, and Magnuson insisted that the Congress was against the bombing and had in fact been instrumental in halting it. Zhou wanted to change the subject after a while but Magnuson, who hogged the American side of the conversation, would not let him. Other members of the delegation were mortified but too supine and seniority-whipped to chime in and talk about something else. Even worse, "Maggie," as he was called, blabbed to the press afterwards. Thus the impression given was of Zhou trying to play Congress off against the president, Congress letting the side down when talking to a world leader, and a world leader visibly annoyed at having to spend time with such lightweights.

On the way out, Zhou told Magnuson (as he duly reported to the press) that he would not visit America so long as a representative of Chiang Kai-shek was in residence there. Zhou, disgusted with the whole interview, told Solomon as they left the room, "You'll have a report to write, won't you?"[16] After the session, the accompanying senators and representatives were ashamed and told Maggie so. He was very contrite and then proceeded to get seriously inebriated.

The delegation left on July 8 but not after more idiot faux pas. At the return banquet, Maggie brought up Taiwan independence with Zhang Wenjin, assistant foreign minister, and refused to let this most taboo of subjects drop. The Taiwanese, he said, had "been foolish to allow themselves to be taken over by a small number of Chinese from the Mainland; had they been more cohesive, they could have prevented this and established an independent Taiwan." He topped it all off by asking how Chiang and his troops got to Taiwan, anyway? "Was it by boat?" Zhang had to tell him that the U.S. Air Force had provided the transport.[17]

Bruce was beside himself, describing the delegation's visit as a "disaster," thanks to Magnuson's "bizarre" behavior, which made him "as petulant as if he were suffering from ptomaine poisoning." Al Jenkins, who escorted the group on their itinerary outside the capital, commented that the visit had "reconfirmed the Chinese belief in the superiority of their own system of government."[18]

My own notes concluded, "In retrospect I'm not sure how bad this all is. We are developing a relationship with the Chinese. They should know us warts and all. This delegation represents warts, of course. Compared to them, the swimmers were polished diplomats."[19]

## Living in the Cocoon

Life for foreign families in Beijing consisted of a pleasant but circumscribed circuit, about three miles in radius. Included were the sights of Tiananmen Square and the Forbidden City; the Beijing Hotel; the Liaison Office; the Jianguomenwai diplomatic compound where we would soon live; the International Club, a grim, cavernous facility with a swimming pool, indoor tennis court, and Western restaurant serving *Jiulebu Sanweiji* (club sandwiches); several favored Chinese restaurants; and the offices and residences of other diplomats in the San Li Tun diplomatic area. At the center was the Friendship Store, where one could buy food, clothing, and a wide variety of Chinese products. Nearby in Wangfujing were the department stores and specialty shops, such as they were. Concession stores, which handled secondhand items, the effluvia of an overthrown bourgeoisie, had intriguing things like old watches to buy. Liulichang, a *hutong* (lane) that specialized in art shops, was a favorite destination, as was the Theater Store near the Front Gate of the city, which to the boys' delight featured lifelike wooden replicas of machine guns and automatic pistols as stage props for contemporary political operas.

Everything was in biking distance, so the family saddled up and hit the streets. At first it was tough going. Oliver ran into a lady whose bicycle fell over while he fell off his. Both were unhurt. He described the experience as "awful," but was soon pedaling again. Earlier, he had burst into floods of tears on his bed at the hotel, telling me that he did not want to go away to boarding school. I explained that there were no schools for foreign children his age in Beijing and that we had no choice but to send him and Adam to the United States in September. Leaving home was part of growing up, I said. Oliver replied that he just did not want to grow up so fast. We had good days and bad. Worry about pending separation hovered over family life. Beijing in July is hideously hot, if it is not raining. We sweated a lot.

Sheila was learning fast about housekeeping, Beijing style. As she told her diary:

July 6. I spent the day at the apartment with a crew of eight cleaning ladies. They were waiting at 8:30 A.M. and stripped to white crepe, somewhat see-through, form-fitting undershirts to start work—no bras, lots of nipples. All seemed in their 40s and had Beijing accents. Some called me *furen* (madam) and others called me *taitai* (Mrs.). None commented on my Chinese. Room by room, we scrubbed down and unpacked and placed the furniture. Local soap and scouring powder from the Friendship Store did not work too well. I was also told to buy a *pan*, a cock feather duster to knock dust down off the walls, a sine qua non of Beijing housekeeping. I ended up borrowing one from … an Armenian neighbor on the first floor.

The ladies took several breaks, including an hour for lunch and a nap, and requested boiled water, although refusing tealeaves. One shared her cup with me and all were solicitous that I was tired. They came from the Diplomatic Services Bureau and did a good job, although the apartment is still filthy. At the end of the day, they all spent a little time hanging off the kitchen balcony exclaiming at the female bathing suits in the International Club pool nearby.

This was the family's first direct experience with Chinese household labor practices. Later we were to discover that naps were *de rigueur* in Mao's China, an almost religious practice, at least in the industrial sector. When the time came to make and install the curtains for the apartment, I was startled, returning home during the lunch hour, to find the women workers asleep on the dining room table with the curtains tucked up under their chins. These were not the short power naps at which Premier Zhou was reputedly so adept, but hour-long snoozes. The habit did not survive Deng

Xiaoping's economic reforms in the late seventies and the surges of economic growth that followed.

Back to Sheila's narrative:

> After dinner, at which there was much fluttering in the dovecotes concerning Senator Magnuson's behavior in his meeting with Zhou Enlai, we went biking under the walls of the Forbidden City, in front of the Meridian Gate and through Tiananmen Square, by the old American Embassy in the Legation Quarter and down "Rectitude Road."
>
> People were singing and playing trumpets under the walls. Couples were snuggling in the strip of bushes that ran down the center of the road. Once, when one of the children looped his bike into a courtyard gateway, a PLA man sprang out. ... Being here seems a combination of outrageous romance and utterly ordinary problems, like keeping the boys going and managing their squabbles.

We took in the great sights of the city and its environs, mounting expeditions to the Summer Palace, the Ming Tombs, and the Great Wall. The boys reacted in fresh and curious ways. When I told Sanhu when the Forbidden City was built early in the Ming Dynasty, all he could say was "Wow, three hundred years older than the Red Lion Inn!" (in Stockbridge , Massachusetts). Months later, visiting the same place, my father, gazing for the first time at the grand scale of the great public courtyards, applied his own Eurocentric architect's comparison, "This," he said, "makes Versailles look like a chicken coop!"

**Where to Go to School**

Primary schooling for USLO dependents was a priority family issue in our cocoon. Sheila and other wives with children who would be staying looked at the alternatives, starting with the "International School" at Fancaodi, China's best effort to provide a positive primary school environment for foreign children. It consisted of two buildings, one for Chinese neighborhood children, the other for foreigners. Both were red brick, three stories, set in a packed-earth courtyard on a tree-lined street of workers' houses. The contrast was striking. Sheila's diary description:

> The curriculum [for foreigners], while strong in Chinese (10 hours plus a week), includes six hours of English using Beijing municipal textbooks for Chinese children, and instead of Social Studies two hours a week of "General Knowledge," science, nature, etc.
>
> We visited classes, encountering shrieking children in the halls, most of whom appeared to be African. In a class of nine-year-olds doing Chinese, about six were from Tanzania, Ghana, Burma, Pakistan, and Nepal. They were working hard with a gentle male teacher, whom they addressed in Chinese. Everyone had little knee desks with spindly legs and patterned linoleum tops in an airy, unadorned classroom. Children were called on and recited confidently.
>
> We were shown artwork: traditional red-paper cutouts, exact copies of a picture of a goldfish with bubbles ... and other efforts at exact reproductions of a sample picture.
>
> Shown the library, a large, airy room, I did not recognize it for what it was immediately. There was a small shelf with stacks of English and French paperback books, illustrated with photographs (*Mine Warfare*) or else charmingly with drawings. All of these were highly political in content and very moralistic, produced for foreign-language studies in the Beijing school system. [Math, we remembered was also political. Take the following word problem, for example: "In a fierce battle, five heroic Vietnamese Air Force jet fighters engage seven cowardly American imperialist bombers over Hanoi and shoot down three. How many imperialist aircraft are left?"]
>
> In contrast to the free-form treatment of foreigners in class and recess, the Chinese section of the school displayed iron discipline. All classes were full, and children sat up straight, opened workbooks and took up pencils upon command, all in unison. Coming out onto the courtyard, Chinese children were drilling on the packed-earth basketball court.

The other alternatives, a French lycée and the Pakistan Embassy School, had relatively stronger curricula but with drawbacks of their own for Americans. In the end, we decided to start a Calvert correspondence school of our own to supplement whatever local school choices families would make. The only space available for our handful of primary school students was a hallway between the Holdridge and Jenkins apartments at San Li Tun. Our first teacher was the Holdridge daughter, Pat, who did a superb job getting us started in the fall.

We decided Sanhu would attend the Pakistan Embassy School. He loathed the place, reporting that all the children started the day crouching on the floor facing into a corner and singing a gloomy song. (Their national anthem, intoned in the direction of Mecca.) His teacher was tough and given to rapping her charges alongside the head. He referred to her, very privately, as "pig-nose weirdo." Their English textbook, published in London in 1966 for use in Pakistan, was quaint and dated. One model sentence read: "A flatiron is an instrument with which one removes the wrinkles from one's clothes, after first having placed it upon the hearth."

## Social Life

Meanwhile, it was still high summer and social life was picking up for the family. The arrival of Don Anderson's wife Blanche, Sheila's close friend from Taichung language school days, and their stunning daughters, Susan and Jean, led to a spike in morale. The girls, exact contemporaries and old friends of Adam and Oliver, had matured in marked and charming ways, adding spark to their relationship.

The Marines opened their apartment and their bar, dubbing it the "Red Ass Saloon" in honor of the Seabees who built it, and threw a lively inaugural ball. Sheila relates: "All three boys thought it the party of the century and came home reluctantly, Sanhu with me at 11:30 and the boys on bikes with the Anderson girls at 12:30. Oliver, who danced with Mrs. Bruce, thinks she's probably the most beautiful woman in the world."

For the rest of us, dancing the frug in the stern, authoritarian heart of Communist China was just another mind-bending experience in an unforgettable time. The Red Ass Saloon was the instant hit of the diplomatic community, attracting wide attention, which doomed it from the outset. Managing membership became a huge headache, and complaints from neighbors who could not get in grew as time passed. For the moment, though, the saloon gave us all a lift.

# 15

# Collecting China

In the tight-shut seventies, geographic access was one of the most valuable gifts the Chinese could bestow on foreigners, and they doled out destinations like party favors. Formal permission to travel followed a strange bargaining process, with first choices traded for fallback cities. "Xi'an is closed but you can go to Tianjin," officials might tell you, the equivalent of saying "No, Chicago is not open, but how about Hoboken?" Foreigners in China collected places the way kids accumulate baseball cards. We did not drop names, we dropped places, the more distant and obscure, the better. Casual mention of a day spent in some grimy hinterland industrial city where no one else had been was the most telling form of one-up-manship. Ploys aside, the more places you went, the better feel you had for this enormous, unknown country. Nowadays, diplomats, journalists, and tourists can go just about anywhere, but thirty years ago, each new town was a pearl of great price.

I was determined to take the family on a trip before the start of school and began the haggling by applying for the most scenic, distant, and historic places—Kunming, Guilin, and Wuhan—with no idea if the Chinese would accept or not. They encouraged me to apply and ended up agreeing on an itinerary that included Wuhan, Nanjing, Suzhou, and Shanghai.

Wuhan was of particular interest to me. Strategically located on the Yangzi River, the city had been the site of the rebellion that overthrew the imperial system in 1911, as well as the scene of notable violence early in the Cultural Revolution. Nanjing, or "Southern Capital," had been the seat of government at various times during Chinese history, most recently the capital for Chiang Kai-shek's

Nationalist government. Suzhou was famous for its gardens and the beauty of its women, and Shanghai was, well, Shanghai.

## Setting Off

In a great state of excitement, Sheila, the three tigers, and I boarded the night train from Beijing to Wuhan on July 23, arriving the next morning after a restless night. Sanhu cut his head on the steps leading to the upper bunk, a tiny cut that bled profusely and brought several service ladies rushing to our aid. They stopped the bleeding with coagulant salts and bandaged him up like a pirate, then called ahead for a doctor from the railroad hospital. He climbed aboard at the next stop, examined the wound, confirmed that the boy had been properly treated, and leapt off the train chirping, "Serve the people."

We crossed the Yellow River before midnight amid dramatic horizon-broad flashes of heat lightening. I guessed that most trains are scheduled to cross this vital strategic point at night. Sheila remembered "a symphony of trains shrieking past us, noisy station stops filled with running women and babies and men all shouting 'Quick! Quick!' as station announcers quacked above it all. Sweating, we awoke to South China and rice growing, with little boys minding water buffaloes and paddy fields in different stages of cultivation."

We settled into the Shengli (Victory) Hotel, an old British pile that was still one of the finest in China. Our room had high ceilings and air-conditioning. The boys were impressed with the bathroom fixtures, British Twyfold "Centaur" toilets. Hankou, the part of the city where we were located, was a former foreign concession. It looked quite European, with dormer windows, brick buildings, arcades, and houses with verandahs, all in a dilapidated state. From our room's two balconies, we could see a large stable courtyard to the west, some lawn surrounded by red tile–roofed buildings to the south, and a patch of misty river.

## We Become a Delegation

Touring with one's children in China was unheard of. There were no American-style children's amusements, no Disneylands, or aquariums with performing killer whales. The Chinese loved their zoos and took their kids to the ones in their cities; but no one went on pleasure trips with children. Unless you were a high-level official with business reasons, you did not go on trips, period. The top leadership used the old missionary beach resort at Beidaihe each summer as a location for important political conferences. Though some took their families, that was it.

But the Chinese were expert at the care and feeding of foreign delegations touring the important sites they wanted to show off—the museums, hospitals, factories, bridges, communes, government offices, and restaurants of the particular place. Foreign delegations were what they knew, and that was what the Platt family became. The China Travel Service in each city assigned us a guide and minder with whom we negotiated an itinerary. Having worked with the U.S. Swim Team, I knew the drill. The sights we asked to see were temples, museums, or historic places listed in Nagels, the only decent guidebook of the day. In fact, we were happy with anything the Chinese wanted to show us—schools, factories, hospitals, whatever. The transformation of our children into dignitaries began right away and proved surprisingly easy. They were genuinely interested in what they encountered, and they grew to enjoy the celebrity status that awaited them in streets full of Chinese astonished and delighted by their exotic appearance and friendly behavior. To gather a crowd of several thousand people in any Chinese city, all that had to happen was for everyone on a given block to stop moving.

## People as Animals

Our delegation's first event was a visit to the Yangzi River Bridge—an iconic landmark of which the Chinese are justly proud. The river is more than a mile wide in Wuhan and had been a formidable natural barrier, flooding frequently over the centuries with disastrous results. Construction of the huge span in the early 1950s had united China physically and politically behind the Communist government.

The head of the bridge maintenance unit, Mr. Xiao, met us and took us into a reception room located deep in the easternmost pylon of the bridge. In a briefing sprinkled with militant slogans, he described the construction process and the victory for Chairman Mao's thought that it represented. The boys, including Sanhu, asked some good questions about building techniques — caissons were not used, apparently, but rather piles driven by works from the surface.

What one saw when crossing the bridge was more striking to us than the structure itself. Sheila's eyes recorded "an absolute stream of men and women and boys harnessed to two-wheeled wagons ... carrying cotton, rice bowls wrapped in straw, bags of wheat and rice. They strained and heaved up the [slope of the] bridge, the boys pushing behind or bent double in harness in front, and then braced themselves against the load coming down, braking it also with large wooden props behind." Our children had never seen people doing the work of animals before.

"You can see why we feel so much the need of trucks," Mr. Rui, our China Travel Service minder told us, embarrassed. I watched a man and a donkey in harness together, sharing the work in front of a cart. The man was outpulling the animal.

Wuhan's summer heat was like a coat you wore with buttons that lock. The city is the hottest of China's "three furnaces," Nanjing and Chongqing being the other two. What made it worse was the lack of relief at night, when people pulled their beds into the streets and onto the rooftops searching for a breath of wind. Our entire visit to Wuhan was suffused with heat.

The cuisine was a match for anything we had found so far in the rest of China. The first evening we dined in Hankou at the renowned Dou Pi restaurant, named after its specialty — shrimps and sticky rice wrapped in egg and flour. The sweet and sour fish — dipped in egg, fried, stuffed with herbs, then refried and covered with sauce of garlic, onions, shrimps, peas, and tomatoes — was to die for. Pig livers and jellyfish — the one tender as a bud, the other a contrasting texture like rubber bands, baby shrimps, and tiny thin chicken strips — filled out the menu. Another Wuhan specialty, soup dumplings — pale green, served in a steamer on a bed of pine needles — became a favorite.

We had tea in an upstairs room. The boys wandered out on the balcony from time to time to wave at the gathering crowd below, like dictators after a coup in a banana republic. Afterwards we toured the kitchen, a grimy hellhole, and congratulated the cooks and waiters, who were delighted with the visit of the young delegates. We walked back through the streets, past people lying in their beds on the sidewalk and fanning themselves slowly, balancing with care the output of energy needed to move the breeze with that which might make them hotter still.

**Salt in the Popsicles**

The next morning, we rose early to take the ferry up the Yangzi to the giant Wuhan Iron and Steel Company, the second largest in China. Sheila's diary recounts:

> The steamer was painted khaki and stopped at five landing stages between ours on the waterfront near the hotel and downriver at the mill landing on the south side. As we swung out, the boat to Shanghai was leaving ahead of us, four decks of passengers leaning on the rails and fanning themselves. The trip takes two and a half days, and we longed to make it. As it was, the river was wide and handsome, a muddy orange color. The foreign concession buildings on the north bank looked very familiar and old-fashioned. One sees so many prints of Hong Kong, Shanghai, and Canton with the same sort of architecture. We sat up front with the crew and talked about the river, which had been high recently. The steel mill landing was flooded into its willow trees. ... A junk nosed up to the bank and unloaded watermelons tossed from hand to hand up the slope. The mill rears darkly out of a green vegetable landscape.

Sweltering but riveted, we toured blast furnaces, the rolling mill, and blowing mill. Workers moved languidly through the heat, sucking salted Popsicles to replace their sweat. The boys, after a Popsicle experience of their own, listened patiently to an official standard political briefing in the cool guest house originally built for Soviet advisors (who had departed abruptly in 1959) and asked questions about working conditions. By now, we had developed a routine with our hosts at each stop, with Sheila asking about the roles of women, Adam focusing on the history of the site, Oliver curious about what people did after work, Sanhu preoccupied about the youngest workers, and me, as always, riveted on politics.

## Acupuncture Kills Pain

For our next entertainment, China Travel Service chose the Number Two Hospital of Wuhan Medical College, which had pioneered the use of acupuncture as an anesthetic. Through windows above the operating amphitheater we saw first a thyroid tumor removed from the graceful throat of a seventeen-year-old girl. Awake throughout, she was wheeled away smiling and praising Chairman Mao. The tumor, Sanhu remarked, looked like a thousand-year-old egg when finally extracted and deposited in a dish. His hosts thought that was funny. The other operation we witnessed involved removal of some particularly unappetizing polyps from the nose of a sixty-year-old worker using wire lassos. Oliver retired for a cup of tea during the procedure.

Moving about the hospital, we saw acupuncture applied to a variety of neurological ills, ranging from paralysis to bad dreams, and a ward for heart patients treated with a combination of Western and traditional medicine. Adam was spooked by a room full of beds on which rows of patients jerked peacefully, their muscles twitching to electrical impulses. He made a discreet visit to the bathroom.

Dr. Ni, a dour political medic, led the reception and inevitable briefing. Sheila, the family medical professional, recorded his explanation of the hospital setup, including "absolute sexual equality, teams of doctors and nurses sent to the countryside, etc. He was at pains to show that the staff served the people and told the story of a doctor, lacking an aspirator, personally sucking mucus from the throat of a peasant child with pneumonia. . . . My own role as a hospital social worker was difficult to explain." She further commented in her diary:

> The mind boggles at the difference between having kidney disease in Wuhan, with two [dialysis] machines available

and no medical fees, and in Washington, with a minimum of $9,000 a year to use a machine. ... My impression was that the doctors and staff are personally very warm and kind. No sign of temperament, hustle bustle, or prima donna behavior.

The technique of using acupuncture as an anesthetic is notably personal. The anesthetist is warmly supportive and strokes, pats, and talks to the patient throughout [the operation]. This ingredient itself is invaluable in a traumatic experience like surgery and must remove so many unknowns and so much fright/anxiety from the situation.

As we left, Sheila said she was impressed and would find it a pleasure to be sick here. Dr. Ni replied that he hoped we would return, but not as patients. Unfortunately, this proved a prophetic exchange.

## Horror at the University

Our request to visit Wuhan University came through the next day. The tour began with my interviewing a member of the Revolutionary Committee office named Chen. My general impression was that the curriculum was a shambles. During our talk, the boys sat around in stuffed chairs and read their books. Oliver talked to one charming girl student who spoke excellent English and had been a Red Guard, gone to the capital, and seen Chairman Mao.

We went upstairs onto the balcony to get a view of the university. I was taking a movie pan of the dilapidated campus and chatting with Chen when Oliver screamed in agony at the other end of the balcony and ran toward me holding his right hand. The tip of his middle finger was gone, the end of the finger mangled and bleeding, his bone protruding. He had been playing with a hand-cranked siren, gotten it going, and then stuck his right middle finger in to stop it.

Chen and I took hold of Oliver on either side holding his wounded hand and rushed him down four flights of stairs and out to the primitive infirmary in the back, Oliver roaring about how it hurt and what a dummy he'd been—"This machine kills! My finger is dead! I'm dead! It hurts! It hurts!" he howled—Sheila and I coo-ing, holding him, blood and sweat getting all over my shirt. The sweat was my own.

A doctor also named Chen quickly put a tourniquet on Ol's fin-ger and covered it with gauze. Mr. Rui, our sitter, called the hos-pital, and we roared off in two Shanghais on a wild ride weaving in and out of trucks on the Yangzi and Hanyang bridges, arriving twenty minutes later at the No. 2 hospital, where the day before we had witnessed the operations.

Sheila relates:

Oliver was semi-hysterical all the way, but very brave, clutching my hand and biting on a knotted handkerchief. The mutilation was shocking to us all, and we kept seeing the exposed bone and hearing his cry. During the ride he said, "I'll never be the same again. I'll have a freak finger. No one will like me." He also, of course, worried about acupuncture and wanted to be put to sleep. "Acupuncture won't work! It won't work!"

In the operating room (the same one in which the young girl had her thyroid tumor removed), which seemed a cool, clean, safe haven, he was given a shot of Dilantin, which made him relaxed and high, so he simply lay back and co-operated with the team, which soothed and patted him. NP and I robed in surgical gowns, masked and scrubbed, sat by his head until, at his request, I went to get Adam and Sanhu and sat in the theater above. Oliver managed a feeble wave and Sanhu watched the repair job carefully, sipping pineapple juice. Adam watched obliquely, and I, thankfully, avoided looking at all.

Meanwhile the tip of Oliver's finger had arrived in another car from the university, where the Chinese had found it jammed in the siren. The doctors were marvelously skilled. They cleaned the tip, cut off the shredded tissue, and made a skin flap. Then they dis-infected his hand, cleaned the finger, snipped the shredded skin, trimmed his bone ("gross clicking," as Oliver described it), fitted the two parts together and sewed them up with sixteen stitches, bandaged him, and gave him antibiotics. Oliver was calmed by the lovely anesthetist who made him feel cozy and relaxed. "I did not even know what she was saying but it was nice stuff—amazing!" he said.

After we returned to the hotel, the anesthetic wore off and Oliver started to hurt badly. We decided then to divide the delegation and send Sheila and Oliver home to Beijing. Just then a knock at our hotel room door announced the arrival of a high-ranking "comfort delegation," including the head of the Wuhan Branch of the China Travel Service, the head of the Wuhan University Revolutionary Committee, Dr. Chen, our Mr. Chen from the university, and Sitter Rui. Oliver, eased by codeine and a Chinese-made drug called Salidin, propped himself up to receive them.

A long exchange of condolences and pleasantries ensued. I told our visitors that it would be hard to imagine the same quality and quantity of medical care in any other country under these circumstances. I told them that I would feel very bad if they blamed themselves in any way, that it was my responsibility to keep thirteen-year-olds of my own flesh and blood from inserting their fingers into unfamiliar machines, that the Chinese reaction to Ol's accident was an even better example of the developing relationship between the two countries than the warm welcome we had received at the university. The delegation smiled and departed. We played Hearts and Old Maid, dosed Ol again, ate, and went to bed. What a day!

Our own Wuhan incident proved to be the effective end of our family delegation. Sheila and Oliver went back to steamy Beijing and several painful sessions at the Capital Hospital (the old Peking Union Medical College founded by the Rockefellers). Adam, Sanhu, and I continued the trip, feeling guilty about enjoying ourselves while Oliver was in pain.

## Collecting Nanjing, Suzhou, and Shanghai

I had been told about the charm of plane tree–lined streets in Nanjing; the exquisite calm of Suzhou gardens, and already knew the noisy density of Shanghai street life. But I was unprepared for the hair-raising dangers of upcountry commercial aviation. The Wuhan-Nanjing plane, an ancient Ilyushin 14 without seatbelts, threaded its way between towering thunderstorms, guided by a pilot whose main flight experience had clearly been fighter aircraft. We decided that trains were better.

A few special moments in my growing collection of Chinese cities remain clearly etched:

—The Precious Belt bridge—53 arches, 1,200 years old, along the Grand Canal straddling the Suzhou River, lots of boats new and old, old men naked as newts hunting for crabs among the lotus and other water vegetation under a hot blue sky.

—Sitting in Suzhou on a hump-backed bridge in the dark, a little light left. In the west, heat lightning around the horizon reflected on the water, three Chinese sitting silently in the swelter watching us, as Sanhu described a ride in Disneyland through an African landscape, with the guide shooting blanks at plastic hippos that threatened mechanically, Chinese music all around.

—Passing one night by a house in Suzhou where a fierce domestic fight was in full swing. One man and two women, lots of swearing and slugging, people bounding off walls, a small crowd of neighbors clustered apprehensively around the front door. I stood on a bridge at the back and listened to the shouts, watching heads flash past the window. In the end the man, thin and past middle life, dressed only in shorts, stamped swearing out of the house.

We returned to Beijing on July 31. Sanhu had come down with the flu in Shanghai, and Adam's fly zipper had broken on the plane. I arrived at the door of our hotel suite with one child clearly feverish, the other gingerly holding his crotch. Sheila was glad to see us, nonetheless. She and Oliver had had a horrible time. The tip of his finger, though healing, had turned black. He would need a new operation and skin graft.

## Settled at Last

The weeks after returning saw real progress in building the family nest. Airfreight and a food and liquor shipment all arrived at the same time as the Diplomatic Service Bureau personnel assigned to install air-conditioners in our apartment. The result was progressive, constructive chaos—piles of dirt, mindless opening of crates, building of shelves and hanging poles, trunks full of excelsior—all in suffocating humidity and no one to rely on but ourselves and people from the mission. The Chinese kindly violated protocol order and put an air-conditioner in Oliver's room so his finger would heal faster. Shortly thereafter a rotund, wall-eyed lady from Shandong named Gang showed up and announced she had been assigned as our cleaning lady. Friendly and straightforward, she went immediately to work scrubbing up the place, doing the laundry, and improving our morale.

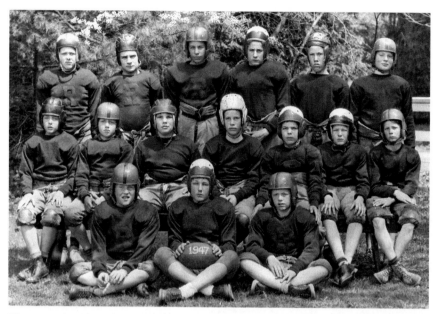

The 1947 Bedford Rippowam School football team (Nicholas Platt is in the back row on the far right).

The Bedford Rippowam Class of 1947 (NP in third row far left).

Welcome banquet, Beijing, February 21, 1972. The Chinese commented on how young President Nixon and his delegation were. The Chinese guests were indeed ancient by comparison.

President and Mrs. Nixon at the Ming Tombs, February 1972.

Counterpart meetings between Secretary of State Rogers and Foreign Minister Ji to discuss practical next steps in U.S.-China relations, February 21–28, 1972.

The Platt family arrives in China: Sheila, Adam, Nick Jr (Sanhu), Nick Sr at the famous Ban Xi Restaurant, Guangzhou, June, 1973. (photo by Oliver Platt)

Madame Mao (Jiang Qing) emerges in public as Mao's successor, here at the U.S.-China basketball game greeting Nick Platt, Beijing, June 1973.

Getting ready to travel, NP at Beijing Railroad station, July 1973.

Nick Platt with his new boss, Ambassador David Bruce, August 1973.

David Bruce with Platt family: Nick, Sheila, and Adam behind Sanhu and Oliver, Beijing, August 1973.

# 16

# Waiting, Watching, and Welcoming

During the summer and fall of 1973, the Liaison Office was preoccupied with the politics of waiting for a Kissinger visit, watching for the Tenth Party Congress, and welcoming one unusual U.S. delegation after another.

The Kissinger visit—initially expected in August—kept being put off for a variety of reasons: Chinese disapproval over our role in war-ravaged Cambodia, leadership differences involved in the scheduling and management of their Party Congress, and finally William Rogers's resignation as secretary of state and Henry's appointment to succeed him. Kissinger did not want to come to China until he had been confirmed by the Senate and had assumed the full authority of that office, along with his duties as national security advisor. The visit ultimately occurred in November after voluminous exchanges with David Bruce, Al Jenkins, and John Holdridge and consultations between Bruce and President Nixon in San Clemente, all against the backdrop of the worsening crisis over Watergate.

## A Meeting Long Delayed

China watchers in general and the Beijing diplomatic corps in particular had developed a cottage industry out of predictions, previews, scene setters, and speculations related to the timing, substance, and outcomes of the long anticipated Tenth Party Congress, the first major meeting since the Cultural Revolution lost its bite. We all scrutinized leadership activities and appearances from every angle and examined every reference in the press for clues. All empirical signs indicated a major conclave in the works—the limousines in front of the Great Hall where the lights had burned late every night since the end of July; the statements of Chinese diplomats abroad; the postponement of most foreign delegation visits; the lack of large-scale leadership turnouts; and reports that Congress delegates had been picked.

Evidence of continuing tension among leadership factions had been there for all to see since our arrival in the capital and before. We speculated now that difficult domestic and foreign policy issues were the reasons it was taking the Congress so long to jell. How to dispose of the ghost of Lin Biao, named as Mao's successor in the current constitution, was particularly pressing. His plane had crashed in Mongolia after an abortive coup attempt in late 1971. Whom to place on the Central Committee and the Politburo, and how to handle educational reform, economic priorities, scientific assistance, youth in the countryside, and culture were among the most controversial questions.

## Calm on the Surface

Our travels in China that summer revealed no evidence that any of these concerns had penetrated the lower levels of the body politic. On the contrary, and in marked contrast to the violent phase of the Cultural Revolution, calm seemed to prevail. I was asked to set the scene for Washington's benefit and wrote the following message, based on an entry in my diary:

> As the Party prepares for its meeting the country seems rather relaxed. My observations are random and fragmentary, based on brief visits to eight cities, but the pattern seems quite pervasive and consistent.
>
> Under enormous posters of the revolutionary peoples of the world clutching rifles and singing fierce revolutionary songs, white-shirted Chinese stroll lackadaisically, fanning themselves with rattan fronds, eating Popsicles and then letting the wrappers flutter gently to the ground. Service personnel with little shovels or, in the bigger cities, riding motorized sweepers, will come along to pick them up eventually.

In Beijing and during visits to Guangzhou, Changsha, Shaoshan, Nanjing, Wuhan, Suzhou, and Shanghai, I have seen only three Mao buttons, one worn by an American Chinese thinking to ingratiate himself with his friends. People play cards openly in the streets and on trains, something done only furtively two years ago and not at all two years before that. The rhetoric of meetings with officials of factories, communes, maintenance units, etc., is toned down, though one or two ritual kowtows to Chairman Mao are a normal feature of every interview.

The shops are crowded with people actually buying things. A walk up and down Nanjing Road in Shanghai on a Monday afternoon in July leads one to wonder if in fact anyone in the city is gainfully employed. The streets and shops are so thronged that you can walk only at a crawl. The pace of work in factories and units is slow, partially a fact of heat. People are less afraid to talk than reported before, but they don't say much. China Travel Service guides relax after a while and often open up a bit.

If politics are not as strident an element of everyday life as before, they are very much there, just the same. The major campaign to "Struggle, Criticize, and Rectify" (*Dou, Pi, Gai*), underway nationwide, is accompanied by exhortations to "Read Books and Study." The Chinese we talked to were not sure at first what these meant and how they related. An official in Nanjing told me that "Read Books and Study" amounted to organized bible study twice a week. The "Struggle Criticize, and Rectify" campaign is vague and started slowly because none of the Chinese at first knew (a) what to struggle against, (b) what they were criticizing, and (c) how they should rectify it, whatever it was. ...

The military plays a much smaller role in civilian life from what one can now see. Representatives from factories, communes, and universities to whom we put the question normally say that PLA representatives still sit on their revolutionary committees. But they are fewer than before and far below the one-third ratio demanded and, in fact, needed during the turbulent order-restoring period of the Cultural

Revolution. There are fewer soldiers on the streets of Beijing now, even than when we first arrived, and they are hard to find in other cities.[20]

## A Communist Analysis

Although the Western and Japanese embassies were well-stocked with competent China analysts, we were all plowing the same sparse field of speculative data available about the Tenth Party Congress, "drinking each other's bath water," to cite a gross metaphor we used. I sought a fresh perspective on domestic politics and found one in the Yugoslav Embassy. Ilja Djukic, an urbane, experienced diplomat with a strong China background, had already become a friend. Through him I met an embassy political specialist named Trcek, a cerebral mole of a man whose close-set eyes sat behind little rectangular spectacles.

Trcek's background included years as a senior lecturer in Chinese affairs in Belgrade and as head of the Yugoslav Party's China section, plus three years now in Beijing. The combination of political, academic, and hands-on experience in China provided him with the most erudite grasp of domestic politics of anyone I had yet met. The Yugoslavs had an edge over the rest of us. They were Communists themselves and understood the workings of party machinery. I called on Trcek, ostensibly for a brief courtesy introduction. But propelled by kindred interests, we talked for two hours, sitting on carved furniture in the Yugoslav Embassy, sweat dripping down beneath our polite jackets and ties.

His analysis: The major policy directions for China were being set now, or have been in the process of being set during the past two years and not during the Cultural Revolution, which in his words was only "a spectacle." The moderates were in control, but the left was strong enough to make itself heard, and to counterattack from time to time. He cited as an example the lead article in *Red Flag* (the party's main theoretical journal) for August, which expressed dissatisfaction with bourgeois tendencies in the "superstructure" (meaning, the top leadership). This, he felt, was in answer to a series of moderate commentaries on culture, which had demanded a higher volume of more entertaining cultural works that paid more attention to local tastes and popular demand.

There were so many unresolved issues that the outcome of the Party Congress could only be a compromise. Deep differences existed over foreign policy, the pace of economic development, culture, and the rehabilitation of officials. The Congress, in any case, was badly needed to confirm policies adopted during the past two years. Government and party cadres (officials) needed an authoritative signal to proceed. Many of them had been recently rehabilitated and were still worried that the more moderate trend could be reversed.

Congress postponements were the work of moderates, Trcek felt. They had enough power to prevent a meeting if preparations were not going their way. In his experience with Party Congresses in Yugoslavia, delays were usually the result of differences over personnel. Policy issues could always be fudged.

The current relaxed pace of society would be difficult to reverse. He noticed large numbers of official cars, filled with the wives and children of cadres, parked for shopping in front of department stores during working hours. In a society where basic standards were so low, the small perks and incremental additions to salaries made a much larger impact on comparative living standards. The spread between 36 yuan (the basic minimum wage) and 150 yuan (what senior cadres earned) as a monthly salary was enormous, much greater than in an affluent society. You could always tell from the numbers of cars in the parking lot whether a political campaign directed at cadre corruption had teeth. If it did, the lot would be empty.

**The Secret Anticlimax**

When we finally learned about the Congress it was already over. August 29 had been a difficult day for our family. With big lumps in our throats, we put the older boys on the plane for Guangzhou, the first leg of their journey home to boarding school (Adam to Middlesex and Oliver to Eaglebrook). That evening we gave a dinner party for C. C. Chang, a visiting Chinese American meteorologist, which included Australian ambassador Fitzgerald, his wife Gay, and Don Anderson.

As we sat down to dinner the phone rang, the distinctive double rings of a long distance call. It was Oliver at the Dong Fang Hotel in Guangzhou sobbing into the receiver. He said he had to come home, he was going crazy, was not going to make it. Sheila and I both talked to him and calmed him down. Adam was cool and collected, but obviously affected. "He's beginning to get to me," Adam muttered. Upset, we returned to our guests. (Years later, Sheila and I still kick ourselves for not having accompanied the boys as far as Guangzhou. Within the week, however, we were comforted by reports from close friends in Hong Kong that they had cheered up. Long term, the separation was a low point for all of us, and left lasting scars.)

The phone rang again, this time a local call. It was David Bonavia, the *Times* of London correspondent, reporting his ticker announcing that the Party Congress had finished yesterday after five days in session! After we said goodbye to our guests, Don and I drove downtown to observe the scene. This is what we reported the next day:

> Atmospherics. Local response to news of the Party Congress has lacked enthusiasm or militancy. As the 9 p.m. August 29 broadcast began to report the results of the meeting, decorative lights on buildings all over Beijing went on. Shortly thereafter, small knots of rather desultory marchers, mostly young people, started parading around the streets of the capital behind red flags, cymbals, drums, and portraits of Chairman Mao. Their patterns of marching were carefully controlled to cover specific neighborhoods, with no large crowds permitted to collect. Tiananmen Square was relatively empty. The largest groups, reaching perhaps several hundred each, were seen in front of the Minzu and Xinqiao Hotels, as if gathered there for the benefit of foreign visitors. There were a few scattered firecrackers and skyrockets. Slogans were muttered en masse rather than shouted in any disciplined or energetic way. Those few Beijing residents who were out on the streets and not marching moved about without joining in. One worker welding a section of pipe near the old city moat did not even stop to look up as the

masses shambled by. The special lights went out promptly at midnight by which time the marchers were well in their beds. Marching activity continued on August 30 on a slightly larger scale, though with no increase in verve.[21]

## Final Assessments

Over the next two days, we sent in a stream of telegrams analyzing the Congress documents that came out. The name lists suggested that Zhou Enlai had managed another tightrope walk. The Politburo ranked Wang Hongwen, the 36-year-old Shanghai labor union radical, at Number 3, but his rise was balanced by rehabilitated moderates, most notably Deng Xiaoping. The Central Committee comprised fewer military men and more women. The State Council (a Zhou stronghold) appeared to have done well. Several officials of the Ministry of Foreign Affairs instrumental in the détente with the United States—UN Ambassador Huang Hua, Foreign Minister Ji Pengfei (William Rogers's opposite number), and Vice Minister Qiao Guanhua (Bruce's favorite)—were honored with membership in the Central Committee.

Specific denunciations of Lin Biao as a Rightist, the worst name a Communist can be called, were a main feature of the Congress's political reports. The people of China were charged to criticize Lin as well as Confucius during their study sessions, which added to the confusion already widespread. That, it turned out later, had been Zhou Enlai's whole point. John Holdridge remembered hearing the premier laughingly tell Henry Kissinger when he visited in November that he had himself taken advantage of the Congress to initiate the campaign to criticize Lin (*pi Lin*). Since Zhou himself had been the Radical's target in the campaign to criticize Confucius (*pi Kong*), the addition of Lin took the focus off him and diluted the impact of the entire campaign.[22]

Congress pronouncements dealt with foreign policy in the broadest terms. The United States was lumped together with the Soviet Union as a superpower whose "hegemonism" was to be opposed. At the same time the Soviet Union was singled out for special treatment with a warning to be on guard against surprise attacks by "social imperialism." We yawned with relief.

The meeting was odd for its brevity. Five days was the shortest congress since the Communists came to power. Defensive references in the documents to "repeated deliberations and consultations" suggested leadership sensitivity to charges of a rushed, put-up job. In addition, this was the first, and only, congress that had not been announced at the outset. We speculated that the meeting planners were worried enough about possible mishaps to forgo the normal, ritual appearances of openness and democratic centralism. In summary, the Tenth Party Congress struck us as a carefully managed production, laboriously prepared and held in secret by an apprehensive leadership, anxious to confirm a new lineup while keeping in hand pressure for further change.

In the immediate aftermath, top officials avoided comment on the Congress to foreigners, even ostensibly close friends. Vietnamese party chief Le Duan arrived in Beijing for a visit the day the Congress ended. At a banquet that evening he was clearly interested in what had happened and asked Zhou Enlai, in effect, "What's new?" Zhou replied, "Nothing."[23]

The arcane outcome of the Tenth Party Congress, and particularly the defensive way it was handled, underscored for all of us living in China at the time the peculiar fragility of leadership relationships in the waning years of Mao's rule. This affected the way Beijing dealt with U.S. leaders, whom Watergate had also made fragile. On practical matters, our relationship on official dealings had reached a plateau. We were in China, and we had set up an office. But the pace of official responsiveness to our requests had slowed, and we were now, it seemed being treated like everyone else. We still lacked apartments, storage space, language teachers, and electric wiring. I supposed that this was what normalization was all about.

## Getting to Know You

But there was nothing fragile about the pace at which people-to-people relations between Chinese and Americans were developing that summer. Beijing was swarming with groups from the United States. The White House Fellows came and went, as did a group from Staten Island Community College, a gaggle of education officials, and the model cities group of young blacks and Chicanos from Chicago, escorted by old friend FSO Charles Hill. Businessmen looking for trade opportunities added significantly to the mix. All were met, briefed, and entertained at USLO.

The groups all wanted contact with American officials, but the thing they seemed to appreciate most was the chance to come to the Liaison Office for an hour and have some real American booze. In Washington, you would probably decline an invitation to stand in a steamy room drinking whiskey with other sweaty Americans, even if David Bruce was giving the party. In Beijing, the idea was compelling. Americans responded to invitations with hoarse croaks of thanks from cracked lips and fat tongues. After weeks of traveling in China with Chinese guides, culture shock, and overeating, the sight of the American flag and a bottle of bourbon brought tears to many an eye.

These groups varied widely in type and quality. The Chinese were clearly targeting a cross section of Americans, and that is what they were getting. The White House Fellows and the educators' group were both attractive bunches of intelligent, reasonably objective achievers who knew what they wanted out of their trips and understood when they did not always get it. A high-powered delegation from the National Council for U.S.-China Trade, representing Westinghouse, Cargill, Deere, and JC Penney, among other companies, came to make commercial contacts that would one day become enormous.

The Staten Island youths were from working class backgrounds, all terribly anxious to be impressed by what they saw, but disillusioned that the Chinese were not practicing what they preached. They were led by some traditional liberals, particularly Bill Birenbaum, a New Yorker transplanted from Iowa; Barbara Thatcher, an old WASP from Bryn Mawr who summered (like me) in North Haven, Maine; and Emile Ji, a starry-eyed young Chinese American professor whose uncle, the interpreter Ji Chaoju, was currently serving in the PRC Liaison Office in Washington.

The model cities group were inner city kids, most of whom were terribly homesick for their neighborhoods and their Motown music. They were being fed well, of course, but hankered for chicken wings, Dr. Pepper, and cream soda from the corner store. One was an avid Black Muslim much impressed with the apparent freedom to practice that religion in China.

Charley Hill, who held the disparate group together, described his delegates as ignorant, unsophisticated, unmannered, incurious, and bright. He found them hilarious and loved being with them. When I finished briefing them, one large, nice-looking kid named Donald came up and said, "Hey man, who is this Bruce you talking 'bout?" As I explained, he asked, "Is that his firs' or his las 'name?" They would go home with a much broader outlook.

# 17

# The Politics of Music

## Dangerous Liaisons

In August, David Bruce had asked me to take over management of the upcoming Philadelphia Orchestra tour. John Holdridge had started the arduous negotiation process in Washington months before. It had become a difficult full-time job, and he had other things to worry about. At any rate, Bruce added, "It's not John's thing." Though flattered, I was deeply apprehensive about the assignment. It was the last major government-sponsored exchange from the United States to the PRC on the horizon and the first one with real cultural impact. The dangers were legion. Culture had torn China apart in recent years. Madame Mao was still in charge of culture, with even the smallest issue referred to her for decision.

Consequently, at the Foreign Ministry, we haggled endlessly over the details of the visit, negotiating music programs as if they were treaties. The Chinese, for example, rejected Strauss' *Don Juan* and Debussy's *Afternoon of a Faun* as prurient and decadent. They came back with Aaron Copland's *Billy the Kid* and any piece by Mozart or Schubert, both of whom they judged politically neuter. Respighi's *Pines of Rome* was fine. The bottleneck at the top meant there was no firm schedule until just before the orchestra was due to arrive in early September. Even then, nothing was solid. Officials were petrified of the chairman's wife and the dire consequences of making a mistake.

Maestro Eugene Ormandy, at least from a distance, could be just as imperious as Madame Mao. No, he would not play Beethoven's Sixth Symphony (the *Pastoral*), as repeatedly requested by the Chinese side. He loathed the piece. Beethoven's Fifth Symphony was fine. So was the Seventh. But the Sixth? Never! Complicating matters further, the orchestra labor union was making sure its rules were carefully followed while the orchestra was in the People's Republic. The usual personality problems within any large creative organization like a symphony orchestra added to my list of worries.

On September 11, I left for Shanghai to meet the orchestra's chartered plane and fly with them to Beijing. I gave myself an extra day in the hope that I would be able to get together with Ministry of Culture officials handling the visit from the Chinese side. Early liaison had been of great help in managing the swimmers' trip. This time, I was held at arm's length until twenty-five minutes before the orchestra landed.

## Beethoven's Peasant Revolution

That was when Mr. Situ, the glum but competent concertmaster of the Central Philharmonic Society, entered the VIP lounge where I was waiting. He sat down and told me with deep apologies that certain revisions in the programs would be required. The leadership now wanted concerts that packaged, with other works, Beethoven's Sixth Symphony, an American composition, and the *Yellow River Concerto*, a wet, romantic piece of program music composed by a revolutionary committee. I pointed out that the agreed programs, which had taken months to negotiate, contained no such combination. Maestro Ormandy's antipathy toward Beethoven's Sixth was well known. The Chinese also wanted revisions in the schedule. I told Situ that I would do my best to work the changes, but feared the consequences of confronting Ormandy with major issues after more than twenty hours of grueling travel.

The orchestra and its entourage arrived, one hundred thirty strong, exhausted but exhilarated. Ormandy, a tiny, hyperanimated man with tufts of fluffy hair, sat me next to him on the plane from Shanghai to Beijing. With trepidation, I related what the Chinese had told me. "You know I hate Beethoven's Sixth, and I did not even bring the scores," he said.

Talking fast, and making a lot up as I went along, I explained the authorities' peculiar predilection for the Sixth in Chinese political terms. The Chinese loved program music, and the *Pastoral* themes represented peasant life in the countryside. Theirs was a peasant revolution, and they identified the storm in the fourth movement with the struggle they had been through. The peaceful, triumphant final movement represented China under Communist rule. It was clear that the request had come from Madame Mao herself.

Ormandy sighed, and said, "If that's what they want, that's what they shall have. I am in Rome and will do as the Romans. I will forget my own rules." His only condition was that scores would be provided by the following afternoon. I almost collapsed with relief.

Ormandy then turned to me. "You should know that I am terribly spoiled," he grinned elfishly. "I only eat in my room, and I only eat steaks and chicken breasts cooked by my wife, Gretel." I had been informed of the maestro's eating habits and had worried how to deal with them. I told him he was sure to like Chinese food and he replied, "I won't." I suggested that he try hard to attend the banquets and just eat a tiny bit, because his hosts would be insulted if he did not. Most Chinese social life went on around the dinner table, and he would be denying himself a major opportunity to meet people. In the event, Ormandy appeared at all important meals, ate nobly, and, to my intense relief, ended up enjoying the food.

I informed orchestra manager Boris Sokoloff of my exchanges with Situ and Ormandy and advised him to keep Ormandy's willingness to play the Sixth in his back pocket during the protracted negotiations that were bound to follow. It was standard Chinese practice to negotiate all details of a visit in advance and then renegotiate the entire program the moment an exhausted delegation arrived in the capital. I told Boris the Chinese would give us anything we wanted as long as the orchestra played the Sixth.

The talks lasted until 2:15 A.M., resulting in a new schedule, which called for four concerts in Beijing instead of three, one of which was a special "leadership program" planned for Sunday, September 16.

## Bravo in Beijing

"The maestro is in a state!" I was told during the intermission of the opening concert. Rushing back to the dressing room, I found Ormandy upset and sweating profusely, his stately Austrian wife Gretel fanning him rapidly with a towel held wide in her ample arms.

"The audience does not like my music," he complained. "They are so quiet. I have never had such a subdued reaction."

I assured Ormandy that the music (Mozart's Symphony no. 35) had been ravishing. The audience response had been as enthusiastic as any I had heard in China. This was not the kind of boisterous ovation to which he was accustomed, but Chinese had not heard Western music for decades and in any case were circumspect in public. This had been a fine start. Ormandy cooled off, with Gretel's help. The concert ended well.

The Central Philharmonic Society presented their visitors a superb concert of Chinese music with traditional instruments. Ormandy was impressed with Chinese musicianship on the *piba*, a gourd-shaped guitar; the *sheng*, a hand-held mouth organ with vertical pipes; and the *erhu*, a two-stringed snakeskin fiddle that sounded at times like a human voice. The musicians told us that yes, they had been sent down to the countryside during the Cultural Revolution. Their special cadre school had been a fruit farm, where they picked plums wearing soft gloves, which protected their precious hands. Madame Mao must have been watching over them.

I never really understood the hands-on impact conductors have on orchestras until I heard Ormandy conduct the Central Philharmonic. Their own conductor, Li Delun, began the exchange, leading his musicians through a ho-hum rendition of a Mozart symphony movement. Ormandy then led the same players through the same piece. The difference was dramatic; the Chinese responded with the strictest attention to the maestro's phrasing, tempo, and dynamics. No one said much for fear of offending Conductor Li, but everyone got it, even I. The musicians then broke into small groups using words and instruments to twitter and warble together, and exchanged gifts. They had much in common and found they could communicate in their own special language. At lunch, we overheard a Philadelphia Orchestra member telling a Chinese musician who was offering him yet more food, "Poco pianissimo, please," to laughter all around.

Banquets and visits to the Great Wall, Ming Tombs, and Summer Palace had their usual impact on first-time visitors and tuned up the Philadelphians. They began as hard-bitten, jet-lagged professionals wondering what they were doing in China. But a crescendo of enthusiasm began to develop, which grew and grew as the visit progressed.

## Madame Mao's Blessing

On September 16, the leadership of the PRC turned out at the highest level ever for a foreign orchestra. Madame Mao led the group, accompanied by politburo member Yao Wenyuan, Peking Municipal Revolutionary Committee Chairman Wu De, Vice Foreign Minister Qiao Guanhua, and PRC Liaison Office Chief Huang Zhen (who was home for consultations). Jiang Qing applauded after every movement of Beethoven's Sixth and led a standing ovation at the end (she later confirmed she had requested the piece). She chatted incessantly and wrote notes to colleagues throughout the *Pines of Rome*, paid polite attention to Barber's *Adagio for Strings*, and seemed moved by Chinese pianist Yin Chenjong's rendition of the *Yellow River Concerto*. Sheila and I sat two rows behind her and David Bruce, watching like hawks. Yin's romantic arrangement of "Home on the Range" and Ormandy's spirited version of the "Worker's and Peasant's March" brought the house down and the music to a close.

Mrs. Mao was wearing a formal black silk crepe version of the gray Eleanor Roosevelt dress she had on for the basketball game in June, white blunt-toed sandals, a white plastic handbag, and a small evening wrist watch set in a circle of what appeared to be precious stones. Full TV and national press coverage were given to her presence at the event in a hall hung with banners reading "Long Live the Friendship Between the Chinese and American Peoples," and "Welcome to China Concert Tour of the Philadelphia Orchestra."

At the reception afterwards, Madame Mao was welcoming, saying she remembered meeting me at the basketball game. She presented Ormandy with an autographed 1870 edition of ancient Chinese songs from her own library, scored in traditional notation, which she said resembled "bean sprouts." To Mrs. Ormandy she gave a large polyethylene bag of Cassia flowers picked from her garden with her own hands. She suggested that the petals be used to flavor wine and cakes for the musicians. The idea of urbane viola players and oboists lacing their martinis with cassia flowers made Sheila and me shriek with laughter later, but it was a genuine gesture and reminiscent of her gift to our women athletes in June.

After a mineral water toast to the continued development of contacts between the peoples and artists of the two countries, the entire party returned to the stage for mass photographs. Mrs. Mao insisted on shaking the hands of all 107 musicians. Ormandy, on the verge of tears by this point, received another jolt when Madame Huang Zhen, who had served in Budapest, approached and addressed him in Hungarian. Coverage of the event was splashed all over the front page of the *People's Daily* the next morning.

The Shanghai stop was a smash. The leadership had blessed the tour, political tension was gone, and the orchestra simply enjoyed themselves. Shanghai audiences were much more alive than those in Beijing. They responded uproariously to Ormandy's closing, blood-racing rendition of "Stars and Stripes Forever" at each of the two jammed concerts. More banquets and a ride up the Huangpu River in a ferryboat serenaded by traditional Chinese musicians. A moving departure, with the entire orchestra boarding a Pan Am Clipper and flying into the Shanghai sunset, closed out an altogether remarkable ten days. One observer noted, "Ormandy really didn't need a plane to get home."

**Dramatis Personae**

The leading personalities involved in the visit added special flavor to the visit's history. Eugene Ormandy himself was, of course, the most piquant. I am not sure why, but we hit it off very well from the start. He had a lot of questions, which Sheila or I were able to answer, and as the trip wore on he kept finding more. As a result we saw a great deal of him. Boris Sokoloff, the manager—a sensible fiftyish Yale man—told me as we parted that we probably had had more contact with Ormandy during this ten-day period than 90 percent of the people associated with him in Philadelphia had ever had. We found Ormandy charming, funny, demanding, egotistical, thoughtful, and childlike. He was narrow in his interests, channeling everything into his music. The results were near miraculous. For example, when the notorious scores for Beethoven's Sixth were given to the orchestra, they turned out to be separate editions from two different musical organizations, the Shanghai and Beijing Orchestras. No one source could supply a group as large as Philadelphia's. Required to work from pages that contained a jumble of different bowing and dynamic instructions, the musicians simply watched Ormandy, and out came a flawless performance.

The maestro was much taken with Sheila, her knowledge of Chinese, and her understanding of music. Given to kissing the cheeks of women he admired, Ormandy made a couple of tries, straining on the tips of his elevator shoes (she was more than a foot taller), then asked her straight-out to bend her knees next time. Naturally she did, and together they formed a new Mutt and Jeff act. Ormandy was held together by his wife Gretel, a warm, solid, long-suffering Austrian lady who wound him up in the morning, fed him, brushed his hair, tied his shoes, patted him, told him when he was out of line, made him take naps, fanned him when he was too hot, wound him down, and put him to bed. She could not have been more friendly, low key, or appreciative to us.

Conductor Li Delun of the Central Philharmonic Society in Beijing, was a fat and expansive politico-musician whose personality was cut from much the same cloth as Ormandy's—obviously the Chinese version of a maestro. Clearly a second-rate conductor, his leadership and political skills obviously made him the ideal honcho for a cultural organization at this stage in China. He knew a great deal about music, had the presence to handle himself well when the national leaders were around, and the managerial ability and sense of humor to run a large communal cultural organization.

Harold Schonberg, the leading music critic of the *New York Times*, was a short, tough, hawk-nosed, middle-aged city boy with a jaundiced ear and the respect of everyone in the orchestra as the most knowledgeable and influential critic in the United States. He was blunt to a fault, making sure to tell Yin Chenjong, the Chinese pianist, that the *Yellow River Concerto* was "trash." Yin happened to have been one of the members of the committee that wrote the piece. When upbraided for his rudeness, Schonberg replied, "I'm a frank guy, I'm a frank guy."

Caught in a white lie in Shanghai, Schonberg was made to pay the Chinese way. When taken along with the rest of the traveling press to the Shanghai Industrial Exhibition (a standard must for all visitors in which he had no interest whatsoever), Schonberg started to limp and told his hosts he could not go on because his ankle was sprained. The Chinese, clucking sympathetically and hovering attentively, took him to the car and started immediately for the hospital. He begged off vociferously and got them to take him to the hotel, whereupon a team of doctors descended upon him and took him to a clinic for an x-ray. Naturally, he couldn't admit he was faking and had to submit, wasting an hour and a half in the process. Later, I asked him mischievously how his ankle was. "Better," came the sour reply.

Yin Chenjong was the most famous pianist in the People's Republic in the 1970s, a roly-poly protégé of Madame Mao's who made his name performing the *Yellow River Concerto*. Born on a small island in the center of Xiamen (Amoy) called Wulanyu thirty-one years before, he started piano at age seven. Local authorities recognized his talent early and sent him to a musical middle school in Shanghai for six years. From there he studied in Leningrad and at the conservatory in Beijing.

Knowledgeable observers from Ormandy to Schonberg on down agreed that Yin had enormous talent. He was used to having his way, however, and Ormandy found him hard to control (musically). "I have never seen such a talented pianist play so badly," he said to me, referring to Yin's irregular counting. He plays with great power and virtuosity, though with an affected style, leading one irreverent onlooker to call him "Ribelace." All that was missing, the wag went on, was a candelabra and mother.

Sheila noted at the time: "The *Yellow River Concerto* played by Yin Chenjong was a great example of 'method' piano playing, with soulful gazes into the air above the piano, grimaces, etc....Mr. Yin played without reference to Ormandy, who kept peering hopefully over his shoulder—in vain because Yin only looked at him after he'd stopped playing."

Yin and Ormandy got along beautifully as people, however. Sharing a common temperament and love of music, the language and cultural barriers between them just seemed to melt.

Personally, Yin came across as a sensitive and friendly person. He knew world music, notably Glenn Gould's virtuosity with Bach's *Goldberg Variations*. Politically, he was a man of his time and place. As we sat together on the plane to Shanghai, he described the Cultural Revolution and its effect on his activities. He never stopped playing, but performances were rare. At one point in 1967, he said, the "Ultra Leftists" led by Lin Biao launched a campaign attacking the piano as an expensive instrument irrelevant to needs of workers, peasants, and soldiers. Yin and his supporters countered by loading a piano on a truck and putting on an impromptu concert in Tiananmen Square, which drew an enormous and appreciative crowd and defended his position. Madame Mao, he said, provided strong support at several junctures, arranging at one point for Chairman Mao to attend one of his concerts. When this was publicized nationwide, attacks on the piano ended.

**Politics Again**

We had not heard the last of Beethoven's Sixth. Two weeks after the orchestra left China, an article appeared in the *People's Daily* attacking Western "program music," especially pieces such as Beethoven's Sixth Symphony and Respighi's *Pines of Rome*. Music such as this "watered down the revolutionary enthusiasm of the masses," the article said. John Holdridge's analysis was that Zhou Enlai had succeeded in gaining enough access to the *People's Daily* to generate this attack on Madame Mao, the originator of the anti-Confucius campaign aimed at him.[24] The sniping between the factions continued, escalating into a full-blown campaign against Western culture that set the diplomatic community on edge for months.

Immediate political maneuvers aside, the long-term impact of the Philadelphia Orchestra's visit was profound. Tan Dun, the world-renowned contemporary Chinese composer (*The First Emperor*) and conductor, told me at an Asia Society event I hosted for him in 2004 that the September 16 Beijing leadership concert was beamed by radio nationwide and heard in the rural village where he was working as a peasant in 1973. The live broadcast thrilled him and changed his life. He and a generation of Chinese musicians his age have since worked to fuse Chinese and Western musical traditions, moving back and forth between Shanghai and New York. Tan also told me that Yin Chenjong had immigrated to the United States, where he was quietly teaching piano in New York.

# 18

# Kissinger Comes

## Sour Reality

Real life in Beijing returned with a vengeance after the Philadelphia Orchestra left China on September 22. Momentous events elsewhere—the Watergate tapes controversy, Kissinger's peregrinations to Moscow and Israel, the Middle East War and a shaky ceasefire, Attorney General Richardson's resignation and the Archibald Cox dismissal, as well as the guilty plea and departure of Vice President Agnew—seemed to soak up the energies of the U.S. government, contributing to a lull in our activity.

As David Bruce told his diary: "In Peking, while Washington burned, we fiddled, walked in the Forbidden City, wrote, read, ate, drank, and saw our unhappy domestic political scene as through a glass darkly. We might as well be, as respects such occurrences, isolated on another planet."[25]

Morale in the mission was low and due for a series of blows. The housing problem came to a head with the news that the Chinese had begun passing out flats in two newly completed buildings, and the Americans were not getting any. To make matters worse, Lin Ping, director of American Affairs, called Ambassador Bruce into the Foreign Ministry and told him that the Marine House Bar had to close. The operation of a bar in which drinks were sold was illegal and the bar had been the scene of raucous late parties, they said. What Bruce did not tell us was that Lin had demanded the total withdrawal of the Marine detachment. Bruce reacted by closing the bar and reducing the profile of the detachment, playing for time until the issue could be discussed at Kissinger's level.[26]

I took it upon myself to inform John Holdridge of the sore feelings among that half of the Liaison Office staff still stuck in the Beijing Hotel. They believed, correctly, that the U.S. insistence on occupying two DCM apartments was holding them hostage. John agreed right away to move to smaller quarters. When the Diplomatic Services Bureau learned of his decision, they allocated the three apartments they had been saving all along. The logjam was broken.

The Kissinger visit to China was postponed once more for a few weeks, giving us more time to prepare. I was placed in charge of the arrangements and, as Bruce put it, "harried" the Foreign Ministry on the details—flight courses, reporters, press credentials, visas, hotel accommodations, and security for a party of more that fifty, including fourteen journalists and three cameramen.

## Low Society

Although correct in official dealings, the Chinese continued to keep their distance socially. Al Jenkins had succeeded in giving a farewell lunch at his apartment for Zhang Wenjin before he took up his post as the PRC ambassador to Canada, but that was a unique special case. I tried in vain to arrange picnics, lunches, and other meals with new colleagues and contacts who had been relaxed and friendly when on the road with delegations. They froze up when they returned to the capital. For example, when I invited four Foreign Ministry working-level colleagues to supper at our apartment, they took five days to answer. When they did, they explained that the most senior invitee had fallen ill. When I pointed out that the event was more than a week away and expressed the hope that he might recover in time, I was told, "He'll still be sick by then."

Sheila, Sanhu, and I did finally succeed in hosting an informal dinner for three interpreter-translators from the office. The guests were Mr. Liu, the relaxed and knowledgeable elder cadre who had arranged for "ox's xxx" to be fed to the American swim team; Mr. Sung, a dour and inexperienced former language teacher, who had been thrust into administrative duties as USLO's first local employee and never quite gotten his nose above water; and Mr. Yeh, a brand new graduate of the Foreign Languages Institute, whose education was interrupted by the Cultural Revolution and whose inexperience was matched only by enthusiasm and political purity.

The evening turned out to be relaxed, entertaining, and educational for everyone. Mr. Yeh, a former Red Guard who had made a pilgrimage on foot to the historic Communist base at Yanan during the Cultural Revolution, was frankly uncomfortable at first. Sitting ramrod straight on his chair, Yeh—who did not really speak English yet, but intoned each sentence full voice as if he were presenting the team lineup on the public address system at a football stadium—announced that this was the first time he had been in the home of a foreigner. He welcomed the opportunity to broaden his sphere of experience, enabling him better to combine the theory he had learned in school with actual practice, as Chairman Mao taught. I suggested that he add a gin and tonic to his sphere of experience. Mr. Yeh said he had heard of gin and would be glad to make an experiment.

This stilted snatch of conversation was considered high humor by all concerned. The manipulation of political slogans to fit odd situations was one of the acceptable ways to make people laugh in the People's Republic during the early 1970s. Along this line, I told my guests that I had locked myself out of my car in front of a downtown bathhouse a few days before. I went to a nearby hardware store and bought a bamboo pole and some wire and proceeded to reach for the car door handle through a slit left open in the back window. A crowd of a hundred or so gathered to watch. To defuse the situation, I needed to explain why this red-haired, tiger-eyed big nose was stealing his own car. A quotation from Chairman Mao rescued me. I told the crowd I had confronted a severe contradiction, analyzed the situation, and was now in the process of conducting a scientific experiment aimed at resolving the contradiction. These lines would not make it on late night TV in the United States, but they broke up the street crowd. All kinds of help and advice were forthcoming. I drove away leaving them buzzing.

We sat down to a dinner of ham, ratatouille, pâté, and vin rosé. Ritual toasts to friendship followed along with more talk about humor and society. I noted that there was no humor published in the papers and wondered if anyone told jokes in the People's Republic. Oh, yes indeed, came the reply, and perhaps we would like to hear some. Well, there followed a story about a dumb general—there seemed to be a genre of dumb general jokes much like our moron or Polish jokes—who came upon a basketball game and, puzzled as to why everyone was fighting over one ball, ordered that nine more be issued so that peace might be restored. There was another story about a father who was so stingy he would not let his sons eat the meat hanging in the larder, only smell it, and would get upset if the kids took more than one sniff at a time. Mr. Sung told a sour parable about a man who starved to death after winning a debate with Confucius. Such was the state of the art.

After dinner we had a long discussion about the differences in our societies stemming from the contrasting emphases we each placed on the individual and the collective respectively—a good solid discussion and useful for the pristine ears of the new graduate. They left at 10:30, having arrived at 6:15, the equivalent of a Western dinner lasting well past midnight.

We continued to batten down the hatches for Dr. Kissinger, even as the dates for his arrival slid further away. USLO prepared briefing papers on every issue likely to come up, including U.S.-PRC Working Level Bilateral Relations, Cambodia, Sino-Soviet and U.S.-Soviet Relations, Taiwan, Japan, Korea, South Vietnam and Laos, and economic issues. It was the first time in my memory that a mission abroad had provided the secretary of state (Kissinger was approved by the Senate on September 19) with a full set of papers in advance.

The news from the United States—the facedown with the Soviets over the Middle East, President Nixon's decision to hand over his tapes—continued to make us reel. Sheila and I will never forget lying in bed at 7:00 A.M. listening to the Nixon press conference live, as hundreds of blue-clad cyclists passed below our window on their way to work, and hearing our president declare, "I am not a crook."

## Kissinger's Visit

Henry Kissinger finally arrived November 10, 1973, bringing a whirlwind of activity off the plane with him. (His entourage included many who would become key officials in the Kissinger State

Department: Robert Ingersoll, ambassador to Japan and soon to be assistant secretary for East Asia; Press Secretary Robert McCloskey; Arthur Hummel, acting assistant secretary for East Asia, later ambassador to the PRC; Executive Secretary Thomas Pickering; Winston Lord, soon to be director of Policy Planning; Roy Atherton, deputy assistant secretary for Near East and South Asia; Oscar Armstrong, director of the PRC Desk; and Richard Solomon and Commander Jon Howe of Kissinger's NSC Staff. Winston Lord's wife, Bette Bao Lord, was also along, visiting the country of her birth for the first time since the revolution.)

The secretary's itinerary spanned the globe. Next stop would be Tokyo, for an Asian Chiefs of Mission Conference. President Nixon was on the decline, with possible impeachment under discussion in the U.S. media. Kissinger, by contrast, was at the top of his game, dealing with crises everywhere, most recently the Middle East.

Arriving at our villa in the now familiar state guest compound, Executive Secretary Pickering, already gray with fatigue, reviewed all arrangements with me. As the delegation settled in, I overheard juicy snatches of conversation. Kissinger, fresh from negotiating the cease-fire between Egypt and Israel, remarked to Bruce, "I would love to put Golda Meir and Nguyen Van Thieu in the same negotiation with each other. They deserve each other. I have always thought that for sheer ingratitude Thieu was unmatched. Now I know better."

The Chinese had arranged the four-day stop like a mini-Nixon visit, including banquets, high-level conversations with Zhou and Mao, Kissinger and Bruce counterpart talks on more mundane issues involving the rest of us, and some sightseeing. On the Chinese side, as before, Marshall Ye Jianying and Vice Foreign Minister Qiao Guanhua played prominent roles. Top radicals like Wang Hongwen were nowhere to seen.

At the opening banquet, Kissinger harked back to early times in our relationship:

> None of us who took this trip can ever forget the sense of excitement when we entered China for the first time. It was not only that we were visiting a new country, and what we thought was the mysterious country, until the Prime Minister

pointed out to me that it was due more to our ignorance than to its mystery. . . . We have made good progress, we have Liaison Offices in each other's capital, and we have increased exchanges between our two countries. But we are determined to do much more and to complete the process we started two years ago.[27]

## In a Holding Pattern

At best, Kissinger's presence in Beijing held the relationship in place during a turbulent time in Washington and the rest of the world. He also came bearing secret offers of security and intelligence cooperation vis-à-vis the Soviets, gifts to which we were not given access. Hours of conversation with the premier and a lively session with Mao, normal treatment for Kissinger, were career high points for Bruce, who sat in on all of them. He told me that Mao was vigorous during his almost three hours with HAK and could have kept going for another two hours had not time intervened—namely, the banquet schedule. He laughed, joked, and dominated the conversation, which was almost a monologue. Cambodia was discussed little at this meeting, or during the entire visit for that matter. The Soviet threat was touched upon, but not exhaustively. "Don't trust them. We know you must have dealings. Watch out." Mao had good recall, and wanted to talk about philosophy.

Bruce was impressed with the personal relationship that apparently existed between Mao, Zhou, and Kissinger. They clearly respected and trusted him. Zhou and Mao were obviously close to each other, Bruce continued. The premier gave not the slightest hint of being in any sort of political trouble whatsoever—being relaxed and confident throughout. The young women, Wang Hairong and Nancy Tang, played an interpreting role and were clearly the chairman's "pets."[28]

By contrast, the counterpart talks reached a grueling stalemate. The Chinese stonewalled on nuts and bolts issues, specifically frozen assets claims. We gave no ground on most-favored-nation treatment on trade matters. The existence of Taiwanese government consulates in the United States was a sore point. The Chinese read a list of ten exchanges they had approved for each side, but that was it. Concrete progress toward normalization was negligible.

Dick Solomon, who was dealing for the first time with the Chinese on their own turf, was disappointed with both sides. The inability to engage in give-and-take, the tightness of the PRC political framework, and the lack of room for maneuver were frustrating. Kissinger, he thought, would have trouble getting support within the U.S. government for the kind of security cooperation he had in mind if the Chinese remained so inflexible. I did not know what HAK had in mind on security matters, but told Solomon that the hard-necked attitude displayed by Chinese bureaucrats was normal. That was the way they dealt with other countries. That was the price of normalization—to be treated like a boarder rather than a guest. Our idea of what could be accomplished day-to-day had been warped by the extraordinary progress Henry's personal relationship with Zhou Enlai had produced. I told myself that I dreaded true normalization.

## Irritating the Soviets

At a private lunch in the guesthouse (Win and Betty Lord, Dick Solomon, Tom Pickering, and Jon Howe were at the table), Kissinger ripped Soviet behavior in recent negotiations. He knew the Chinese were listening, but this was not just for their benefit. I got the strong impression that he believed everything he said and found the vituperation relaxing.

Labeling the Soviets an "extraordinary bunch of shits," he went on to describe their crude negotiating tactics, social rudeness, and general boorishness. Once, near the end of negotiating a recent agreement, the Soviets gave him their latest draft, describing it as very close, with only minor changes to what the United States had wanted, and then left immediately for lunch (after which signing was to take place). HAK discovered the document had many changes and was miles away from what the United States wanted. He told the Soviets no dice—no change, no agreement. Later the Soviet ambassador commented, "I told them it wouldn't work."

During the Brezhnev visit to Camp David, Brezhnev never arrived on time, lounging conspicuously in front of his cottage at times when he was supposed to be meeting or eating with the president. He tried to see the president alone without Kissinger by saying he was tired, pretending to take a nap, and then bounding up when he thought Henry was out of range and asking for an appointment with RN. The Secret Service alerted Kissinger, who appeared at the meeting, to Brezhnev's discomfiture. The Soviets are able to swear, call names, heap invective on the president's head (while he was bombing Hanoi), and then be sweetness and light at dinner, while getting drunk, as if nothing had happened.

Kissinger loved to play the U.S./China/USSR triangle. One morning at the Liaison Office after a session with David Bruce, he saw me reading the Chinese papers and asked me to show him what had been quoted from his toast the day before. He was particularly interested in his statement on U.S. aversion to hegemonism, not just in Asia but worldwide.

When I read the *People's Daily* account to him he asked, "Do you think that will drive the Soviets up the wall?"

I answered that I thought it would.

"I think so, too," he replied, happily.

## A Thousand Cups among Friends

The visit was, if anything, a subtle success. The meetings, especially with Mao and Zhou, bespoke a strong relationship, at least between the principals. Relations at lower levels could be sour and testy. The communiqué itself was a bland document around which one had to peck vigorously to find kernels of new substance. Clear Chinese conditions for normalization were glossed over. There would be more frequent talks "at authoritative levels," and the liaison offices would be upgraded "qualitatively and quantitatively." That was Kissinger's phrase and no one knew what it meant. Bruce liked the mission small, and Kissinger agreed. He had called our office "in many ways a model for a revitalized Foreign Service." In any case, there was no physical room for new bodies. Secret security arrangements were not mentioned at all, of course. Nor were the Marines, who would be allowed to stay, at least for a while.

The secretary of state, with his entourage hovering about like so many gray flannel helicopters, departed on the morning of November 14, taking their private whirlwind with them. During a last chat at the airport Kissinger commented on some of the material I had supplied for his final toast to Zhou Enlai. In his staff office he had stood over me impatiently while I finished it and tore it from the typewriter.

Looking at it, he had pursed his lips, said "It won't be one of my greatest," and given it back.

Win Lord, at a desk nearby, said this amounted to an A-minus. The more standard reaction, Win said, was to shout "garbage," tear it up, and stomp away.

For this particular toast I had given him a traditional Chinese saying: "When among close friends a thousand cups are not enough." Kissinger told me that, after hearing it, Zhou had gone back to him asking if he knew the second half of the saying, which translates roughly "Among those who do not understand each other half a sentence is too long." Henry reported he had laughed and replied that he was incapable of delivering only half a sentence.

At the airport he asked me if I knew the second half. I said I did, but that I had thought only the first part right for a toast and appropriate for those who had developed the kind of relationship he had with Premier Zhou. It would not have been right for his first visit, but was just the thing for his sixth. Kissinger, happy on balance with the outcome of his visit, bounded up the ramp of the plane and was gone.

# 19

# Death and Departure

## A Fatal Accident

Our life changed in the blink of an eye. As I wrote Adam and Oliver on December 2, 1973:

> Last Sunday, we were all driving toward the Great Wall in the little red Toyota—your mother, grandmother, grandfather, and Sanhu along with me. It was a lovely clear blue day and our spirits were high. We had given a large and delightful party for the parents the night before at the Mongolian barbecue restaurant on the North Lake. Suddenly, out of nowhere, a young teenage girl cyclist coming in the opposite direction swerved in front of us. I jammed on the brakes, trying desperately to stop, but could not. We hit her bike and she flew over the hood of the car, hitting and smashing the windshield and landing in a heap off to the side, seriously hurt. We flagged down a truck, and I took her to the hospital, where she died that afternoon. Needless to say, we all feel terrible about this, especially me who was at the wheel at the time. ... No one in our car was hurt, though there was glass all over the place. The car suffered a broken windshield and some minor dents.

I remember vividly the bumpy, freezing ride on the back of the flatbed truck watching the poor creature, never to regain consciousness, convulse slowly. The first hospital we came to specialized in bone sets and could only send us on to another hospital in the same jarring truck, but this time with two doctors and a stretcher bed.

The Xuanwu hospital specialized in brain surgery and took her in, said she was in very serious shape, and started operating immediately. She died four hours later.

Sheila's diary, written the day of the accident, provides her own poignant perspective:

> 11:20 en route to the Great Wall, lovely morning.
>
> Our accident. Skid, crash, feeling that life was completely changed, all our happiness gone. Stood in the road surrounded by a crowd of 200–300 country people, enjoying the spectacle as we tried to get help for the girl we'd hit. She bled heavily from her right ear and twitched right outside our window. Helen [Nick's mother] stood between her and Sanhu, who busied himself in the car reading. Got a flatbed truck to help, lifted her on straw mats, and N took her off down the road. . . . The Bonavias and a French couple stopped, and the latter phoned USLO. Eventually Herb Horowitz arrived and the big station wagon took Helen, Geoff [Nick's father], and Sanhu away to an agonizing afternoon of waiting in the flat. . . . The Public Security Bureau took photos and measurements, and we all stood about until 4:30 P.M., when Nick got back and signed a statement of facts about the accident after having it interpreted.
>
> We drove the car, shattered windshield and all, to the Public Security Bureau (Foreigners' Division) on the street east of the Forbidden City. Another statement taken in a curtained room by a big cop. John Holdridge was present and a little PSB interpreter named Ma. I was allowed to call Helen and Geoff. Got home, trembling, at 5:30. We spent an appalling evening of apprehension and shock, going over the circumstances in our heads. . . . Sanhu drew a picture entitled "I am proud to announce that Nicholas Platt is innocent! with judge and cheering crowds."

### The Investigation Turns Hostile

Sheila stuck close to me as the Public Security Bureau, increasingly hostile, continued their investigation. Her journal describes a disturbing interrogation on December 9:

NP and I were called again to PSB. More questioning, this time with a stout, senior cadre sitting in. The tone of the proceeding was accusatory and unfriendly. They suggested NP's "mind wandering, mind numb, not paying attention," or he would have seen the girl. NP patiently stated her action, crossing our path from the left, was too sudden and unexpected to avoid hitting her. Inconclusive and frightening session suggesting they wish to pin responsibility on us. Nothing said about speed. Hostile reaction when NP stated that he did not understand why the girl was in his path. What was she doing there? The response from the cadres was that it was not our role to cross-examine them. . . . Most upsetting was their statement that we could have seen the girl before the crossroad and avoided her, but didn't because of carelessness. . . .

PSB required next that we view the corpse. We were driven slowly to the hospital, kept waiting in a yard outside next to an incinerator. Inside the hospital morgue, we were shown the body, dressed in new clothes, with a red scarf around the lower face, wrapped in a pink blanket. We requested the scarf be lifted and made positive identification. A scar on her forehead marked the site of the unsuccessful operation. . . . A brutal morning leaving both of us very upset, unconfident of the fairness [of the Chinese authorities].

In the difficult days that followed, Sheila held the family fort, moving my parents through the familiar sights of Beijing and accompanying them on a short trip to Shanghai and Suzhou. I was not permitted to leave the capital. My mother and father left for the United States, as scheduled, on December 7.

My USLO colleagues and other members of the international community crowded around to provide what comfort and support they could. Jim Lilley, whose ear was perpetually glued to the ground, cheered me up with a report from Beijing's super-efficient grapevine. Word of the accident was all over the capital within twenty-four hours. Popular opinion, for what that was worth, judged me not at fault and a good person for having made the effort to take the girl to hospital.

## Harsh Judgment

David Bruce reported the real PSB judgment to Washington in the following cable I drafted for him:

> 1. Peking Public Security Bureau Traffic Section rendered decision December 21 on Platt accident, which decreed withdrawal of his driver's license and payment of 25,380 Yuan to family of deceased. Decision laid no blame on victim but charged Platt with ignoring PRC laws and serious violations of Municipal Traffic regulations. That mother of deceased had been rendered unable to work as result of accident (due to mental breakdown as subsequently alleged) added to seriousness of case, decision said.
>
> 2. Upon hearing decision, Platt asked what appeal procedures were available, and requested full documentation behind finding of traffic violations, including PSB diagrams of accident scene. Public Security officials replied that such documents not normally made available, that facts of case were "irrefutable" and that "indignation of masses" could not be held in check much longer. Platt asked for and received permission for adjournment to discuss case with me and my deputies.
>
> 3. We all agreed that there [was] nothing to gain by rehashing with the Chinese the circumstances of the accident, although there was no conclusive evidence that Platt had been exceeding official speed limit (which is 60 kilometers per hour or 37.5 MPH), or that victim coming from opposite direction had not swerved suddenly into his path. Moreover, not mentioned in final statement was that victim might not have reached hospital at all had it not been for successful efforts of Platt to commandeer a truck and accompany her first to one hospital and then another.
>
> 4. Our assessment was that grave consequences of accident and desire of authorities to provide compensation to bereaved parents decided them to place full blame on foreigner driving automobile. Rather than work forward from the facts, the PSB had worked backward from the results in

accordance with practice often followed in adjudication in PRC.

5. We agreed that it would be in best interest of both USLO and Platt if he accepted penalties but refused to sign any documents suggesting admission that he had violated PRC laws and regulations.

6. During afternoon meeting December 21 with Traffic Section, Platt presented letter to PSB accepting withdrawal of license and payment of indemnities, but nothing else. When Chinese asked that he sign decision, he demurred, asking that letter be considered sufficient. PSB agreed and declared case closed. PSB refused final request by Platt for PSB diagram of accident.

7. Indemnity, under Platt's policy with Ming An Insurance Co. (Hong Kong), paid promptly December 22 by their Peking agent, the People's Insurance Co.

8. We assume that Chinese declaration that case closed means precisely that and that both USLO's and Platt's future relations with PRC officials will not be affected.[29]

## Sentenced to Leave China

In fact, my ordeal was far from over, as the next cable reported:

> *Subject:* PRC Request Platt Recall
>
> MFA/Oceanian Affairs Director Lin Ping called Jenkins to MFA December 29 and delivered following statement from prepared text:
>
> I have asked you to come here today to discuss the unfortunate accident of November 25 in which the car driven by Mr. Platt on the way to the Great Wall caused the death of a fifteen-year-old schoolgirl. The Traffic Control Division of the Peking Municipality has made a decision on the case and Mr. Platt has undertaken to indemnify the relatives of the deceased.
>
> However, this is a case of irreparable loss which no indemnity can replace. Even now, the girl's mother is in an abnormal mental condition due to the shock.

As the American side may be aware, previously when deaths have been caused by diplomats stationed in Peking, the diplomats have invariably been recalled on their own initiative.

The U.S. side will understand our wish that this matter be handled the same way.[30]

"There was something eerie and upsetting, " I noted in my diary,

about being the note taker at my own sentencing. Lin Ping seemed to rather enjoy it all. Tang Lungbin, the protocol man with whom I had worked closely on the Kissinger trip and other projects looked positively ill (to his everlasting credit). Zhao Jia, the lady interpreter whom I had first met on the Nixon trip, did her job with gusto. [Now a lawyer in Chicago, she told me recently that Lin Ping had warned her before the meeting to behave in a strictly professional manner.] It was a beautiful day outside. Tea and cigarettes were offered, just like any other time. The weather discussed, and then—wham!

## Backing from Bruce

Ambassador Bruce, whose support and wide sympathy were crucial to Sheila and me, cabled Henry Kissinger the same day:

You will already have received telegram regarding PRC decision to have Platt leave the country at an unspecified date because of automobile accident. We had hoped affair was closed as a result of acceptance of license revocation and payment of indemnity.

I have no knowledge, nor likelihood of obtaining, accurate facts about cited reference to recall being "invariable" outcome of traffic deaths caused by foreign diplomats in PRC.

It seems to me best not to argue further, or try to appeal this arbitrary decision. I consider this determination unfair to Platt, and prospective loss of his services a severe blow to the future efficiency of our Mission.

I do, moreover, feel deeply concerned over the possible connection of this action with other recent picayune incidents such as refusal to issue TDY (Temporary Duty) visas for USLO replacements, obviously exaggerated complaints over Marines, long delays in answering requests for appointments with officials, and various indications of a marked lack of reciprocity here for our sensitive treatment of PRCLO representatives in the United States.

My personal recommendation is that if practicable concurrently with Platt's leaving it should be announced that he has been assigned to another position in Washington or elsewhere of a grade and importance that would be judged as constituting a promotion.

In my estimation Platt is a man of exceptional ability and high character. He had behaved during the whole of this recent painful period with admirable dignity and compassion. Such an appointment as I have suggested would signal to the Chinese that although we had complied with their own sovereign rights to demand a recall, we do not ourselves regard this as a reflection on the officer to whom it was applied, but on the contrary maintain entire confidence in him.

I believe this requires speedy handling.[31]

We now slid off one tenterhook onto another, from waiting to know what the police would do, to waiting to know what the Foreign Ministry would do, to sweating out the department's decision on a new assignment. Bruce had been assured that the secretary of state was fully aware of the problem and would not let it get lost in the bureaucracy. That was a comfort, as was the knowledge that the director general of the Foreign Service, Nathaniel Davis, had had exactly the same problem in Bulgaria when he was chief of mission, with exactly the same results.

The following weeks were trying beyond words, but correctly handled. I was my own action officer throughout, both a cruelty and a blessing. At least I had something to do. None of us had planned for such a contingency. As in so many other situations, Don Anderson and I made it up as we went along, supported by our bosses. One thing we all agreed on. USLO, not Washington, would make the decisions. The accident must not be politicized and become a football thrown around in the bureaucracy at home.

Washington reluctantly acquiesced in the Chinese action. Our research with other missions, in fact, confirmed Lin Ping's assertion that diplomats involved in traffic fatalities had "invariably been recalled on their own initiative." We were right to yield. Other missions who fought the ruling ended up with the offending diplomat declared *persona non grata* and given hours to leave. Departing "on my own initiative" preserved, I later found out, options for future dealings with the Chinese. It also permitted me to set the date for going, providing a decent interval to pack and say goodbye.

Six years later in 1980, around a hot pot in our kitchen in Washington, a Chinese diplomat described the private reaction within the Foreign Ministry to our accident. Several people had defended me, he said, maintaining I had acted honorably in stopping the car, hailing a truck, and taking the girl to the hospital. Other foreigners involved in accidents had behaved differently. He intimated that the same ruling would not have been made now, with the new emphasis on legal procedures in the PRC and more relaxed politics under Deng Xiaoping.

Media treatment of the accident and our impending departure was worldwide but brief and smoothly managed. Everyone knew what to say and said it. My father called from New York to report that reaction had been sympathetic. Our final weeks saw an emotional round of farewell parties, capped by a big reception given by the Bruces, who were saintly throughout the entire affair.

### David Bruce's Prophecy

I called on David Bruce at four o'clock in the afternoon the day before I left China. The weak January sun straining through the Beijing dust barely lit the room. The old ambassador looked at me through his hooded, droopy eyes and said, "The accident was awful for you, but a great break for your career."

I was astonished. I had killed a Chinese girl. My career as a "China Boy" was over. How could this be a great break? Smiling his warm, wrinkly smile, Bruce explained that the China specialty was narrow. I would now be forced to branch out, with opportunities to climb a broader and taller ladder in the State Department. "Beijing is a dead end," he said.

As we parted, Bruce told me he was coming home for a spell. He had "done about as much window dressing as he could." His house in Georgetown was open. Huang Zhen had a big lead in consultation time. Henry wanted to see him. Bruce invited me to come and pay a visit.

## The End of the Beginning

We left Beijing the morning of January 19, 1974, on Air France bound for Paris. I had asked David Bruce to authorize departure via Europe, knowing that passing through Hong Kong bore high risks for me and for future dealings with the Chinese. Too many friends, particularly in the press, would lead inevitably to a press conference. Sore and vulnerable, I was bound to say something that I, and USLO, would regret. No one knew us in Paris except for our lifelong Foreign Service friends, Allen and Marilyn Holmes, to whom we were bound for two weeks of comfort and diversion en route to Washington. Bruce approved, and we traveled without public notice.

Leaving Beijing was difficult and emotional. As Bruce reported to Washington:

> Nicholas Platt's departure from Beijing January 19 provoked one of the largest airport turnouts we have seen since arriving. A score of diplomats including New Zealand ambassador and counselors from (British), German, Soviet, Polish, and other missions turned out at 7:00 A.M. along with sizeable American contingent. While this was primarily a demonstration of the high regard in which they hold Nick Platt, several members of the diplomatic corps commented privately that they wished to show a sense of solidarity with him in response to the Chinese handling of the entire affair.[32]

Saying goodbye to the original USLO couples—the Jenkinses, Holdridges, Andersons, Horowitzes, and Lilleys, families with whom we had lived as close as on a nuclear submarine—was particularly hard for us. I was happy to note a few tangible benefits for some. Don Anderson got my job and Jim Lilley my apartment, but the event was indelibly sad. Lucille Zaelit, my irrepressible secretary, British diplomat John Boyd, a close friend since Hong Kong days, and Canadian journalist John Burns, who had shown special compassion after the accident, were also difficult to leave. In due course the flight was called; we climbed the stairs to the plane, and flew away.

## Charting a New Course

I was pondering a flurry of excellent job offers, including my original onward assignment to the political section in the Tokyo embassy when a message came from General Brent Scowcroft, Kissinger's deputy at the National Security Council. He said the secretary was interested in having me on the NSC staff and that I should wait.

Arriving in Washington, I called on General Scowcroft to ask whether he really thought I could be effective dealing with the Chinese in Washington, given the circumstances of my departure from Beijing. He replied that Kissinger had instructed him to contact PRCLO deputy Han Xu to explore, privately and informally, the answer to this question. Han told him that the Chinese side would have no problem dealing with me whatsoever.

While this news was a relief, I had discovered while in Washington that I was just not ready to return, for the time being, to working on Chinese issues. The bad memories were still too fresh and would warp my judgment for some time to come. I told General Scowcroft that I would prefer the assignment to Tokyo, a job that had been in my sights for years, which I had given up to go to Beijing. He agreed and released me.

I have always been grateful to Henry Kissinger for taking a personal interest in my fate. I was told that he insisted on clearing the cable listing my assignment options and scratched off a number of jobs that had no China content. He did not want the Chinese to conclude that they had put me out of their business. My friends in personnel revealed that they had beefed up the description of the China aspects of the Tokyo job—I would be covering Japan's foreign policy, particularly in Asia—so he would accept it. His interest insured that the options remained open and that when I made my choice it would stick.

At the end of February 1974, I left for Yokohama and five months of Japanese language training prior to reporting for work at Embassy Tokyo. I would be alone until June, when Sheila and the children, released from loathed boarding schools at the end of the academic year, would join me.

The accident in Beijing had a profound effect on our professional and family lives. It forced me to grow from a "China Boy" into an Asia Hand. For Sheila, our personal wounds spurred an intense interest in post-traumatic stress that led her to a lifetime specialty as a counselor and trainer to international institutions whose personnel abroad confronted the same kinds of shock. The accident, Sanhu told me recently, turned him into a fearful hypochondriac for a time. Memories of the windshield shattering, turning opaque white, and the rank smell of soybeans kept flashing back. Thereafter, for some years, whenever there was a thunderstorm with lightning, he slept in rubber boots. "You had a boring childhood," he commented. "But you made sure your children did not."

# 20

# Renewal in Japan

## Language Therapy

The shock of leaving Beijing began to dissolve under total immersion in the Japanese language. The training was therapeutic. The process—repetition, with a tangible result—was like sawing wood, a comfort and a distraction. Not that it was easy. On the contrary, I wrote home,

> The first missionary who ever studied this language reported to his bishop that it was an invention of the devil designed to prevent the spread of God's word to the people of these islands. He was right. . . . In any case, I am up at 6:20 A.M., . . . ride the train from Tokyo to Yokohama—sardined among hundreds of Japanese—to be at class by 8:45. I have a small tape recorder (all our lessons are on cassettes), which hangs around my neck connected to my ear by a plug and a wire, and I study all the way, mouthing the phrases pumped into my ear. It must be a surprise to my traveling companions to be near a towering foreigner who seems preoccupied and from time to time utters irrelevant snatches of language like "I would like two copies of that big red dictionary, and three sheets of white paper, too." The schooling lasts from 8:45 to 3:20—very intense but so different from the work I have been doing that it seems almost a holiday. All I have to worry about is whether I can memorize the next dialogue in the lesson, or master a practical new grammatical pattern.[33]

Being right there in the culture helped me learn. The same day I studied the phrases needed to guide a taxi—"stop here," "straight ahead," "turn left," "turn right"—I tried them out on a bemused driver. He responded obediently to this form of linguistic dressage, patiently performing the maneuvers again and again as I barked the commands.

The language training revealed the strength of Chinese culture in Japanese society. The Japanese borrowed and adapted the architecture, lifestyle, and culture of China wholesale during the Tang Dynasty (600–900 A.D.), an era when China really was the center of the known world, a vibrant, open, and technologically advanced society. The grandeur of Tang wooden buildings is best preserved in the ancient capitals of Kyoto and Nara. Tang Chinese lived on the floor. Japanese still do now. Confucian values, Zen Buddhism, Tao intuition—all Tang exports—are at the center of Japanese philosophy. Japan's complicated mix of attitudes toward China, contrasting a strong sense of cultural inferiority with the confidence and competence to assimilate and master foreign technology and art, date from seventh-century China

More to my immediate concern, during Tang times the Japanese created their writing system around Chinese characters, an extraordinary feat given that Chinese grammar lacks the tenses, declensions, possessives, particles, articles, and other troublesome inflections that riddle the Japanese language (and ours, too). Japanese uses a different verb form to address the various ranks and stations in society. There's a special form for use with the emperor, your wife, child, dog, boss, equal, inferior, or barbarian colleague. This explains the extraordinary importance of name cards to Japanese. If you do not know the rank of the person you are addressing, you cannot communicate correctly.

The Japanese created two separate systems of phonetic symbols (Hiragana and Katakana) to deal with their inflections and words of Japanese and foreign origins. These they mixed with Chinese characters to create the most infernal writing system any foreigner could confront. Those who master the language as children or native speakers find it an exceptionally efficient and incredibly fast reading method. Those from abroad who start late find hell.

The Japanese talent for making foreign words their very own helped me understand the ease with which they adopted foreign ideas. *Waishatsu*, from "white shirt," meant any dress shirt. *Sebiro*, from "Saville Row," meant a Western suit. *Hutoboru* was, simply, a football. My favorite slang expression, *bakshan*, a combination of the English word "back" and the German word *schoen* ("beautiful"), meant, "she looks great from behind, but not so hot when you get round to the front." The Chinese, whose language is sacrosanct, could not abide such practices. Faced with the challenge of rendering the term "parachute," they put together the three ideograms for "descending," "life-saving," and "umbrella." The Japanese version was *parashuto*.

## Comfort at the Survival Level

I left language school in Yokohama with survival-level Japanese. I could manage travel, train schedules, maps. Many place names use Chinese characters, which helped me navigate. I could feed myself, buy movie tickets, shop, drive the back roads of Japan, and convey polite greetings.

Happily, my job at Embassy Tokyo would not require the foreign language level that I had needed in China. My beat was the Foreign Ministry (Gaimusho), tracking key elements of Japan's foreign policy, including China, Korea, Southeast Asia, the Soviet Union, and the Middle East. My contacts and counterparts were Japanese professional diplomats whose English was far better than my Japanese would ever be. So we conducted our business in English.

This practice yielded special dividends. My Japanese colleagues were much more candid in my language than in theirs. Spoken Japanese, my months in Yokohama had taught me, is a language shot through with equivocation, precise in the service of obfuscation, its purpose to avoid giving offense, rather than to communicate bluntly. Day-to-day usage serves more as a verbal lubricant in a crowded and tightly regimented society than as a vehicle of clear expression. As a result, I was thrilled to discover my Japanese contacts felt free to tell me things in English that they would not have said to their own countrymen, providing sharp insights and private thoughts that spiced my reports to Washington.

I had had a parallel experience when speaking Chinese in Beijing, and found myself being more blunt and candid than I would have been using the nuances of my own language. In part this was because I didn't know many ways of saying things differently. In part it was the sense that my own countrymen could not listen in that gave me a license for candor.

## A Perfect Plug-In

I was also lucky with the level at which I connected with official Japan. As a first secretary of embassy I was expected to deal with the directors of the ministry's different "desks" (China, Korea, U.S.S.R., U.S., etc.), the perfect place to plug into the foreign policy establishment. My counterparts, some of whom I had known for years, were expert on their areas of responsibility and welcomed the chance to exchange information. More important, the office directors were charged with devising solutions to whatever problems arose and encouraged to think for themselves. In the Japanese system, their seniors on up the line spent most of their time developing consensus around the ideas that their unfettered directors sent forward. As their careers progressed, my counterparts would become consensus managers, too. But for now I had open access to the freshest thinking in Tokyo's foreign policy establishment.

Over the next three years, I practically lived at the Foreign Ministry, sometimes visiting two or three times on a given day. With traffic jammed solid in downtown Tokyo, I soon resorted to traveling the half-mile from the Embassy to the Gaimusho very discreetly by bicycle, a diplomatic conveyance hardly used in status-obsessed Japan.

Frequent contact bred lasting friendships. Japanese diplomats, unlike their arm's-length Chinese counterparts, loved to come to American homes and would sing after dinner without coaxing. Their renditions of American folksongs were even worse than mine. Initially reserved and impenetrable, they relaxed and warmed up over time.

The decision that you were a friend brought with it lifetime responsibilities. There was something quite familiar about the way Japanese handled their relationships; it later dawned on me that they behaved like Bostonians. My old schoolboy relationships with Ben Makihara and Tatsuo Arima, now established figures in Japanese business and diplomacy, gave me credibility with the Japanese. More effective was that the link between Great Grandfather Alpheus Hardy and Nijima Jo, the founder of Doshisha University (see chapter 1), enabled me to say that my family ties with Japan went back to 1865, three years before the Meiji Restoration. That blew them away.

## The Family Takes to Tokyo

Sheila and the boys arrived during the summer. The older boys, Adam (16) and Oliver (15), took one look at the facilities Embassy Tokyo had to offer and the attractions of a huge, safe city and begged to stay. An ample house in the Azabu district with a small garden came with my job. We moved in happily after a few months in a temporary apartment on the Embassy compound, hired an eccentric, moody, middle-aged maid named Setsuko-san, and confronted the problems of getting settled.

Decisions about schools fell into place. Adam and Oliver would go to the American School in Japan, enjoying the freedom of an hour-plus, multiple-train-change commute each way. The peripatetic Sanhu, whose tenth birthday cake featured nineteen flags, one for each city he had visited, would stay in the neighborhood, attending Nishimachi International School, founded and run by Tane Matsukata, the sister-in-law of former U.S. ambassador Edwin O. Reischauer. Sanhu said it was a big improvement over DTS ("Dining Table School") or his Pakistani alma mater in Beijing. He also felt special because the entire nation took the day off on his birthday, the same day Emperor Hirohito celebrated his birth.

Sheila put her social work degree to professional use for the first time, managing adoptions for a Japanese social service organization. After Beijing, the family reveled in the cornucopia of activities Japan offered its people and shared with foreigners: travel, music, movies, theater, temples, Sumo wrestling, skiing. We did not make history, just had fun.

## Work in a Big City Embassy

In contrast to USLO Beijing, a small, isolated pioneer settlement, Embassy Tokyo was like a long-established city, large and well organized. Deputy Chief of Mission Tom Shoesmith was the de facto mayor. The ambassador, Robert Hodgson, a political appointee, had been a vice chairman of Lockheed Corporation. Untainted by the bribery scandal involving Lockheed that shook the Japanese political structure over the next several years, Hodgson's low-key and unassuming style made him an effective envoy during what would emerge as a tricky time in the relationship between the United States and Japan. (Also on the staff were key figures who were to become important colleagues and friends: Michael Armacost, who was ending a tour as aide to Hodgson's predecessor, Robert Ingersoll, later served as ambassador to the Philippines and Japan. William Clark, a future assistant secretary for East Asian and Pacific Affairs and later ambassador to India when I was in Pakistan, was also finishing up his tour in the political section).

My immediate boss was Political Counselor Richard Petree, a wise and calm Japan hand with several tours under his belt. The political section that he led was roughly the same size as the entire Liaison Office in China. My job was to help him manage the whole section, in addition to my own External Affairs Unit. The Japan hands welcomed me and my family into their community. I had not gone through the full two-year language-training ritual required for entrance into what envious outsiders called the Cherry Blossom Society, but that did not seem to matter. My deputy, Desaix Anderson, later prominent as the first U.S. chargé in Hanoi, was an indefatigable legman whose extensive network of close relationships throughout the Foreign Office provided tons of grist for our reporting mill. Howard McElroy, a feisty former Marine from Long Island, managed politico-military affairs. (He later became, in effect, the town manager of his native Southampton.) William Breer, who rose to become deputy chief of mission in Tokyo, was in charge of covering the labyrinth of Japan's domestic politics. I began to sense that David Bruce had been right about the benefits of a broader career.

Wags in the embassy joked that following Japanese foreign policy was a non-job, because Japan did not have one. You could have fooled me. As I worked my way into the Foreign Ministry, I found Japanese diplomacy tightly focused on:

1. Security, which relied for protection against the Soviets on the nuclear umbrella under the treaty with the United States and the conventional shelter provided by our Pacific Fleet. The Japanese paid minute attention to developments on the neighboring Korean Peninsula, strategically regarded as a "dagger pointed at Japan's heart." The half-million Koreans living in Japan ensured that domestic politics were hotly intertwined. China was then seen as less of a threat, but an object of close scrutiny.

2. The development and maintenance of reliable sources of raw materials, which drove relations with the Middle East, Africa, Latin America, the United States, and the Soviet Union.

3. Access to markets throughout the world, of which the United States was the most important.

Looking back, Japanese foreign policy in the 1970s was a more reticent and less confident version of China's diplomacy today, with domestic growth objectives the paramount determinant of behavior toward the outside world. The oil crisis in 1972 had sharpened Japan's sense of dependence internationally—on the Arabs for oil, on the United States for security, and on the rest of the third world for raw materials.

## President Ford Pays a Visit

These trends and pressures formed the backdrop for the visit of the new U.S. president, Gerald R. Ford, in November 1974. President Nixon's resignation that August had riveted Japan's attention. The final hours of Nixon's presidency on August 9 were broadcast live on Armed Forces Radio and Tokyo media. The Japanese had felt betrayed by Nixon's failure to inform them in advance of his opening to China, but the "Nixon Shock" was now past. Local analysts saw the Ford visit as a tactical gesture of amends by Henry Kissinger, still secretary of state. Kissinger's memoirs make scant mention of the trip.

Whatever the motivation, this was to be the first visit to Japan by a sitting U.S. president in history. Remembering that riots against the Mutual Security Treaty had forced President Eisenhower to cancel his Tokyo stop in 1960, government authorities were hypernervous. To make matters even more intense, news of a huge bribery scandal involving Japanese officials and the Lockheed Corporation had just broken, and Prime Minister Tanaka had been implicated. The result would be a period of turmoil in Japanese politics. The power brokers in the Liberal Democratic Party, which had led the government since 1948 (and continued to do so until 2009), agreed that Tanaka could stay in office for the Ford visit but that this would be his last hurrah.

The process of organizing the activities abroad of our top leader is as complex and arcane as the choreography that governed the movements of a Chinese emperor. Having worked in the Executive Secretariat and taken part in Nixon's visit to China, I was assigned as the embassy coordinator for the Ford operation. I was to learn the hard way the huge difference between simply going on a presidential trip and assembling one from the ground up. My first job was to mobilize embassy support for the White House and State Department planners who set up the visit, make sure that the embassy was working smoothly in harness with these people, and see that they were properly plugged in to their counterparts in the Japanese government.

A president's personality determines the way his staff behaves. The advance men who managed President Nixon's visits had been arrogant and overbearing, reigning with terror over embassy underlings around the world. Ford's people were every bit as precise in their requirements but friendly and accommodating in manner and willing to learn and adjust to local conditions. Astonishingly, many of Ford's men were same people who had advanced Nixon's travels. Same guys, different boss. Result: different behavior.

I realized from the beginning that the only way to keep track of the things I needed to know was to attach myself like a pilot fish to these people. So during three weeks of sixteen-hour days, I made my office a dressing table (with a built-in sink) in the Okura Hotel suite that the advance team used as headquarters. Propinquity is power in situations of this sort. Luckily, the head White House staffer, a freckled, friendly Irishman named Red Cavaney, welcomed all the help and advice I could provide and did not find me intrusive.

Two weeks before the arrival of Air Force One, with the schedule firm, we designated two groups of embassy officers to act, (1) as project officers responsible for ongoing functions like motorcades, motor pools, baggage, hotel rooms, security, gifts, and thank you letters, and (2) as events officers, whose activities were focused on making a particular event go well. Thus we had an officer responsible for airport arrival and departure, one for all events at the Akasaka Palace (the rococo home away from home that the Japanese use for a guesthouse), one for Imperial Palace events, and so forth. DCM Tom Shoesmith and I picked the people and set up meetings for them with their temporary White House and State Department masters, and the whole machine started to move.

There was a lot to do. About five hundred visitors were involved, including Gerald Ford and the eight who made up his official party. The bulk of the visitors were from the press, the White House Communications Agency, and the Secret Service, some of whom began to arrive early. Several hundred hotel rooms had to be reserved and a motor pool of about ninety cars assembled for their use.

While the projects officers were making these arrangements, the events officers went to work visiting the sites the president would be in, diagramming every room he would pass through and every step he would take. They did this several times, refining each scenario, making sure for example that the doors he was supposed to enter opened (disasters occur when such details are not checked out) and in general assuring that there would be no surprises. All this information was funneled to Red Cavaney, who together with his friendly pilot fish would discuss the details with the Protocol Department at the Foreign Ministry. After these discussions Red would rewrite the general program and telephone the changes to Washington. The end product of the process was a little book, which all members of the official party carried—their guide for every step of the gigantic minuet that was to begin the moment the president emerged from his plane.

Once the organization was set up and at work, my job was to oversee its operation, notice problems, and solve them before they got big. If events or projects officers were not being responsive, I had to find out why, talk to them, and get them back on the track. If the Japanese government was sticking on a point and the normal negotiating process was breaking down at the working level, I had to make sure that Shoesmith took it up with the chief of protocol or higher. Our desire to land a plane with presidential communications gear at Osaka, for example, met with strong opposition in the Japanese bureaucracy. Osaka airport had a leftist labor union, and they feared that the landing of a U.S. military aircraft would touch off demonstrations.

Permission could be arranged only after Foreign Minister Kimura had had a word with the minister of transport. For several hours, however, there was no minister of transport with whom Kimura could have a word. The cabinet was reshuffled just as the plane in question was taking off from Washington. By the time a new minister had materialized, the plane had left Alaska and was inbound without permission to land. To our relief, the plane landed at Osaka without incident. Japanese sensitivity to military presence of any sort provided a cornucopia of negotiating topics. Military markings on all cars used at the Akasaka Palace had to be removed, as did the markings on helicopters.

Communications were a special headache. The president is expected to run his government from wherever he is, so he travels abroad with an electronic retinue that virtually strews telephones in his path, (I had used such a phone in Beijing's Great Hall of the People during Nixon's visit). In addition, a coded communications system for paperwork must be set up. A balding Alabaman named Melvin Barefoot, who headed the White House Communications Agency advance team, became the first American to install a phone in the Imperial Palace.

Barefoot was a sophisticated negotiator. Confronted with the clash between his own requirements and a Japanese law that forbade foreigners from operating their own radio stations in Japan, he worked out a scheme whereby the U.S. government would give the Japanese the White House equipment for a few days, during which time the Japanese would kindly lease it back to us (for $3,000), and then return the title to us after the trip was over. It was Kabuki Theater all the way, for the equipment never changed hands for a minute, but at least the Japanese would be able to tell questioners in their Parliament if the matter were ever raised, that they were renting Japanese communications gear to the Americans for use during the president's trip.

By the time the president arrived on November 18, everything was ready for him and the four planeloads of courtiers, guards, media people, and communicators in his train. We knew his schedule to the minute, which we had plotted to the foot, and the layout of the Akasaka Palace and all the places he would visit. His helicopters and his armored car were waiting at the ramp, along with seven trucks, eight buses, and twenty cars for the rest. From there it went like a great big clock.

During the visit itself, I took advantage of my broad bureaucratic mandate to rubberneck unabashedly. I had the requisite passes to be a fly on a lot of walls and made the most of it. In the courtyard of the Akasaka Palace, I watched the president move stiffly, though with natural dignity, through the arrival ceremonies with the emperor and saw him walk right by the crown prince and the imperial family (they were just too short for him to see) until called back by the emperor. Ford's cutaway trousers were a good three inches too short, and his ankles froze in the brisk fall wind as he took the salute from the guard of honor.

I stood discreetly at the foot of the grand staircase in the palace as Kissinger swept down, followed by a cloud of dignitaries.

"Platt, what are you doing here?"

"Oh, just keeping track of things, Mr. Secretary."

"Well, if you're keeping track of things, for God's sake find me a bathroom."

The next day at cocktails before the president's banquet, I had a chance to thank the secretary for his help after my accident in Beijing. He replied that he had appreciated what I had done in Beijing and had hoped to get me on his staff in Washington. I told him that I was happy with the Tokyo assignment.

The president's dinner produced a number of small vignettes:

• Former prime minister Kishi, whose handling of the ratification of the Mutual Security Treaty in 1960 had led to the furor that snuffed out the Eisenhower visit, standing absolutely alone during cocktails, as if no one could think of a thing to say to him now that, almost fifteen years later, an American president had finally come to visit Japan.

• Prime Minister Tanaka, seated well below the Imperial Family and the salt at the head table, looking bored and preoccupied as the final hours of his stay in office ticked away.

• Emperor Hirohito and President Ford, chatting away like magpies, a diminutive, aged representative of the oldest ruling family on earth and a clean-cut American jock-politician who had lucked his way into the world's most powerful job. At the dinner he had hosted earlier in the visit, Hirohito had expressed, for the first time, historic regret over the "recent unpleasantness," i.e., World War II.

The Kyoto portion of the visit was all pleasure and no real pressure. Kissinger's hang-up bag was lost for about three hours, wrinkling administrative brows and fluttering the Secret Service dovecote (they found it on the plane), but that was the only glitch. The geishas at Tsuruya, the renowned traditional restaurant where Ford dined, drew heavy U.S. media attention but did not stand up to close inspection. From a distance they danced delightfully, but proximity revealed acne beneath the thick white make-up, which in turn accentuated yellow teeth.

Politically, the trip broke new ground. The main message of the communiqué was that the security relationship between Japan and the United States was much more than military. Security also depended on the extent to which the two countries could cooperate to solve the global economic problems (energy, food, finance) that threatened world stability and, by implication the strategic balance. This broadened definition of security, codified and sprinkled with holy summit water, has guided our relationship ever since.

The symbolic and ceremonial aspects of the visit were equally important. The presence of an American president in Japan after postwar decades of Japanese prime ministers traveling hat-in-hand to the United States added reciprocity to the relationship. The Japanese could now begin to think more closely in terms of partnership with the United States, as opposed to the one-way subservience of the past.

The Japanese responded to Gerald Ford's sincerity. He had the knack, born of a politician's training and his own personality, of convincing you that you were the only person in the world at that moment you had together, even if it was only for a few seconds. Ford clearly developed a relationship with the emperor, one that resulted in one of the few decisions Hirohito made during his lifetime: to make his own visit to the United States the following year.

As a newcomer to Japan, I had difficulty understanding the emperor's place and role in society. In preparation for the Ford visit, I asked an elderly Japanese political commentator to explain it to me. We were lunching at the restaurant atop the New Otani Hotel, which commands a panoramic view of downtown Tokyo. My guest took me over to the window and said, "The center of power in Japan lies before you. To the east is the business district and the entertainment center, to the south the government ministries, to the north the universities and publishing houses, and to the west the courts and the residences of the key government officials. In the middle is a big green empty space where the emperor resides. It represents no power at all. But like the hole in the donut, it gives the rest of Japanese society its shape. Does that help?" It did, I said.[34]

After the Ford visit, Takeo Miki replaced Tanaka as prime minister. His choice by LDP elders came as an almost total surprise to observers in Tokyo, locals and foreigners alike. The contrast with political analysis in China was striking. In Beijing no one could be blamed for bad guesses, given our pathetic diet of information, the few crumbs that fell from the table of a secretive society. I was privately relieved to learn that Japan's free press, accessible politicians, and plentiful pundits could be just as wrong.

# 21

# Becoming an Asia Hand

## The Fall of Saigon

When Saigon fell in April 1975, Washington wanted to know anything and everything we could find out about the impact of our defeat on Japanese assessments of American power and influence in Asia. Tokyo was the crossroads between the West and the rest of the region. The constant flow of American officials, military officers, politicians, and policy planners gave me plenty of opportunities to supplement my own analytical soundings on all sides of the Japanese policy community.

I knew from my first months at work that the Korean Peninsula was Japan's principal preoccupation. Relations with the neighboring Republic of Korea were terrible, the delicate, difficult legacy of decades of war and Japanese colonial domination. The people of both countries hated each other, and still do. Tokyo's ties with North Korea, already frozen by Cold War hostility and Soviet influence, were complicated by the presence in Japan of half a million Korean residents who supported Pyongyang politically and financially. The overall U.S. nuclear deterrent and conventional military deployments along the Demilitarized Zone between the two Koreas and further south were crucial to Japan's security. All that the Japanese cared about was whether the U.S. failure in Indochina would affect our policy and posture in Korea, where the power of the Soviet Union, the United States, and China converged.

They concluded that it would not. The security of the United States and Japan depended on deployments in the western Pacific rather than those on the Asian continent. Japan could live with the U.S. defeat in Indochina as long as it did not lead to any force reduction in the western Pacific. By midyear it was clear that Japan, in the words of one American official, had "rolled with the punch."[35]

Prime Minister Miki visited the United States in August and assured President Ford that an active American role in the western Pacific was still welcome. That assurance, in itself, was a mark of our diminished stature and of Japanese worry about our staying power. In October, Emperor Hirohito made a high-profile visit to the United States that included a trip to Disneyland and a heavily photographed meeting with Mickey Mouse on a park bench. The pictures astonished the Japanese. Disneyland was another of Hirohito's own unique personal decisions, the result of a long and deeply held wish. It struck a relaxed if bizarre note during a tense year.

Although Tanaka had left office after the Ford visit, the Lockheed case was still hot and getting hotter. American payoffs to Tanaka and other Japanese officials had the potential to ruin our relationship. Tanaka would be indicted in August of 1976 and ultimately go to jail. To contain the damage, we created a separate legal channel between the attorney general's office in Washington and the Japanese judicial authorities. This enabled us to refer the flood of press queries on the Lockheed case to tight-lipped court officials, who could say nothing about it. This kept explosive material out of sensitive political and diplomatic channels.

In March and April 1976, Embassy Tokyo sent me on a trip throughout Southeast Asia to assess the balance of influence post-Vietnam. Ostensibly traveling to represent our embassy at a regional narcotics conference in Kuala Lumpur, I paid calls in all of the countries of the region on my way there and back. I found that Southeast Asian policymakers wanted the United States to be the strongest power in the region, but failing that would be perfectly content with a roughly equal U.S.-China-Japan-Russia balance, with no single power in a position to dominate. Beijing was the beneficiary of the fall of Saigon, but its gains were offset by a pervasive fear throughout Southeast Asia of China's size and looming power. The countries of the region were, in general, more preoccupied with each other than with the great powers, I concluded.[36] Washington liked the report.

## Changes in China

China, another major concern of the Japanese, was the original reason for my assignment to Tokyo. With the conclusion of the Sino-Japanese Air Agreement in 1974, Tokyo replaced Hong Kong as the as the main transit point between the United States and China. I set up shop at the crossroads, took care of a stream of major American visitors, and kept my ears open. Americans, including Secretary of State Kissinger, now bent over backwards to keep the Japanese informed of their China contacts and assessments. I was in constant touch with Japanese China watchers.

Change was the watchword of the years 1974–77. With Nixon out and Tanaka going, the Chinese had lost their original champions in Washington and Tokyo. U.S. Liaison Office chiefs came and went. George H. W. Bush replaced David Bruce in 1974, and Thomas S. Gates took over from Bush in 1976. The Chinese guard was changing, too. Vice Premier Deng Xiaoping had replaced Zhou as Kissinger's interlocutor in the spring of 1974. The secretary of state remained the one constant throughout the Ford years, but his relationship with the Chinese changed after Nixon's collapse and the fall of Saigon.

Beijing officials assessed the United States as weak. They branded Kissinger's efforts to achieve detente with the Soviets "appeasement," infuriating him in the process with references to a "latter-day Chamberlain." U.S. unwillingness or inability to move ahead on normalization of relations further soured Chinese officials. China, for its part, was divided internally, as jockeying for the succession to Mao intensified with the chairman's growing frailty. On the surface, both sides made efforts to maintain the façade of normality. Kissinger visited China regularly, and in December 1975 Gerald Ford traveled to Beijing and met a physically feeble Mao. The magic of 1971–73 was gone.

Zhou Enlai, in poor health and under attack from the left, died in January 1976. Deng Xiaoping was purged yet again in April. Mao's long-scheduled "meeting with his maker" occurred in September 1976, presaged by the massive Tangshan earthquake and followed by a leadership upheaval in Zhongnanhai. Madame Mao and her "Gang of Four" were arrested four weeks later after launching an abortive coup. Mao's anointed successor, Hua Guofeng, described by one of the first Americans who met him as "effete and effeminate—even a bit gay,"[37] took the reins of a transitional coalition while the able Deng Xiaoping, rehabilitated once again, began the process of strengthening his hold over Chinese politics and economic reform. In their day-to-day relations, Beijing, Washington, and Tokyo treaded water, waiting for new leaders to be elected or consolidate their power, while slowly building the practical economic, cultural, and social links that would dominate the future.

## The MiG-25 Crisis

Meanwhile, I found myself in the eye of a three-sided storm involving Japan, the Soviet Union, and the United States. On Labor Day, September 6, 1976, a MiG-25 "Foxbat" fighter landed at Hakkodate airport in Hokkaido. The Soviet pilot, brandishing a pistol from his cockpit, requested political asylum in the United States. As the embassy duty officer of the day, I was paged off the courts at the Tokyo Lawn Tennis Club to deal with the matter. And as the action officer in the political section responsible for the diplomatic handling of defectors, I sent Washington an immediate request to grant defector status to the pilot, Viktor Belenko. Washington quickly agreed. Then the trouble began.

The Japanese, deathly frightened of the Soviets, wanted to return the aircraft to the Soviet Union at the same time they released to pilot to us. The Ministry of Justice claimed jurisdiction over the case, arguing that Belenko had violated the National Sword and Gun Act when he waved his pistol. They maintained that they had no power to hold the plane. It had only served as the vehicle for the violator.

Washington was astonished and furious. The plane that had carried Belenko was neither sword nor gun, but one of the deadliest weapons in the world. We needed a long, careful look at the Foxbat. No one in the NATO Alliance had seen this most advanced fighter in the Soviet arsenal up close. I took the matter to my friend Yukio Satoh, the Foreign Office official in charge of security relations with the United States, explaining the very grave consequences to U.S.-Japan relations if the plane were released at the same time as the pilot. Yukio, one of my closest and most candid contacts, reported an intense tug-of-war underway between the Ministry of Justice and the Japan Defense agency, which demanded to examine the plane. In postwar Japan, the Defense Agency remained bureaucratically one of the weakest in the government. Yukio went to his superiors and persuaded them to manage release of the pilot and the plane as separate matters.

Japanese public interest in this case was white hot. The Japanese authorities sequestered Belenko at the Suijo police and fire station on a peninsula next to Tokyo's Haneda airport, from which Belenko would fly to America. A wall of fireboats was deployed around the peninsula to keep curious media craft away.

International protocol regarding defectors required that an American official first interview Belenko, to determine face-to-face if he wished to go to the United States. Then the Soviets would have their turn to try to make him change his mind. On the appointed day, Friday, September 10, I appeared at the Suijo Police Station and was shown into a small office, where I sat down next to pilot Belenko, a compact, muscular man with a big nose, sandy hair, and a wide smile. In halting English, he described his desire to go to the United States and to someday fly again, even if only a plane that carried freight or sprayed crops. He understood the implications of his act for his family and could accept the consequences. I handed him his airline ticket and left.

On my way out the Japanese showed me the room in which Belenko would be interviewed by the Soviets an hour later. In contrast to the cozy office in which he and I had met, this was a large room with doors at either end. Two lines of conference tables had a narrow slot in between that was filled wall to wall with Japanese police riot shields. Belenko told me later that he appeared at one end, the Soviet officials at the other, and they shouted back and forth across this barrier for only a minute. He was prepared for the possibility that a letter from his family might be shown. "I have left, so it doesn't matter," he said.[38]

Half an hour later, Belenko departed Japan aboard Northwest flight 22. The airline had arranged for the entire upper deck of their 747 to be set aside for Belenko and his bodyguard, a CIA agent, specially flown in, known for his expertise with both handguns and his hands. He had earned a black belt in judo and had the high squeaky voice of a person who, like many sumo wrestlers, had been hit in the throat many times. The meetings at the Suijo station were covered extensively in the media, limited to pictures of me and my Soviet counterparts going in and out the door.

The easy part was over. Pressure from Washington to inspect the aircraft mounted. We were instructed to tell the Japanese government that members of Congress and top officials in the White House were beginning to question the value of our security treaty. If Japan could not make available this most important weapons windfall since the beginning of the Cold War, what kind of an ally was it?

In the end, Mr. Satoh and his colleagues devised a special, very Japanese solution. The Foreign Office explained to the Soviets that the Foxbat's landing gear had been damaged (not true), making it impossible simply to fly the plane back to its base in Vladivostok as the Soviets demanded. Instead, the aircraft would have to be taken apart for shipping back to the Soviet Union. Lacking expertise of their own to dismantle the MiG-25, they would have to hire a contractor located at Chitose Air Base (which the United States operated jointly with the Japanese). The contractor would be—surprise, surprise!—the U.S. Air Force.

In the event, it took a month to complete the meticulous dismantling. The parts were then placed in handsome, custom-built wooden crates, as if packaged at a fancy Japanese department store. Plexiglas windows were installed helpfully to show what was in each box (wings, fuselage, engines, and so forth). These were then loaded onto a freighter and shipped back to the Soviet Union.

The Soviets were livid, insisting Belenko had been drugged and hustled onto the U.S. airliner. Later that September, Soviet foreign minister Gromyko complained to the Japanese in Tokyo that they had "preyed on the plane like a mountain dog." The affair roiled Soviet relations with the Japanese for months to come.[39] In fact, we got a very good look at the plane. A month later, the U.S. Air Force had the temerity to submit a bill to the Japanese government for their services as a contractor.

## The Guard Changes—Mondale Visits Japan

With the November 1976 election of Jimmy Carter, Henry Kissinger was out after eight years of powerful influence. Tokyo, Beijing, and now Washington had undergone a complete change of leadership since the original opening to China. Vice President Walter Mondale's first act after inauguration would be a trip to Asia, with Japan the first stop. Accompanying Mondale would be the newly appointed assistant secretary for East Asian and Pacific Affairs, Richard C. Holbrooke, a longtime friend from our early days in the Foreign Service who possessed a mixed reputation for brilliance and brashness. Rumors, especially upsetting to the Japanese, that Carter was bent on pulling U.S. troops out of Korea preceded the Mondale delegation.

Preparations for Mondale were assigned to me. His lead advance man, a gum chewing former Michigan State football-player-turned-lobbyist named Bob Beckel was low key and easy to help. The visit, from January 30 to February 1, 1977, gave me a good look at Mondale, and I liked what I saw. As I wrote to my father later:

> I participated in five hours of briefings Mondale used to prepare himself for his talks with Prime Minister Fukuda. These were relaxed sessions in Mondale's hotel room attended by the top policy people who accompanied him (including Holbrooke and Mike Armacost) and our DCM, Tom Shoesmith. Mondale was dressed in jeans with a hole in the knee that had been repaired, Tretorn sneakers without socks, a wooly shirt, and a huge cigar. He sat on the sofa with his legs tucked up under him and went over his talking points with great care, making sure that he understood everything he was supposed to say, approved of it, or had anything he wanted to add. Throughout, he kept bouncing questions off the people around him as to why we wanted to say this or that, what this meant, why that would look stupid to people back home if he put it that way. All in all, it was a very efficient and good-humored performance by a man who seems very comfortable with himself and his role. He showed that a relaxed approach can get good results—the talks with the

Japanese were successful, and Mondale flew home radiating satisfaction with the Tokyo stop.[40]

U.S. troop withdrawals, Armacost told me later, were not discussed.

An important by-product of the visit was my next job. As Holbrooke bounded off the plane, he asked if I would like to come back to Washington next summer and take charge of Japanese affairs in the East Asia Bureau. The man currently in the job, Bill Sherman, wanted to come out to Tokyo as deputy chief of mission for the new ambassador (Senator Mike Mansfield was about to be nominated). I told Holbrooke I would be delighted. Country director for Japan was an exalted job for a person in my rank, one usually held by a career Japan hand and never before by a "China Boy."

I cemented my ties with Holbrooke soon after. I was sitting in his hotel room chatting about the transition in Washington while he unpacked. In a few minutes, he was scheduled to accompany the vice president to meet Prime Minister Fukuda. Rummaging through his luggage, Holbrooke reported in panic that he had forgotten the pants to his blue suit. Traveling in khakis, he had nothing appropriate to wear for the most important event of the visit. Desperate, Dick asked if, by any chance, I had a suit handy and, as it happened, I did. Like all seasoned visit managers, I had taken a room at the hotel and quickly produced the clothes, which fitted quite well. Relieved and properly clad, Holbrooke went off to the meeting, assured that somehow I was a useful person. He wore my suit the entire time he was in Tokyo.

The assignment to the Japan Desk took several months to clear a bureaucracy dead set against what amounted to a double jump in rank for me. In the end, Holbrooke and his new deputy, my old mentor and colleague, William Gleysteen, prevailed. We returned to the United States in June 1977, fully renewed after the Beijing setback. David Bruce had been right. I left Tokyo with a broader background and a new set of skills. It would be three more years before I would get back to work on relations with China, but I was now qualified to deal with Asia across the board.

## New Work in Washington

As country director for Japan at the State Department, I spent a year plowing the furrows of a huge, established relationship. Hardy perennial frictions had to be handled with meticulous care—defense spending that was too small; trade surpluses that were too large; a currency that was too cheap; a U.S. military presence that was too noisy or hormonal for neighboring Japanese communities; the existence, or not, of nuclear weapons on visiting U.S. Navy ships; choppy postwar relations with Asian countries, particularly Korea. A generation of Japan hands had developed time-honored ways of dealing with all of these. My job was to master the techniques and apply them smoothly, and with speed where necessary. What was new was the ballooning volume and importance of our relationship, a function of Japan's rapid economic recovery and growth.

I got important help from two sources. One was Mike Mansfield, who began in Tokyo as ambassador just days before I left for home. I had served as his control officer when he visited Japan in early 1977 while still Senate majority leader. Easy to like and trust (the only member of Congress I ever took care of who returned his counterpart fund (local currency) allowance unspent), we developed a relaxed relationship. The Japanese revered Mansfield for his age, his dignity, and his unassuming accessibility. Visitors to his office never forgot that the ambassador personally made them a cup of coffee, which he served himself, even though the taste was quite bad. Washington hung on his every word, especially during the first year of his long tenure in Tokyo before he developed a reputation as an apologist for Japan. I played the role of forward spotter for Mansfield's heavy artillery. I could arrange overnight for a cable from the ambassador making the points I needed on any aspect of our relationship, which I would then make sure hit the desks of all affected cabinet officers the next morning.

One such barrage endeared me to Robert Strauss, the special trade representative, whose negotiating style kept the Japanese on constant edge. His assistant, Richard Rivers, got himself into severe trouble during a visit to Tokyo in which I participated. He was quoted as daring to suggest to the prime minister during a courtesy call that Japan could solve its trade imbalances with the world by controlling its growth rate. The Japanese press uproar was so loud that State Department and National Security Council officials asked me to cut Rivers's visit short and bring him home. I knew this would ruin Rivers and turn our trade relations more sour than ever. After assuring that Rivers's private meetings went well the following day, I drafted a cable for Mansfield to sign that described the exchanges as constructive and the Japanese press reaction as overblown. Curtailing Rivers's trip would be a mistake. Washington cooled and Rivers's bacon was saved. Thereafter, I was able to see Bob Strauss whenever I needed to, a handy privilege during a period of trade stress between Japan and the United States that lasted for years. Strauss, very privately, described trade negotiations with Tokyo to me as "wiping your behind with a wagon wheel—an endless process."

The other special source of assistance during my time on the Japan desk was Tatsuo Arima, my old Saint Paul's classmate, who just happened to be assigned to Washington as the Japanese embassy political counselor at the same time I was put in charge of relations with Tokyo. This was hardly pure coincidence, as Tatsuo so stoutly maintained. Japanese men are closer to their schoolmates than anyone except their mothers, a sensibility that clearly influenced the Foreign Office's decision. American priorities may be different, but Tatsuo and I knew each other quite well and could communicate easily. Together we could defuse brewing crises in advance, particularly in the security field. I could be sure of a direct line to the leaders of the Japanese foreign policy establishment, if I needed it. Visits by prime ministers were frequent, carefully choreographed, and observed in minute detail in Japan. It helped me to have Tatsuo at hand to explain how every tiny arrangement would be interpreted in Tokyo.

## The White House Calls

In the summer of 1978, Zbigniew Brzezinski invited me to join his National Security Council staff in a position that covered U.S. policy toward Japan, Korea, Southeast Asia, Australia, and New Zealand—in short, everywhere in East Asia but China. I had become one of a rotating interagency group of Foreign Service officers who replaced each other in key subcabinet policy positions in State, Defense, and the White House. These included Michael Armacost, William Gleysteen, Morton Abramowitz, and Roger Sullivan, my fellow language student in Washington and Taiwan. Richard Holbrooke managed the musical chairs and used what became known as the "East Asia Informal Group" to mesh interagency policy toward Asia. We were all capable of writing the talking points for each other's bosses (Vance and, later, Muskie at State, Brzezinski at the White House, and Brown at Defense) before they met, and frequently did.

Working at the center of American power was heady. The NSC staff worked next to the White House in grand and comfortable offices, with high ceilings and fireplaces that contrasted with the modest scale of the mansion across the way. NSC staff had access to the White House, which provided poignant glimpses of history. I remember walking along the underground passage between the East and West Wings one day and seeing President Carter jogging forlornly around the Rose Garden, the prisoner of his unfortunate pledge not to leave the White House grounds until our hostages, taken in September 1979 had been released from Iran.

My immediate boss was Zbig Brzezinski, who thought, spoke, and wrote in broad conceptual brush strokes. His boss, Jimmy Carter, loved detail, perhaps to a fault. Any NSC staffer who repeatedly left a safe open in the Executive Office Building got a stern personal note from the president of the United States. We thought there could be better uses for his time.

No staff study was too arcane for Jimmy Carter. The only paper of mine he really liked was an extract of Emperor Hirohito's poetry that I prepared for his visit to Japan in 1979. Knowing that Carter would appear with Hirohito several times, and understanding the emperor's stature in Japanese society, I had picked excerpts from several poems Carter could quote on themes that would come up in his speeches—the search for peace, the beauty of nature, the strivings of mankind, and the like. In this instance the combination of Carter's decency, moral sense, and attention to minutiae paid off. He used the quotes. The Japanese press took note and raved.

During that Tokyo visit, I stood in for Brzezinski, who stayed home to deal with a crisis in Nicaragua. Carter accepted the substitution without comment, introducing me to the emperor matter-of-factly as his "national security advisor." That status had entitled me to a seat in the cabinet room aboard Air Force One, from which I observed the interplay between the president, Mrs. Carter, Secretary of State Vance, Treasury Secretary Mike Blumenthal, and Dick Holbrooke. Carter appeared frequently for discussions, seated in shirtsleeves on a low stool in the center of his compartment, engaging in easy give-and-take, with his advisors around him. In such a group, thirty thousand feet above and miles away from the Congress and the rest of Washington, policy could be made on the spot.

Room at the top, I discovered, could be extremely uncomfortable. The cabinet space, next to the president's suite, resembled a cocktail lounge, with a high-backed, U-shaped banquette placed around a worktable. The excitement of frequent meetings with the president wears off, to be replaced by the mounting back pain that would afflict anyone who spends eighteen hours in a cocktail lounge. In the end, all the cabinet officers, led by Secretary Vance, who had a bad back to begin with, were sleeping on the floor, a fitful school of beached whales, snoring gently. Amy Carter would walk by from time to time, her passage marked by the signature fragrance of thirteen-year-old feet.

Work in the NSC was also scary. Zbig's staff was tiny, and all of us reported directly to him. I was unnerved at first to discover that he often sent my recommendations on other agencies' policy papers concerning Asian issues straight to the president, without comment. With the exception of Carter's desire to withdraw U.S. troops from Korea, which no cabinet officer wanted to touch, most of my issues were outside Zbig's area of interest or expertise. There was little time in his job for editing or feedback in any case. I learned early that I had to be right, had to know precisely what the policy players in other agencies thought, and that they had to be aware what I would recommend. Misuse of NSC powers was a sin punished by a quick push from the White House perch, I knew from the fate of others.

### Korea on Our Mind

U.S. troop withdrawal from Korea was the issue that absorbed most my time at the NSC. No one knew where precisely President Carter got the idea, but he held it strongly. When the proposal surfaced at the beginning of his administration in 1977, it upset our Asian allies, especially the Japanese, more than any U.S. act since the end of World War II, including our defeat in Vietnam. The strategic interests of Japan, South Korea, the Soviet Union, China, and the United States intersected in the Korean Peninsula. Any weakening of our position threatened the stability of the entire region. Asians had two main fears about the United States—that we would bully them, or that we would desert them. Of the two, desertion was by far the most frightening and fueled the strong reaction against withdrawal from Korea.

U.S. government professionals dealing with Asian issues in the State Department and the Pentagon were united in opposition to troop withdrawals, but reluctant, as were their superiors, to confront their president directly. So, in 1978, we put together an elaborate three-stage plan designed to change the mind of one man, Jimmy Carter. The first stage was to be a National Intelligence Estimate examining the latest evidence of North Korean military strength. Next—and this would be my responsibility to organize—would be a major interagency study (Presidential Review Memorandum NSC-45) laying out the policy options informed by the NIE. The finale would come during a presidential visit to Korea in the summer of 1979, during which, we hoped, Jimmy Carter would tell President Park Chung Hee he had changed his mind.

The initial stages proceeded according to plan. The intelligence estimate concluded correctly that we had underestimated the North Korean ability to attack and damage the south. The policy study, equally laboriously assembled, favored a recommendation to postpone troop withdrawals. But the findings were never discussed directly with the president. Holbrooke at State, Armacost at Defense, and I at the NSC all recommended that our bosses meet with the president to hash out the issue before he traveled to Seoul, but the subject was not discussed. Then came the visit, right after the Japan G-7 meeting in June 1979.

The Korean welcome for Carter was tumultuous, with hundreds of thousands cheering along his route, while high school bands dressed in American style football halftime uniforms blared numbers including "Onward Christian Soldiers." Carter could not help but notice the Christian steeples and crosses that dotted Seoul's hills. As we arrived at the Blue House for discussions with President Park, I thought the stage was set for a success. I was wrong.

## Bad Chemistry

For days leading up to the trip, we had worked with Blue House officials to choreograph a smooth interaction. If President Park did not raise the issue, we told his National Security Advisor Kim Kyong Won (later ambassador to the United States), the chances of Carter's postponing withdrawals would improve greatly. As we filed into the conference room, the U.S. president was still glowing from his welcome. Vance, Brzezinski, Brown, Ambassador Bill Gleysteen, Dick Holbrooke, and I followed and sat down. Park and his entourage were already in place.

After greetings, disaster struck. Park Chung Hee led off immediately with a long lecture on the strategic drawbacks that would stem from U.S. troop withdrawal—a heightened threat from Pyongyang, a weakened U.S. strategic posture in Asia and the world, a stronger Communist China, and on and on. He could not understand how the United States could even contemplate such an action. Park punctuated his presentation with snaps of his fingers, a habit he had when he was ill at ease.

Carter's own stress mannerism, seen frequently during press conferences, was to open his mouth wide with a snap of his jaw. Clearly furious, he began to do this, and then passed a handwritten note to his colleagues that said, "If he keeps on like this, I am going to withdraw all troops tomorrow!" Brzezinski was alarmed, and called for a coffee break. The plenary never resumed. Instead, the two men retired at Zbig's suggestion to Park's office for a private meeting, just the two of them, to discuss other issues on the agenda. The Koreans provided an interpreter, and Zbig sent me in as note taker, to balance the sides. Arriving shortly after the talking began, I found both men still snapping away, Park his fingers, Carter his jaw. I had never seen such a bad chemical reaction between two leaders. But the subject had changed, and the conversation that followed on economics and human rights was substantive and serious, if not cordial.

I rode back to our ambassador's residence with Holbrooke in the car just behind the presidential armored limousine carrying Brown, Vance, Brzezinski, and Gleysteen, some on jump seats, shoehorned in together with the president. When the cars arrived at the residence, Dick and I, seasoned motorcade veterans, jumped out poised to follow at the heels of our leaders into lunch. But the doors to the big limo did not open. Holbrooke and I waited, peering into the rear window. We could see the president pointing his finger at each of his advisors, who sat looking sheepish. The only other mouth that was moving was Gleysteen's. Dick said to me, "I guess they are finally having that meeting."

Gleysteen told me later that a fuming Carter had laid into his advisors in the car, pointing at each and saying that all of them had been against him on Korean troop withdrawal from the outset. Gleysteen spoke up to tell him why, outlining the consequences of pulling out. Carter listened.

The car doors opened, and a grim lunch ensued. The president cooled down. He agreed to postpone withdrawals on condition that President Park made a commitment to increase significantly the ROK defense budget and release a number of political prisoners. I retired to write up the report of the Park-Carter conversations, and Holbrooke sallied forth to repair the damage.

He succeeded. In fact, by the end of the of the visit two days later, President Carter saw fit to tell Park Chung Hee in the car as they rode to the airport that he thought it might be best to put U.S. troop withdrawals from the Korean Peninsula on hold for a while. Thirty years later, an American military presence in Korea, reshaped and repositioned, continues to remain a key factor in the stability of Asia.

# 22

# The Pentagon Meets the PLA

## Normalization at Last

I was in the White House the day President Carter announced that on January 1, 1979, the United States and China would establish full diplomatic relations. A fascinated bystander, I had only been a spectator in the process, which turned out to be fortunate. Policy toward China had been the responsibility of my NSC colleague, Michel Oksenberg, a distinguished professor at Michigan and leading expert on PRC domestic politics. The East Asia interagency mechanism had worked fine for all issues except China. Instead, fierce competition between State and the NSC over stewardship of China policy had plagued the Carter administration from day one.

The intense, secretive rivalries of academic life prepared both Oksenberg and Brzezinski well for the constant guerilla warfare that broke out with Holbrooke and Vance over the day-to-day management of the normalization process. I had been friends with Oksenberg since he was a research scholar in Hong Kong during the 1960s. From my adjoining office in the Executive Office Building I could overhear vicious arguments that fed what became lifetime ad hominem hatreds. Mike had never worked in a big bureaucracy and had little time for the consultative process. A marvelous lecturer and lucid writer, his interpersonal skills were less developed. Fully occupied with the rest of Asia, I stayed firmly out of the way.

## Back to China with the Secretary of Defense

At the end of 1979, after six years on the periphery of U.S.-China relations, I was given one more chance to work directly on a new link with Beijing. The job in the Office of the Secretary of Defense responsible for East Asia policy, most notably nascent military ties with the PRC, came open, and I jumped at the chance.

Almost immediately, in January 1980, I found myself on Defense Secretary Harold Brown's plane bound for Beijing on another high-profile visit in the history of U.S.-China relations. The Soviet Union had made it so by invading Afghanistan six days before Brown took off from Andrews Air Force Base. Planned since the summer, the U.S. secretary of defense's trip to China became an urgent focus of world attention. I was still technically a member of Brzezinski's NSC staff but was asked to join Brown's delegation to prepare for my new job, which would formally begin after we returned from China. I would serve during the trip as Brown's note taker and assistant, as if I had already assumed the post. This first visit to the PRC by a secretary of defense would start the process of forging the last unfinished link in the U.S.-PRC relationship, that between the Pentagon and the PLA.

Our relations with China developed rapidly during the year following normalization. Vice Premier Deng Xiaoping, now back for good at the top of the heap in Beijing, visited the United States in January 1979. I attended receptions given for him in Washington and saw firsthand how skillfully he bonded with the American public. Deng's four feet eleven inches topped by a ten-gallon hat during a stop in Texas was a signal hit. Vice President Mondale reciprocated with a trip to China in August of 1979. Old deadlocks on issues involving trade and consular operations began to ease. Consulates were opening in different parts of the United States and China to support the work of the embassies in the capitals. Also that fall, Congress approved Most Favored Nation trade arrangements for the PRC.

Military-to-military ties were still in their infancy by late 1979 and perhaps the most fragile of any strand in our relationship. Defense attachés were assigned to Beijing and Washington but had not settled in. The question of military contact with the PRC had been controversial from the outset, questioned by China scholars wondering what the United States stood to gain, Soviet experts concerned about the impact on U.S. relations with the Soviet Union, members of Congress who supported Taiwan, and Asian allies apprehensive about a strengthened PRC.

I had not been privy to the clandestine foreplay regarding military relations with the PRC. Exchanges on intelligence- and technology-sharing with Chinese officials, including Deng Xiaoping, had been secret features of visits by Kissinger, in 1975, and Brzezinski, in 1978 and 1979.[41] But events of 1979 preceding the Soviet invasion—mostly in the public domain and easily visible from my NSC perch—added both complexity and urgency to the process of linking the two militaries.

In February (reportedly with tacit U.S. approval), the PRC had launched a border war against Vietnam. Irritated over Soviet-backed Vietnamese gains in Cambodia, Beijing wanted to "teach [Hanoi] a lesson." Instead, second-string Vietnamese divisions gave PLA units a bloody nose in a tussle called off after only seventeen days. Beijing learned the hard way just how old-fashioned Chinese equipment and logistics really were. The Soviet invasion of neighboring Afghanistan only intensified Chinese desire to modernize their military through closer ties with the U.S. armed forces.

The Taiwan Relations Act, passed by Congress in April 1979, would make military relations more complicated for Harold Brown and, for that matter, every secretary of defense since. The Congress was angry over the way the executive branch treated Taiwan when it normalized relations with Beijing. The act mandated that the United States should supply "such defense articles and defense services as may be necessary for Taiwan to maintain a sufficient self-defense capability." The legislation provided more protection for Taiwan than the administration wanted and infuriated Deng Xiaoping. In practical terms, the act meant that we were arming Taiwan to protect itself against the PRC, while at the same time strengthening the PRC to protect itself against the Soviet Union.

Finally, the September 1979 capture of U.S. hostages at the U.S. Embassy in Iran shocked the American public, shook the priorities of the Carter administration, and further shaped Harold Brown's instructions.

## Tightrope Instructions

We took off from Andrews AFB on January 4, 1980, in the secretary of defense's windowless converted fuel tanker—we called it the "tube." As soon as we reached cruising altitude, Secretary Brown asked me to convene his large interagency delegation in the conference area. This was the "East Asia Informal Group Plus," with representatives from warring factions sent by their superiors to keep an eye on one another.[42]

In contrast to the careful compartmentalization of Kissinger delegations, Brown took pains to share in detail with the entire group the carefully qualified instructions he had received from President Carter that morning. As would occur throughout the visit and, in fact, my entire year with Secretary Brown, I took the notes (on which these chapters are based).

His objective, he told us, would be to broaden and deepen the defense/security dimension of the U.S.-China relationship *without* forming an alliance or any formal anti-Soviet arrangement. He wanted to coordinate policies where our interests were parallel, but avoid establishing a "big brother–solve everything" relationship. He would cite Chinese devotion to self-reliance. Carter was prepared to schedule a visit by Party Secretary General Hua Guofeng in June and announce it, if the Chinese so desired.

Our consultations would cover the world strategic situation, regional issues, and bilateral cooperation. Brown said he was authorized to consult privately on assistance to Afghanistan and Pakistan. We could mention transportation and logistics arrangements (even though this was beyond the instruction), but not contingency planning. We could tell the Chinese of our plans to funnel aid to the Afghans through Pakistan.

On technology transfer, we would indicate ways in which we differentiated between China and the Soviet Union, discussing what we made available for Beijing that we did not allow for Moscow. We would engage in technical discussions on items under foreign assets control. While we had no plans to sell arms to the PRC, a point we wanted to stress in public, we could discuss the availability of military equipment on a case-by-case basis. Over-the-horizon radar, Landsat D, and site surveys could also be topics. (Landsat D was a ground receiving station for the Landsat photoreconnaissance system, ostensibly for civilian use on oil exploration and agricultural production.) Technically, Landsat D would provide the means for major improvement in the resolution capabilities of Chinese intelligence satellites.[43] The president, Brown continued, drew a firm distinction between arms and military equipment but wanted to retain the option of changing policy to include defensive weapons.

On arms control, the president wished to establish a hotline with the Chinese using a full-time circuit. We were to urge the Chinese to do more testing underground, and sound them out on acceding to existing multilateral arms control arrangements.

## Talks in Beijing

The four days of conversations in Beijing were long, meaty, and often difficult. Members of the delegation from all U.S. agencies attended whichever meeting they wanted. The old games of exclusion that had marked the Nixon/Kissinger–Mao/Zhou era were over. In more important respects, U.S. foreign policy was undergoing a tectonic shift. As Under Secretary Komer put it later, "U.S. policy has changed more in three weeks than in the past two years." Détente with the Soviet Union was dead. Just as we arrived in China, President Carter announced a series of measures curtailing U.S. relations with the Soviet Union, including grain sales, civil aviation flights, fishing allocations, consular relations, technology transfer, and sports contacts (leading ultimately to the boycott of the Olympic Games).

The Chinese could barely conceal their delight. At a tea reception before the welcoming dinner on January 6, General Xu Xiangqian delivered a diatribe against the U.S.S.R., ranting on for fifteen minutes without letting the interpreter speak. Like all Chinese generals, Xu was very old. My notes describe him as "borderline gaga."

Brown hit the themes of his instructions during his banquet toast, assuring the Chinese that the combination of the United States, NATO, and Japan would provide strength sufficient to contain Soviet expansion, praising China as a great and self-reliant country. The United States had no intention to act as its tutor.

Brown's discussions with China's new leadership focused on (1) perceptions of the Soviet threat and how best to counter it in Afghanistan; (2) vexing international problems, including Chinese help to free U.S. hostages through support for UN sanctions against Iran and different approaches to countering the Vietnamese in Cambodia; and (3) ways to expand bilateral military ties and technology transfer.

## Strategic and International Issues

Both sides saw eye-to-eye on the Soviet threat. Brown told Defense Minister Geng Biao, "It sounds as though our staffs wrote the papers together."[44] Brown emphasized that the combined weight of the United States, Europe, Japan, and China would be more than enough to deal with the global threat from the Soviet Union.

Deng Xiaoping described Soviet moves in Asia as aimed ultimately at the United States and the West and was pleased that the United States had finally seen the light. Brown agreed with Deng that their objective should be to "turn Afghanistan into a quagmire in which the Soviet Union is bogged down for a long time." Deng approved explicitly of new U.S. measures to project power in the Indian Ocean, including expansion of facilities at Diego Garcia; increased naval capability; discussions with Oman, Somalia, and Kenya on air base access rights; and broadening security discussions with Saudi Arabia and Oman. They "would have been better done earlier," Deng said, but added, "Don't take this as criticism, understand."

Brown and the Chinese leaders agreed on the need to provide confidential assistance to Afghan refugees and insurgents. Aid to Pakistan would be a crucial next step. Deng described the U.S. decision to help Pakistan despite its efforts to develop nuclear weapons as "a very good policy." The Indians would be annoyed, he acknowledged, but they did not play a stabilizing role in the region. The size and substance of support for Islamabad would remain an issue. Brown said that the Pakistanis were reluctant even to discuss the subject.

The secretary of defense carried a personal letter from President Carter to Party Secretary General Hua Guofeng urging China to join the United States in an upcoming UN vote to sanction Iran. In all his meetings, Brown argued forcefully that international solidarity would pressure Tehran to return our hostages. The Chinese listened carefully. They deplored the taking of our hostages but expressed concern about the effectiveness of sanctions (as they do to this day) and the long-term impact on their relations with Iran. They said they would think about it—in effect, a polite no. For our part, Brown disagreed flatly with Foreign Minister Huang Hua about the best ways to counter Vietnamese military action in Cambodia. The Chinese urged us to back Pol Pot as the only effective resistance force and to postpone support for Prince Sihanouk. Brown demurred.

### Bilateral Military Relations

During his meetings with Defense Minister Geng, Brown presented proposals to increase contacts between the two defense establishments, including:

> 1. an invitation to Geng to visit the United States, followed by a schedule of regular meetings;
> 2. expansion of the respective attaché offices on a reciprocal basis, as soon as adequate working and living accommodations became available in Beijing;
> 3. an invitation to a delegation from the PLA military academy to visit the United States; and
> 4. establishment of a hotline between the Pentagon and PLA Headquarters.

Brown indicated his willingness to discuss communications and medical support, as well as transportation and logistics "without implying that we were in a supply relationship or engaged in joint planning for military contingencies." He wanted to announce any or all of these proposals at the end of the visit.[45]

Geng welcomed an expansion of attaché offices and accepted the military academy invitation. He would consider the other proposals and reply through diplomatic channels.

In fact, at this point, the Chinese were leery of committing to regular consultations between the ministers of defense or to publicizing their contacts in advance, at least in detail. They were agreeable to a general statement that Secretary Brown had invited a series of military defense delegations and the Chinese side had accepted the invitations.

## Technology Transfer

The Brown visit provided the first opportunity for direct talks between Chinese and Americans on technology transfer. Current restrictions were particularly galling to Beijing. Brown and Assistant Secretary Gerald Dineen led the Chinese through the thickets of U.S. technology export control mechanisms relating to the sale and licensing of arms and dual-use technology. They offered to explore, case by case (a term that became a mantra), the export of items to China that the United States did not provide the Soviet Union, including elementary forms of integrated circuits and the technology to produce them. In addition, we were willing to discuss licensing technology associated with Landsat D, over-the-horizon radar (OTH), and high-speed computers used in Western Geophysical's system for oil exploration, all topics clearly off-limits to the Soviets.

The morning of January 9, after clambering briefly on the Great Wall, Brown's party visited the headquarters of the 6th Armored Division, where a military exercise featured old Soviet-model tanks rushing around firing at each other. The Chinese seemed to be trying to impress us in a spirited way with how rudimentary their equipment and tactics were.

In the afternoon, Brown met with Party Secretary General Hua Guofeng, Mao's successor. The cordial meeting focused on President Carter's invitation to Hua to visit the United States. We recommended June 1980, before our presidential campaign would begin in earnest. Hua had scheduling problems of his own and promised a response through diplomatic channels. Otherwise the conversation covered familiar topics—action in response to the Soviet attack on Afghanistan, levels of assistance to Pakistan, UN response to the Iranian hostage crisis, military relations, technology transfer, Cambodia, and so on. By now, we knew each other's talking points by heart.

Hua's reception of Brown was widely publicized in domestic and international media, marking attention to his visit at the highest levels of the Chinese leadership and another milestone in the normalization process. A banquet and a press conference filled the evening. We left Beijing the next morning bound inland for the city of Wuhan and its shipbuilding plant. Naval headquarters for the East Sea Fleet in Shanghai was our final stop before departure for Tokyo January 13.

## Assessments, Atmospherics, and Personalities

Brown's presence in Beijing so soon after the Soviet invasion gave the Carter administration a sense of at least doing something in response and the Soviets a foretaste of the international consequences of the their action. The invasion had killed détente and tilted the United States toward China.

Strategic symbolism aside, Brown's visit marked the wary beginning of the formal relationship between two military establishments whose most recent view of each other had been over gun sights in the Korean Peninsula twenty-seven years before. A generation had passed since the armistice agreement in 1953. But China's military leaders were the same men who had fought that war. Ours had been lieutenants in the units facing them. The year ahead would see this odd couple become better acquainted. At least they had introduced themselves.

Substantively, the gains were mixed. The Chinese did not grant overflight rights, perhaps reckoning that the paltry level of assistance that the United States was then willing to provide the Afghans and the Pakistanis ($100 million in Foreign Military Sales funds and $100 million in Economic Support Funds) was not worth the intelligence our airborne cameras might gain in the process. The PLA could not get used to the idea of a Pentagon hotline in their midst. (They got around to it in 2009.) Technology transfer, hedged and limited, made a start, with General Liu Huaqing handing Gerald Dineen the first detailed Chinese wish list of items before we left Beijing. Such lists would be the stuff of endless future meetings during 1980, as well as the basis, ultimately, for some significant transfers, including anti-tank munitions technology, air defense radar, electronic countermeasure devices, radio and communications equipment, and transport helicopters. Brown and Dineen, my notes record, both left Beijing feeling that the Chinese did not understand either the potential military implications of either Landsat D or Western Geophysical's computers, or the scale of the concessions the United States had made in offering them.

Briefing Prime Minister Lee Kuan Yew at a meeting I attended in Singapore a month later in February 1980, U.S. ambassador to the PRC Leonard Woodcock gave his own assessment of Brown's conversations on technology transfer. "In the two and a half years I have been in Beijing," he said, "this was the most useful exchange, aside from normalization itself, and the most useful of all the high-level visits."[46] Woodcock's other ranking visitors had been Vice President Mondale, National Security Advisor Brzezinski, and Presidential Advisor Clark Clifford.)

For me, Brown's visit was an important return to a familiar, if at the end, bitter, scene. Our time in China let me meet the new post-Mao leadership face-to-face and, equally important, get the measure of my new Pentagon bosses in circumstances familiar to me and helpful to them. I could not have asked for a better debut.

### Harold Brown

Harold Brown was easy to help. My predecessors, Mort Abramowitz and Mike Armacost, had proven to this secretary of defense the benefits of having his own personal Orientalist close at hand. He called on them, and now me, for direct advice, bypassing several bureaucratic layers, and causing some envy in the process. I would need to brief my immediate superiors with great care, particularly Under Secretary Bob "Blowtorch" Komer and the more reserved, lawyerly Assistant Secretary David McGiffert, on the details of my private meetings with Brown, which were to occur frequently.

Brown loved substance, but there was not an ounce of small talk in him. After long, strained silences sitting together in cars, I found the secretary of defense instantly responsive and engaging once I raised an issue of policy or technology. His scientific mind processed information and ideas as quickly as anyone I had worked with, particularly because it was always open. He was notably cautious and careful in his dealings with foreign leaders, relying on detailed talking papers from which he rarely departed. By contrast, he performed with ease and precision in front of the press, with few notes.

In the mornings during this trip, as I always had during earlier travels in China, I listened to the Voice of America and the BBC on a shortwave radio. I would then brief Brown on the headlines first thing while he was going through his cables. One day he asked me for my personal view as to whether the Soviets could prevail in Afghanistan.

Moscow appeared to have bitten off more than it could chew, I replied, begging lack of expertise and only limited reading on the subject. I neglected to tell Secretary Brown that my assessment was based almost entirely on having just finished reading *Flashman*, George McDonald Fraser's rollicking and raunchy novel describing the British debacle in Afghanistan in 1840. A history fanatic, Fraser always took pains to place Flashman's antics in accurate settings. His main sources for Afghanistan were the diaries of Lady Sales, the wife of the general in charge of the expeditionary force that was slaughtered almost to a man in Jalalabad. Flashman described in detail the ferocity and duplicity of the Pashtun tribes involved in the fighting. (I came to know Pashtun leaders a decade later when serving as ambassador to Pakistan and learned firsthand how little had changed.) Brown took my observation without comment.

## Deng Xiaoping

I had read about Deng Xiaoping for more than a decade and shaken his hand during a reception in Washington following normalization in 1979, but had never had a long, close look. He did not disappoint. A tiny man less than five feet tall, he was brisk, blunt, and funny. Deng hawked and spat like a peasant in the field, startling visitors with frequent, loud, and wet offerings to the spittoon by his feet, a practice all the more striking in the formal grandeur of the Great Hall of the People. Expectorations aside, he kept his guests guessing with a mixture of light humor and blunt, heavy substance. Greeting Brown for the first time, he lamented, "China is backward. We don't have anything to export. Perhaps we can export these hot towels [which were being passed around]." Meant as a joke, this was Deng's least accurate prophecy.

We would soon gain early insights into his profound impact on modern China. Two questions from the PLA dominated the initial months of our new military relationship: (1) How can we extract from you the most sophisticated technology possible? and (2) How do you retire from a military career? Both reflected Deng's new policies. We knew that upgrading military technology was one the "four modernizations" preached by the post-Mao leadership (the others: agriculture, industry, and science). But the intense Chinese interest that was to surface in all aspects of American military retirement procedures was our first indication that Deng had ordered all officials across China above a certain age to retire. This was a momentous decision and arguably Deng's most important.

By 1979 the Chinese communists had been in power for thirty years, an entire generation. But there had been no significant changes in the leadership, except through death or political purge. In effect, the same people who came to power in 1949 at the provincial and national levels, and even the county level, were still in office but thirty years older. The entire Chinese body politic was stuck, constipated by layers of elders who could not contemplate the loss of power and perks.

This condition applied to the military leaders we had already met, an extraordinary parade of geezers, including the dignified but, many believed, irrelevant defense minister Geng Biao; the crusty but politically still potent vice chief of the PLA staff, Zhang Aiping; the near-senile General Xu Xiangqian; and the energetic General Liu Huaqing, who was both cheerful and smart. Liu emerged as the key Chinese official operationally involved in docking the Pentagon and the PLA. But he, too, was in his seventies.

For Chinese senior generals, retirement was unthinkable. The freefall from four-star rank to life in one's home village was just too far. China lacked the afterlife infrastructure American officers had — think tanks, beltway consultancies or business opportunities, and generous pensions — that could make retirement busy and happy. They have them now. In the months to come, on the fringes of formal meetings, the Chinese peppered us with questions about annuities, promotion rates, and jobs in industry. We answered every one and provided all the material that we could. We also suggested that they be in touch with the South Koreans, whose military establishment was closer to theirs culturally. The Koreans had created positions for their retired generals that came with houses, cars, and the all-important "face" attached.

Vice Premier Deng chose not to promote himself to higher rank and would later resign from all formal positions, though he remained China's top leader until he died in February 1997, at age 92. He did not move against those around him immediately, but he had put the handwriting on the wall for them. He broke the generational logjam, freeing the way for fresh generations of leaders to manage China's rise.

## Hua Guofeng

Party Secretary Hua Guofeng, Mao's chosen successor, was not to be one of these. "With you in charge, I'm at ease," the chairman had famously said, an assessment greeted by snorts of derision throughout China. We were to find out why. A low-common-denominator functionary who wielded little effective power, Hua was still tolerated in office in January 1980, but would last only a few months more. I found him articulate and in command of his brief, but commented in my notebook, "He's benign, smiling, soft and cuddly, sort of weak and effeminate." It was hard to believe Hua could survive in the same arena with the likes of Deng Xiaoping. Come to find out, he couldn't.

# 23

# America Greets the PLA

Once back in Washington, developing my own channel to the Chinese military was the crucial next step in shaping the growing relationship with the PLA. General Xu Yimin, was the brand-new Chinese military attaché in Washington. He called on me at the Pentagon in late January and presented himself as my opposite number, smiling broadly from an almost perfectly round, humorous face. He came from the same part of Shandong Province as Confucius, he told me, and was clearly a person of broad education. Xu, like most military attachés, had a long intelligence background. Together we would become the day-to-day managers of our expanding military dialogue. Visits by General Liu Huaqing and Defense Minister Geng Biao in May were next on our agenda.

## Life in the Five-Sided Building

Meanwhile, I had moved from my ornate, high-ceilinged office in the Executive Office Building to a space shaped like a railroad car on the E-Ring of the Pentagon. This august outer layer of the "Five-Sided Building," especially those sides with windows on the capital city across the Potomac River, is where power resides, both civilian and military. The transition from the smallest to the largest bureaucracy in the U.S. government was a shock. At the NSC, I could move a memo to the president with only one stop in between, Brzezinski himself. In the Pentagon, policy documents moved in great, languid circles, printed on a different color of paper at each level of approval, until finally signed off on at the top. At the State Department, where all ideas for consideration must be put in writing, the secretariat machinery ensures that papers move to decision. In the Pentagon, the way to slow an idea down is to put it on paper.

I soon found out that the military assistants to the secretary and his deputies were the keys to action. Short phone calls and brief chits funneled through the MAs made things happen. The U.S. military produces the best bureaucrats in America, many of whom, like Colin Powell and Alexander Haig, have moved to high civilian office. (While I was in the Pentagon, Powell was the military assistant to the deputy secretary of defense.) The military assistants (usually two- or three-star generals) are savvy and fast and make sure that the offices of the civilians who rule the military are properly managed.

The Office of the Secretary of Defense/International Security Affairs (ISA), my new home, was and still is an unstable compound. Unlike the permanent ziggurats of the armed services, the civilian structure serving the secretary is struck like a tent every time an administration changes. An air of impermanence, of competition, of jostling for the ears of the mighty, prevails. Moving into this environment, I was comforted by knowing that I, too, was a guest, and that the substance for which I was responsible was a top priority for both civilian and military alike. These helped me through the initial skirmishes on office space, bureaucratic turf, and access to the top officers. Deputy assistant secretaries of defense normally do not have direct access to regional military commanders like the commander in chief of the Pacific Command (CINCPAC), but I did, thanks to the skills and clout of my predecessors, Abramowitz and Armacost.

The most useful perk that came with my job was membership in the Pentagon Officers' Athletic Club, a vast underground complex of the finest sports facilities in the land—squash courts, basketball floors, an Olympic-length swimming pool, saunas, steam baths—you name it, it was there. My own dependence on exercise matched that of the U.S. military establishment as a whole and helped me penetrate that jock culture. Sneaking off for an hour to play squash, unheard of in the State Department, was normal practice in the Pentagon. Urgent conversations with four-star generals anxious to visit China took place under the showers at the POAC. Friendships with key staff officers were cemented on the squash courts.

During my year-plus at the "Five-Sided Building" I spent most of my time docking the PLA and the American military establishment. Other important duties included (1) squeezing more defense spending from Japan, (2) preventing the new dictatorship in South Korea from killing opposition politician Kim Dae Jung, and (3) managing bilateral military sales relationships with Australia, New Zealand, and the countries of Southeast Asia. As the defense secretary's man on Asia, I traveled widely throughout the vast region, on a varied menu of tasks that I enjoyed as much as any before or since.

## General Liu Comes to Washington

General Liu Huaqing and his PLA advance delegation arrived in Washington May 6, 1980, for talks at the Pentagon and a look at the facilities in Indiana, Colorado, California, and Hawaii that Defense Minister Geng Biao would visit later in the month. Dr. William Perry, then under secretary of defense for science and technology (with responsibility for weapons systems procurement, research, and development) welcomed Liu. Perry would become a key figure in the search for ways to improve China's defense capability without threatening others. A former mathematics professor from Caltech, Perry would later return to the Pentagon as defense secretary under President Clinton.

Perry told Liu that the United States was prepared to help the PRC both to build its technical infrastructure and to modernize its armed forces, step by step, subject to the political constraints of the day. Meeting later with Gerald Dineen, Liu said he understood the constraints on technology transfer and the need for self-reliance on China's part. He outlined new Central Committee guidelines. PRC imports of foreign technology and equipment could take several forms: (a) purchase of technological data, (b) invitations to foreign experts, and (c) formation of joint ventures. The goal would be to train PLA officers and technicians in order to improve Chinese weapons. Imported technologies need not be first-rate. China understood other countries' reluctance to export their best systems. But the technology had to be better than China already had. "We have to consider our own level," Liu concluded. "Even if we could get the most advanced technology, we could not absorb it. We need to be able to use what we buy for practical purposes."

What Liu wanted most was help in improving China's F-8 high-performance jet fighter plane. "We need advanced radars, electronics, and guidance systems. If you can give us the engine, we would want that. Then the aircraft would be the best. If you could give us the pulse Doppler (radar), the F-8 would be equivalent to the MiG-23. This is one of our most urgent demands. We hope you will take it as a special case and consider it again. The Vietnamese have acquired the MiG-23. We will produce the aircraft." Liu invited American experts to come to China immediately.

Dineen did not respond.

Liu Huaqing then took off for his inspection of Defense Minister Geng Biao's upcoming stops in Colorado, California, and Hawaii, the routes all carefully arranged by the Pentagon to avoid aerial photography of sensitive military installations. He returned two weeks later bubbling with enthusiasm, delighted with the briefings he had received, the frankness of the talks, the visits to so many corporations and installations, the friendly attitude of the officers and men. He had made a real effort to see everything; high-precision weapons, army armaments, naval weapons, electronic countermeasures. Liu was most impressed with U.S. efforts to develop new weaponry and our experience in administering research.

Liu and his delegation concluded that U.S. emphasis on research, development, evaluation, and testing assured its leading role far into the future. The trip was a valuable experience for the Chinese in developing their military technology. As for training, Liu was impressed with the quality of American bases and academies. "You are strict, well equipped, and highly efficient," Liu beamed. "Everywhere we went, we met people from different walks who spoke to the importance of our relationship. We believe our relations will flower. We are also looking for fruits," he concluded with a smile.

The most important "fruits" Liu sought were not to drop from the tree any time soon. Dineen told Liu that none of the requests related to the F-8 could be approved, including advanced engines, radars, and guidance systems. On the brighter side, Dineen reported approval to transfer several significant items of dual-use technology and military support equipment. These would include "read only" memory chips; Bell commercial helicopters, which could be made in the PRC; disc drives, serial printers, and computers. All of these items would benefit the economy as a whole, Dineen concluded.

Swallowing his chagrin (my notes report him "disappointed and pissed"), Liu closed his meetings with a graceful review of the relationship since Harold Brown's visit. He expressed satisfaction with progress so far, and invited Perry and Dineen to visit China. But he made it clear that F-8 improvements would remain high on China's agenda, whatever problems they gave the United States.[47]

## A Chinese Defense Minister's First Visit to Washington

On May 25, Sheila and I went up to New York to meet the Chinese defense minister and his wife, Zhao Lanxiang, and escort them to Washington. Geng was wearing a light gray Western suit, of which he turned out to have a regular supply, with a blue and silver necktie, also part of his uniform. He dyed his hair brown, using some kind of henna rinse. During our weeks together, the person that emerged was shrewd, polished, controlled, and materialistic. Here was one Long March veteran ready for Deng Xiaoping's opening to the rest of the world.

Harold Brown was at Andrews Air Force Base to greet Geng and drive into the city. In the car together, Brown reviewed the visit schedule, the division of labor between them, and who would talk about what. Brown described the good impression General Liu had made during his preparations for the defense minister's tour. Searching in vain for small talk with our secretary of defense, Geng raised the subject of Alaska, over which he had flown en route to the United States. How sorry the Soviets must be that they sold it to us in 1867, he mused.

Five months had passed since Harold Brown's discussions in Beijing. Significant international developments during that time would dominate Defense Minister Geng's conversations in Washington. Failure of the U.S. attempt in April to rescue the Iranian hostages had led Secretary of State Vance to resign and Edmund Muskie to take his place. Student opposition to General Chun Doo Hwan's seizure of power in the Republic of Korea was coming to a head in the city of Kwangju. The United States, blamed for tacit support of Chun, was under pressure to intervene. On the eve of Geng Biao's arrival, I had attended a meeting of senior U.S. officials that decided to support the restoration of order in Korea in the short term and worry about democracy later. If Chun made it to the Blue House, we would reluctantly have to accept him.

In the car, Brown described our policy on Korea and the climaxing situation in Kwangju. Our emphasis was on stability. We had warned the North Koreans, encouraged moderation in the ROK, and expressed our desire for political liberalization as a means for maintaining long-term stability. It was Seoul's own decision to make. Geng asked how the DPRK was responding. Brown reported that Pyongyang was maintaining readiness and perhaps preparing for hostilities. Frankly and privately, Geng commented that China for its part would not encourage unilateral action by the North Koreans, noting pointedly that the North Korean economy was not independent.

## A Cozy Chat

The next day, the two men held an unusual, informal warm-up in Brown's office, and later that evening watched the movie *The Empire Strikes Back* at the White House (a big improvement over *Red Detachment of Women*). At the Pentagon, the two men chatted easily about what they would say about strategy toward the Soviet Union; ways in which they could coordinate action; the failure on both sides to predict the Soviet action in Afghanistan, and the difficulty the Soviets would have in conducting a war in China. Even with forty-seven Soviet divisions massed along the border, Geng believed, China's sheer size would seriously challenge the Soviets. They were having enough trouble subduing the Afghans in a much smaller area. Their surrogates, the Vietnamese, had planned to wipe out Pol Pot's forces in one dry season offensive in Cambodia, but they had_failed.

Brown and Geng wound up their chat touching on ways in which Chinese and American military-to-military relationships could develop, including technology transfer. Geng understood that supplying certain items to the Chinese during an American election year could create political problems. The PRC would go slow, not press, and take satisfaction in the gradual improvement of relations. Geng said he was delighted to be in America and happy with the hospitality he had received so far. He had not seen anything yet.

## Full Honors

During the next three days, Washington gave China's defense minister the full treatment, starting with a top-pomp military arrival ceremony at the river entrance of the Pentagon; formal talks with Secretary Brown; a welcome dinner at the National Gallery of Art; talks and lunch at the State Department with Secretary Muskie; White House conversations with President Carter and Vice President Mondale; a session on Capitol Hill with congressional leaders; dinner and entertainment at the Kennedy Center; a separate White House meeting with National Security Adviser Brzezinski; and lunch with the chairman of the Joint Chiefs of Staff. The symbolic point of the visit—the defense minister of China for the first time comparing notes on the Soviet threat in the U.S. capital with America's national security elite—was made with style.

## Substantive Issues

In their discussions, Geng and U.S. leaders acknowledged Moscow's problems subduing the Afghans and noted worldwide revulsion to the invasion, including the Olympic boycott. Support levels for Pakistan were still a question. President Zia refused to engage with the United States and spurned our aid offers, despite proposed increases. Because the rescue mission had failed, the United States was as preoccupied as ever with the Iran hostage crisis, and the Chinese as politely reluctant to impose sanctions as before. Pol Pot had survived the Vietnamese onslaught, but the United States would not help this "criminal" take power, Chinese entreaties notwithstanding.[48]

President Carter greeted Geng warmly, expressed regret that Party Secretary Hua Guofeng's schedule would not permit a visit to the United States during the rest of 1980, and hoped to visit China as president of the United States after the election. Vice President

Mondale cited the phenomenal progress in U.S.-China relations since normalization, including trade, international monetary fund membership, and Most Favored Nation treatment, but looked for progress in four areas: textiles, a maritime agreement, civil aviation, and diplomatic housing.

At the State Department, Geng attacked the imposition of martial law and the violent suppression of dissent in Korea by Chun Doo Hwan's "fascist military dictatorship," actions that would alienate popular support, jeopardizing the North-South talks and threatening peace and stability in East Asia. Geng asked Secretary Muskie and Assistant Secretary Holbrooke to exert their influence on Chun to oppose dictatorship and further democracy. He assured them the DPRK had no intent to invade the south or become involved in ROK politics. The PRC would work to bring about reunification through peaceful dialogue, step by step.

Muskie replied that he shared China's interest in peace and stability on the Korean peninsula. During the past week, the United States had worked to exercise a stabilizing influence, but his estimate of the prospects for political liberalization in the Republic of Korea were not encouraging.

At the White House, Brzezinski assured Geng that the United States would not permit the Soviet Union to gain military superiority or alter the balance of power in Southwest Asia and the rest of the world. Our goal was a total withdrawal of Soviet troops and a neutral Afghanistan. "We hope that [with] the normalization of relations with Iran, which we hope will come after a few months when the hostage crisis is solved [*sic*], to be better able to assist the Afghans."[49]

Brzezinski asked Geng if the Chinese military action against Vietnam in 1979 had, in fact, taught Hanoi a lesson. The defense minister replied that China's military pressure had drawn thirty first-line Vietnamese divisions out of Cambodia to face the Chinese, making it possible for Democratic Kampuchea to survive Hanoi's dry-season offensive. "Will there be advanced education?" Brzezinski asked (meaning more "lessons").

"Definitely," Geng replied. Beijing planned to keep tensions high on the border and resist Vietnamese pressure for disengagement.

In parting, Geng and Brzezinski complimented each other's tough, politically astute wives, neither of whom had been shy about expressing their views during conversations at social events. "She influences me not to capitulate," Brzezinski informed Geng.

At his final meeting at the Pentagon, May 29, Geng offered to sell the United States some rare metals, which could be of use militarily. These included titanium, molybdenum, vanadium, rare earth elements, and tantalum. Brown responded that the United States used all of these and would examine our needs. The two men agreed to China visits by William Perry and Joint Chiefs Chairman David Jones and to exchanges between the logistical services and the military academies. CINCPAC Adm. Robert Long would go later, they decided.

After years at daggers drawn, suddenly everyone in the two military establishments wanted to visit each other. The Geng visit made me very popular. I was now the "go to" person on China, and everybody in the Pentagon knew it.

## A Grand Tour

Spectacular military tourism is a Pentagon specialty, crafted and refined over decades of congressional travel designed to influence members responsible for the military budget. On May 30, Defense Minister Geng and his delegation departed on a tour of the United States fit for the chairman of the Senate Armed Forces Committee.[50]

Secretary Brown saw Geng off at Andrews Air Force Base. "I've not had a chance to congratulate you on your successful missile shot," Brown told Geng. (The test had occurred while Geng was in Washington.) "Ten years ago I would not have believed I would be congratulating a Chinese for such a thing."

Geng thanked him and said, "Well, you know what direction it's pointed in. We won't fire anything first, but we want the Soviets to know that we have something, especially one that can strike back." The two men then bear-hugged awkwardly, and we boarded the special Air Force VIP aircraft that would fly us across the continental United States and to Hawaii.

It was an extraordinary trip, carefully contrived to impress the Chinese and demonstrate the strength of America. As the ranking U.S. escort, I saw everything at Geng's side, and to some extent through his eyes. That morning, the delegation climbed in and out of all-terrain vehicles at an American Motors plant in Indiana. In the afternoon, at a massive firepower demonstration staged for them by the 4th Infantry Division at Fort Carson, Colorado, they stood transfixed as Apache gunships popped up from behind hills to fire wire-guided missiles at doomed targets. A sunset barbecue among the cottonwoods at Turkey Creek Ranch provided the PLA visitors with scenery and chow straight from the Western movies they had all seen.

The Colorado stop included eye-goggling missile-tracking displays at North American Air Defense (NORAD) Command Headquarters in the bowels of Cheyenne Mountain and a tour of the sparkling, futuristic campus of the United States Air Force Academy.

En route to San Diego, we dipped and circled over the Grand Canyon and refueled at Luke Air Force Base near Phoenix, Arizona, where the Chinese got an eyeful of American fighter aircraft. At least eighty F-15s and many more of the older F-4s and F-104s stood in rows on the runways. In San Diego, a visit to its famous zoo yielded memorable photos of PLA generals in their floppy hats and baggy uniforms bonding with the giant animal mascots who ran to greet them and walking with gingerly delight among a crowd of penguins. The next day, aboard the USS *Tarawa*, a helicopter carrier, the elevator carrying the defense minister got stuck, causing considerable consternation among the Navy brass, but widespread hilarity among the Chinese. The Americans were human after all.

At Third Fleet headquarters, the Navy briefed the Chinese on the main features of modern naval warfare, emphasizing the ability to coordinate their "platforms" (carriers), stay at sea, and operate. To demonstrate, they treated Geng Biao and his group to a morning at sea aboard the USS *Ranger*, observing flight operations. This was the climax of the entire visit, a show of teamwork and technology that stunned the visitors. In San Diego, our quarters at the magnificent Coronado Hotel, a huge, cozy, old-fashioned wooden structure that dominates the bay, provided relief from the relentless modernity of the U.S. military establishment.

Assistant Secretary of Defense Dineen flew into San Diego for a last meeting with General Liu and one more look at the technology transfer lists. Liu was most grateful for this special gesture and looked forward to welcoming Dineen, Perry, and me to China later in the year. As the conversation closed, Dineen asked questions about the form and purity of the strategic metals that the Chinese had offered during Geng's last conversation with Harold Brown.

The Chinese defense minister ended his visit in Honolulu, where he toured Pearl Harbor and held one last substantive session, this one with Admiral Long at Pacific Command headquarters. A lengthy discussion of comparative strengths of the Soviet and American navies led the Chinese to conclude that the United States was ahead but the Soviets were catching up.

The concrete results of Geng's visit were a modest collection of dual-use computers, radars, and rolling stock and a start on transferring munitions technology. But the first-class tour he and his PLA colleagues were given of official Washington and U.S. capabilities nationwide set the scene for William Perry's visit three months later, which turned out to be the most revealing and significant of all the exchanges during that first year of military relations between the United States and the PRC.

## New Thinking from a Veteran of the Long March

For a new China hand like me, chances for informal chats with a Long March veteran like Geng were not to be missed. He made a point of telling me he had served on the international commission (to us the Marshall Mission) in Beijing in 1946. One of his Kuomintang counterparts then, a special intelligence officer named Cai Wenji, had since moved to the United States. The two met again at a private dinner hosted by Cai in Washington the night before we left.

Geng had spry, modern views for an old Communist. He told me that the Chinese Constitution was an incomplete document, flawed by a lack of provisions governing investment. The earlier emphasis on politics in education (namely, Mao's) had been wrong. The current focus was on economics and modernization, with some political studies, but it stressed performance. More pay for more work. Students must study and pass exams. Good students at the high school level could now be moved ahead a year or even two if particularly talented and take college entrance exams early. Workers should receive bonuses for good performance on a monthly basis. Cadres would be selected and trained with more care, rotating the young ones to different jobs to see what they were good at and to give them a variety of experience.

The three thousand Long Marchers who, like him, remained in the government would retire in accordance with a plan to bring forward younger cadres. The old men "have experience, but lack energy," he said. China's biggest problem was population growth, but the government was determined to limit families to one child or two through sanctions and incentives. America's biggest problems were its trade deficit and the propensity to waste energy, particularly oil, Geng noted. Thirty years later, they still are.[51]

# 24

# The Perry Mission

## Getting Practical

William Perry's tour of China's military/industrial complex laid the foundation for practical cooperation between the Pentagon and the PLA for years to come. He had asked to see China's defense industry from the bottom up so that he could work out a way to help within the narrow space permitted by U.S. rules and politics. His delegation of three-star generals and civilian experts, including Gerry Dineen at the top, consisted of three groups. The A group would be responsible for studying weapons systems, the B group electronics, and the C group strategic materials and metallurgy. For two weeks in September 1980, they got an eyeful of Chinese capabilities and weakness, from the research institutes of Beijing and missile launch sites in the Gobi Desert to aircraft factories in Xi'an, tank plants in Inner Mongolia, satellite tracking facilities in the mountains of Shanxi, electronics institutes in Nanjing, and submarine pens in Shanghai. I stuck close to Perry, attended all his events and meetings, and took notes.

## Perry's Political Commissar

Perry introduced me during this trip as his "political commissar." During my months in the Pentagon, we had developed a good and easy relationship, which lasts to this day. Then as now, I found him brainy, low key, precise, and courageous. But Perry really did need a political commissar. He frequently departed from his script, pushing his guidance to the limit and beyond. His principal toast in Beijing, for example, looked forward to concrete results in Sino-U.S.

military cooperation, including "weapons." He did this on purpose, knowing that he was creating a dynamic for policy change.

"How do we make Chinese military forces, particularly along the Siberian border, more formidable without harming our own national security?" Perry asked Ambassador Leonard Woodcock in Beijing on September 6. He answered his own question. "We help them with short-range antitank missiles, ground and air, modern avionics, and support equipment. This last one we can work on now, but it is the least important. Policy guidelines preclude us from the first two. We expect to recommend changes next year."[52] Perry told Woodcock he did not expect to discuss antitank weapons this trip, but in fact he did. While I agreed with his analysis and objectives, I became the keeper of the constraints, joined in this function by Roger Sullivan, who had moved from State to the NSC China job. We spent our time making sure that Perry knew what the agencies had agreed to and what would cause problems—what was new and what was not, what Bill could say to the Chinese and what not. He did not always listen, but knew that our role was to protect him.

The sights of the trip were rare and special: camel caravans plodding by deserted rocket gantries in Gansu; sunrise over submarine pens in Shanghai; the serried ranks of the terra cotta army guarding the tomb of the Chin emperor near Xi'an; and the elaborate bathtub of the enchanting Tang Dynasty courtesan Yang Guifei at the Hua Qing hot springs close by. The springs were where Generalissimo Chiang Kai-shek was betrayed and captured by the "Young Marshal" Zhang Xueliang in 1936, losing his false teeth in the humiliating process. (See chapter 3.)

The itinerary was punctuated with jolly banquets and hundreds of toasts in Maotai, the lethal liquor that burns with a blue flame when lit. We all lit up, too, and in the process, began to bond with the soldiers of China, our bitter foes in Korea. Our hosts were only too ready to tuck in to the special rations that came with the foreigners. Sea slugs—warty, squishy, cucumber-shaped organisms considered extremely honorific and therefore required fare for distinguished delegations—followed us everywhere, even in the desert thousands of miles from the ocean. I imagined a little man with briefcases full of the things dogging our footsteps.

## Changing Times

The Chinese leaders Perry met were all confirmed members of Deng Xiaoping's evolving post-Mao team. Li Xiannian was promoted to premier the day after he met our delegation. Crusty old PLA chief of staff Zhang Aiping became a vice premier shortly thereafter. Genial host Liu Huaqing remained where he was, the architect of the Sino-U.S. military relationship and the planner responsible for Perry's extraordinary itinerary. The visit took place against the backdrop of massive (15 percent) cuts in the Chinese military budget, as Deng moved to modernize the economy. The conversations compared Western and Soviet strength, laced with Perry's expert assessments of weapons technology and punctuated with the usual mantras—"case by case" and "step by step." To make that point he used a traditional Chinese saying I had taught him: "Fat men are not made in one mouthful." (*Pangzi bushi yikou chide.*)

It was clearly a new day in China, even on the street. On Sunday, I rented a bike and pedaled under incandescent blue skies to my old haunts—the department store in Wangfujing, Tiananmen Square, and the diplomatic compound at Jianguomenwai. The mood of the city had changed and seemed more relaxed. People were more willing to talk. A sign of the times, Mao's designated successor, Hua Guofeng, announced his resignation as party secretary while we were in Beijing.

I spotted a familiar figure walking along the street near the International Club (now the St. Regis Hotel). It was my son Adam, visiting from Hong Kong, and his friend Mimi Oka, whose father was the correspondent for the *New York Times*. We did an affectionate double take. I had no idea Adam was in Beijing. In Cultural Revolution days, foreigners could not just "turn up."

## What We Learned

The balance sheet for Bill Perry's visit contained pluses for both sides. The United States gained a direct, firsthand feel for China's military capability. Bill Perry was able to stand under the bomb-bay doors of the S-6, the "Badger bomber," look up, pace the dimensions, and observe, "Hmmm. This could hold about six cruise missiles." We were struck by the enormous scale of Soviet assistance to China in the 1950s. All the designs for China's planes, tanks, and guns came from the Russians, along with entire plants to produce them. To be sure, the Soviets did not give the PRC their top-line weapons. Using automobiles as an analogy, they provided the capacity to make Pontiacs rather than Cadillacs, more than adequate for Chinese purposes.

At the same time, we could also see that there had been no advances in the design of these weapons during the twenty or so years since the Soviet advisors had left, probably because there had not been that much opportunity. In our briefings at various factories, an historical pattern of six stages in Chinese defense production emerged: (1) Soviet help; (2) Soviet withdrawal; (3) recovery from the damage done by Soviet withdrawal; (4) the Cultural Revolution, during which production was halted for two years or more while engineers and managers engaged in "labor" in their factories; (5) recovery after they returned; and (6) the current financial squeeze.

The Cultural Revolution damaged national security as well as the education of a generation of China's youth. The disruption was particularly severe in the research institutes, which Perry told General Liu were ten to twenty years behind.

The plants we saw were working well below capacity, the drab gun and tank lines side by side with brightly colored baby carriages, children's bicycles, and toys produced for profit.

More recent efforts to upgrade weapons technology had not yielded much result. Four years of work with British help to produce the Rolls-Royce Spey Jet aircraft engine in Xi'an had produced only four engines, each assembled from imported military components. Perry told his hosts that that the plant—a sprawling complex with 10,000 workers and 40 workshops—was up to world standards; but privately our experts concluded that Rolls-Royce had not given that much to the Chinese, who now had to manufacture their own components and had a long way to go. Our hosts in Shanghai took pride in showing us their Y-9 jet transport, a laboriously reverse-engineered Chinese version of the Boeing 707, representing years of effort to create technology already thirty years old.

The missile pad at Shuangchengzi, where China launched its first satellite in 1970, was deserted and ghostly. Our experts likened the level of its technology to our pioneer Mercury project. We knew, however, that a more advanced site existed. Missiles and nuclear weapons must have absorbed the bulk of the resources Beijing was clearly not spending on tanks, planes, and guns.

## What the Chinese Learned

"We need to know," Perry told Woodcock in Beijing, "how to convince the Chinese that the progress has been worth it so far, that we are proceeding in a significant way, without their becoming discouraged." Perry's approach was to expound on every subject raised with candor and expertise. The Chinese constantly asked Perry and Dineen for their advice as private sector scientists and business authorities, sat at their feet, and genuinely valued their assessments.

### Technical Levels

In meetings at Hangzhou and Shanghai at the end of the visit, Perry and Dineen gave General Liu their final judgments. China had a good technical foundation on which to build, they said. The facilities and staffs of the research institutes had been well grounded but severely set back by the Cultural Revolution. Unless China made big long-term investments in education and high-speed computers for design and analysis, the institutes would fall further behind.

Perry recommended specifically that the Chinese:

a. Send a substantial number of Ph.D. candidates from the institutes and universities to the United States and Europe to return as the teachers of a new, self-sufficient generation of Chinese scientists.

b. Accelerate and expand scientific and exchange programs now underway with U.S. companies and defense labs.

c. Give research institutes access to modern high-speed computers, including a large computer in Beijing with access from the institutes throughout the country by phone lines.

d. Send substantial numbers of bachelor's degree candidates for computer technology and sciences to the United States.

e. Establish links, now totally lacking, between designers, institutes, and production engineers in factories. We had solved this problem in the United States by arranging for production engineers to work in design institutes.

f. Create in the Defense Ministry and each military service the position of armaments director, responsible for research, production, and logistics, to support weapons systems. This person, with no additional responsibilities except technology transfer from other countries, would pull together design and production functions. He was describing his own job, Perry said.

### Manufacturing

The factories he had seen had the facilities, staff, and tools to build good-quality equipment, efficiently and to schedule, Perry judged. But the volume of government orders was too low for the plant capacity available, designs were thirty years out of date, and small-scale computers were not used in the production process. He recommended that the Chinese:

a. Build on what they had rather than starting over; modernize existing designs rather than introduce new ones; improve the plants, machines, jigs, and personnel; and modify components to create large changes in performance with small changes in technology.

b. Initiate at pilot plants small computers to use in production-process control. Computers provided opportunities for major technology transfer at low cost. Hardware, software, and training were readily available from computer companies.

### Modifications

Perry gave some examples of product modifications that could be useful for the Chinese to introduce. PRC aircraft engines were unreliable and short-lived, leading to big maintenance expenses and high rates of failure in flight. Simply replacing the engine blades and discs with high-alloy equivalents would bring big improvements.

Chinese gun designs were adequate, but their ammunition was old-fashioned, Perry continued. Adopting cluster munitions for artillery shells, proximity fuses for anti-aircraft munitions, and long-rod penetrators in antitank rounds would make a huge difference. He explained that conventional antitank bullets simply bounced off Soviet armor, which, like ours, was made of layer upon layer of Kevlar fabric. The kinetic energy of a long-rod penetrator could pierce tanks like an arrow.

This turned out to be the most significant observation of the entire visit. Perry would later recommend transfer to the PRC of a technical data package to manufacture long-rod penetrators. The modification would allow the Chinese to improve their defense against Soviet armor using existing gun tubes and factories, with minimal threat to their neighbors.

### Electronics

Dineen's assessment of China's electronics industry, a prime factor in the modernization of both the military forces and the civilian economy, followed Perry's themes. He described Cultural Revolution damage to research institutes and engineers and a shortage of good standardized test equipment, recommending that the institutes buy cheap test equipment abroad rather than make their own.

Clean rooms and other specialized facilities were in short supply and scattered inefficiently, even if in the same area. Contact among university professors, institute people, and production managers was lacking. Dineen agreed that production people should be brought into the research institutes, and research facilities placed in factories. Increased production of semiconductors at lower cost was another challenge. Joint ventures with the United States, Europe, or Japan could help with the assembly of 16-K chips. At an appropriate time in the future Chinese would be involved at the front end of the process, but not now.

General Liu and his colleagues were genuinely grateful for Perry and Dineen's frank judgments. He acknowledged that their recommendations had been made without considering whether China could afford to implement them, or whether the United States could help. He agreed with their analyses.

## The F-8 Again

Detailed discussions with American experts on how best to upgrade the F-8 fighter were another plus for the Chinese. At their first meeting in Beijing, Liu had raised the F-8 matter. "Without weapons, talk of military cooperation does not make much sense," he had said, bluntly. Support equipment was useless without the weapons that went with it. Perry warned throughout the visit that the United States was limited to transferring only dual-use technology related to the plane, but he agreed to discuss the issues.

We actually saw the aircraft at an airfield in Xi'an. After clambering all over it, U.S. Air Force attaché Bill Webb commented to me, "This is a flying cigar, very hot at one end." The wings were tiny. He expressed doubt about the plane's maneuverability except at high speed, which proved prophetic. (Twenty years later, an F-8 flying parallel with a U.S. reconnaissance EP-3, both going only 250 miles an hour near Hainan Island, collided with it, crashed, and caused a crisis in the relations between Beijing and the new administration of George W. Bush.)

After viewing the Chinese F-8 in Xi'an, the American expert on our delegation suggested a two-phased program: first, concentrate on extending the F-8's radar range, communications range, engine life, and infrared air-to-air missiles; and second, focus on making new engines for the F-8 and adding look-down radar. Before leaving, Perry proposed a visit to China by U.S. turbine engine and electronics experts to study in some detail the F-8 engines and radar and to identify shortcomings and what technology needed to be transferred. Decisions on policy exceptions would come later.[53]

## Following Up

Returning home to a capital beset with concerns about the imminent election and the war between Iran and Iraq, our briefings with other U.S. officials, diplomats, and members of Congress were purposefully ho-hum. This had only been a survey trip that involved no policy changes or weapons sales. There was nothing new to report. No press releases were made or planned.

Nevertheless, during the months between President Carter's defeat and the beginning of the Reagan administration, PLA delegations continued to arrive, requiring my care and feeding. Grizzled Long March veteran Xiao Ke and his logistics team dined in their shapeless green uniforms on my Oliver Street lawn, a bizarre sight for residents of Chevy Chase D.C. Patterns of scientific exchange mapped by William Perry began to take shape with the appearance at U.S. conferences of Chinese military intellectuals from a variety of think tanks. What Stanford University's John Lewis described as the beginnings of a "big groping exercise on the part of China's scientific, technological, and strategic elite" had begun and continue to this day.[54]

Dr. Perry met on December 15 with PRC vice defense minister Zhang Zhen, whose delegation had spent a month touring U.S. facilities and plants. Zhang made specific requests for U.S. experts to visit Chinese installations and give lectures on antitank-weapon and night-vision technology. Perry said he would do what he could under current guidelines. For the future, he was preparing a paper recommending broad cooperation with the PRC on tech transfer. Approval would be up to the new administration.

I jumped in at this point to warn how long policy decisions took to emerge during a transition between administrations. I told Zhang that Defense Secretary Brown and his successor, Caspar Weinberger, had already met and that Brown believed the discussions had been productive. I said I would work hard to insure a smooth transition. Perry added his hope that "Mr. Platt educates Mr. Weinberger as well as he educated Brown and me." General Xu Yimin expressed the desire to maintain our contact and friendship.

## A New Roadmap

As it turned out, Dr. Perry had set the course for the development of military relations between the United States and China until the Soviet Union collapsed ten years later. The findings of his report were frozen by the result of the election, but only for a while. In due time, the Reagan administration took action on much of what we had discussed, including a program to develop the F-8 fighter aircraft. Future Chinese tank rounds would change from balls to arrows, manufactured with the help of a U.S. Technical Data Package. Dual-use items, among them high-speed computers and chips, helicopters, military trucks, and over-the-horizon radars, all would find their way to China. The military attaché offices in both capitals would expand, exchanges of specialized delegations (logistics, military education, and others) would multiply, and the stream of Chinese B.A. and Ph.D. candidates in the sciences would widen.

## Then and Now

PLA suppression of student demonstrations in Tiananmen Square in 1989 brought the expansion of military links between the United States and China to an abrupt halt. The end of the Cold War shortly thereafter further undercut the rationale for interaction between the two military establishments. Since then, ties between the PLA and the Pentagon have moved in fits and starts, the casualty of a series of crises. Military contact has been the first element of our relationship to be cut as a sign of displeasure or concern by either side.

Ironically, the growth of China's power has revived ties between the PLA and the Pentagon. The combination of curiosity and mistrust that marked our earliest dealings, when China was weak, remains today. So does the wide gap between U.S. and Chinese military capabilities first confirmed during Perry's visit. But the realization that the more we know about each other, the safer we both will be, is once again pushing the "two armies" closer together. What we forget, of course, is the extent to which we helped shape China's military modernization to begin with.

Asia Society president Nick Platt, Henry Kissinger, and Asia Society
chairman Maurice R. "Hank" Greenberg, New York, 1993.

Riding a tiny Mongolian pony, Asia Society Caravan, Karakorum,
Mongolia, May 1996.

With PRC President Jiang Zemin in Washington, October 1997.

With PRC
Premier Zhu
Rongji in
Washington,
April 1999.

Interviewing UN Secretary General Kofi Annan at the Asia Society, June 1999.

With Shanghai mayor Xu Kuangdi, Shanghai, 2000.

Delivering the Lincoln Lecture at Fudan University, Shanghai, 2001.

Welcoming the guest of honor, Secretary of State Colin Powell, at the Asia Society Annual Dinner, New York, June 2002.

289

Welcoming Yang Jiechi, PRC ambassador to the United States
(later foreign minister), December 2002.

A frank and free exchange of views with Richard Holbrooke,
New York, 2003.

290

With President Bill Clinton at the Asia Society Annual Dinner, New York, May 2003.

Receiving a traditional greeting from a Maori warrior at the Asia Society, May 2004.

With Nobel Laureate Shirin Ebadi, Iranian human rights advocate, at the Asia Society, June 2004.

# 25

# Change and Move On: Fast Forward

## Election Shock

The interregnum following President Carter's resounding defeat at the polls in November 1980 was a time of tension, depression, and anticipation, with major mood swings from one day to the next. Democratic political appointees mentally packed their bags while soldiering on at work. Professionals like me, who had some chance of keeping their jobs, sniffed the wind for signs of who their bosses might be. Rumor ruled.

News of new appointments began to seep out—Alexander Haig to be secretary of state, Jim Lilley to the East Asia job at the NSC, John Holdridge to be assistant secretary of state for East Asia and Pacific Affairs, Dixie Walker to replace Bill Gleysteen as ambassador in Seoul, among others.

## China Angst

Policy toward China was a major topic during the transition months. The incoming Reagan administration was clearly critical of the normalization deal Carter had made with the PRC, angry at the treatment Taiwan had received, and determined to make a clean sweep of all China policy jobs. In private meetings with incoming officials and at public conferences, people debated the continuity of current policy, levels and nature of weapons sales to Taipei, and degrees of official versus unofficial relations with Taiwan.

One of Alexander Haig's first actions upon being named secretary was to fire the entire conservative transition team at State, rocking Reagan's core group and delighting the professionals at Foggy Bottom. Rumor had it that China policy was one of the reasons.

Defense intellectuals from China appearing at conferences I attended displayed serious angst of their own. They worried that Reagan did not understand PRC sensitivities toward the Taiwan question and would use the issue as a way to check and manipulate China. They also feared that U.S. policymakers perceived the Chinese communists as still bent on overthrowing capitalist America and regarded China as a potential enemy. More fundamentally, one of them told me, the United States might have a "wrong estimate of Chinese potential, a weak and unworthy friend, unable to play a role when necessary. It would be tragic if American policy were based on this principle."[55]

My farewell conversation with David Jones, the chairman of the Joint Chiefs of Staff whom Reagan had invited to stay on, was all about China policy. The ten-minute ceremonial call originally scheduled by Jones's aides turned into forty-five minutes, one on one. Jones had frequently approached me at the Pentagon Officers' Athletic Club for informal advice on the prospects for his planned trip to China. We were on easy terms. Jones began by saying he enjoyed a close relationship with the new secretary of defense and had been accepted into the new president's inner circle. They discussed their intimate opinions of political figures in front of him in a way that suggested they trusted him completely.

At the most recent cabinet meeting (February 11, 1981), Jones continued, the president had asked the government to stop pretending that the relationship with Taiwan was not official, as he had promised in an August campaign statement. Specifically, Reagan had asked for suggestions on things that could be done in the military relations field. Jones had said that the U.S. military would like to visit "both countries" and have ship visits to "both countries." Jones related this to me somewhat sheepishly.

What, he asked, could be done to improve the atmosphere of the Taiwan relationship and respond to the president's wishes without destroying or harming our relationship with the PRC. I replied that any action taken by the U.S. government that appeared to give a more official nature to our relationship with Taiwan would injure our ties with the PRC. It was a matter of face and symbolism on both sides. Appearances mattered more than reality. The United States could make weapons sales to Taiwan (armored personnel carriers, helicopters, standard missiles), currently considered "non-controversial." The PRC would complain bitterly, but as long as we did not officially upgrade our relationship with Taiwan, the PRC would accept it in due course. Any such upgrading would prompt Beijing to retaliate by reducing its ties with us.

More official military relations with Taiwan would mean a freeze on military cooperation with the PRC. Neither General Jones nor Admiral Long would be able to visit the PRC, as they had been invited, and as both wanted, to do. I added that critics inside the PRC now described Deng Xiaoping as a dupe of the United States, a country that was willing to sell weapons to Taiwan but not to the PRC and that now appeared to be backtracking on its commitment to treat Beijing as the legal government of China.

Jones said he understood the issues better now (he had taken notes throughout) and would be discussing the matter with Admiral Long.

This was to be my last opportunity as a government official to provide advice on U.S. policy toward China. The Reagan administration ended up continuing established, constructively ambiguous guidelines governing official/unofficial relations with the PRC and Taiwan. The issue of weapons sales to Taiwan and the management of our relationship with Taipei would continue to rile our relationship right up to the present, but I would be working on other things.

## Moving On

I learned my own fate early in the New Year when Richard Armitage, head of the DOD transition team, called on me in my office. His appearance was striking—a huge, muscular, weight lifter's torso with no neck, topped by a bald, bullet-shaped head, which emitted words in a gravelly voice. The words were friendly, humorous, and smart. I liked him instantly, but remained wary. I asked him simply to tell me if I had a chance of staying on at Defense under the new administration. If not, I needed to hustle and find a new job. Rich said I was OK with the Reagan people, but someone had his eye on my job, and that someone was he. It was the only post in the government that he wanted.

I thanked Rich for being straight with me and offered him advice on how to operate in the Pentagon. I explained the treacherous facts of bureaucratic life in the civilian side of the secretary's office and described some important tricks. It did not matter, for example, how well he knew the new secretary; it would be vital for him to be the first Reagan appointee to report for work at the Office of International Security Affairs (ISA) and the first person to put his name on a memorandum. This would establish his seniority within the organization, which in turn would help him get the right office space on the E-Ring and the pick of the staff assistants who would serve him. Early arrival would provide a leg up in the constant competition that marked his level on the bureaucratic food chain. I explained the importance of the military assistants to the secretary and deputy secretary, the men who really ran the bureaucracy and managed the tricky relationships between military and civilians. My own deputy, Rear Admiral Don Jones, was particularly skilled, and I urged Rich to keep him.

Rich Armitage probably knew all this already, but took it all in and acted accordingly. Colin Powell, the military assistant to the deputy secretary, was to become his closest friend. Rich and I bonded, too, a relationship that became important later. When I served as George Shultz's executive secretary from 1985 to 1987, Armitage had risen to be head of Weinberger's ISA. Shultz and Weinberger were enemies, but I could always phone Rich and make sure messages got through. In 1990–91, Rich negotiated the final U.S. Bases Agreement with the Philippines, a drawn out and delicate task with a weak and emotional government. I was ambassador in Manila at the time, and we worked closely to create an effective "good cop (me)-bad cop (Rich)" team.

Armitage told me I would have no trouble getting work back at State. Paul Wolfowitz wanted to talk to me about a job on the Policy Planning Staff, which he was to head. I had gotten to know Wolfowitz during the past year at the Pentagon, where he was a systems analyst. He became engrossed in Asian affairs and had needed some teaching. Elliott Abrams, who would be named assistant secretary for International Organization Affairs (IO), his first government job, was looking for a principal deputy with experience in navigating the bureaucracy at State. After discussions with both, I took the IO job, seeking broader, if not greener pastures, in which to graze.

The afternoon of February 13, 1981, the Defense Department bade me a formal farewell. Every civilian who completes a policy-level assignment and is still *compos mentis* receives a Distinguished Civilian Service Medal and a flowery citation in front of a group of close colleagues in the secretary's office on the E-ring. It is a fine send off by a military establishment that loves such ceremonies and excels at arranging them. In Pentagon slang, medals are known as gongs, a noun that is also used as a transitive verb. So, appropriately gonged, I departed the Five-Sided Building once and for all.

## Fast Forward

For the next twelve years, the China Boy who became an Asia Hand was forced to stretch much, much further. Sixteen turbulent months in the State Department's Bureau of International Organizations compelled me to deal with a broad universe of foreign policy issues amid contending senior personalities in a new administration just starting its learning curve. China issues occupied only a tiny place on my plate. Secretary of State Alexander Haig's staff meetings kept me up to date on the status of our ties with Beijing, as did regular informal contact with fellow China hands. But despite the angst of the transition period, there was to be more continuity than change in the policy of the new administration. The same themes that preoccupied the Carter administration after normalization—Chinese focus on U.S. ability to counter the Soviets, anger over U.S. arms sales to Taiwan, snail's-pace U.S. technology transfer to the PLA—were features of Haig's feedback on his contacts. Frankly, I was content to be doing something else.

Day to day, most of the work in the International Organizations Bureau involved cleaning up after the Israelis and the South Africans in the Security Council and supervising the fine diplomatic needlepoint that occupied the UN's specialized agencies in Geneva. Creative policy making centered on African affairs. When not serving as the suffering synapse between Secretary Haig and Jeane Kirkpatrick, Reagan's strong-willed UN ambassador, I was working closely with African Affairs Assistant Secretary Chester

Crocker to move the South Africans out of Angola and Namibia. This led to two absorbing years (1982–84) as U.S. ambassador to Zambia, where I developed a close relationship with the tearful but politically astute president, Kenneth Kaunda, and acted as Crocker's roving representative to the Frontline States in the conflict with South Africa. I remember that Kaunda revered Nixon's imagination and courage in opening relations with China and regularly urged visiting American officials, from Vice President Bush on down, to do likewise when dealing with Pretoria.

The relationship with China was complicated. Although the Zambians were grateful for the Tan-Zam railway the Chinese had built to Tanzania to provide an alternate route to market for Zambia's copper, they complained that Chinese locomotives were too weak to pull their trains. The private reaction of Beijing's ambassador in Lusaka was derisive. At a dinner he hosted for me, the crusty Long Marcher snorted that the Zambians had subjected 70 of the 100 engines donated by Beijing to the "three destructions"—derailing, colliding, and burning. The grease fires that resulted from poor maintenance were as scorching as the Mongolian hot pot we were eating, he said. Chinese raw material investments in Africa get headlines today, but we forget they have been there for decades spending billions in support of their political and economic goals.

I kept up with developments in China during my time in Zambia—a frenetic stint that was followed in Washington working as executive secretary to George Shultz (1985–87); four hair-raising years (1987–91) in Manila as chief of mission, dealing with coup attempts, volcanic eruptions, earthquakes, typhoons, and base negotiations, while working to support Cory Aquino's fragile democracy in the Philippines; and a last ambassadorship in Pakistan (1991–92), observing at close hand the Soviet collapse in Afghanistan and Central Asia.

## China Expands and Explodes

During these years, Deng Xiaoping's reforms opened large portions of the Chinese economy to free enterprise, foreign investment, and international trade. China joined the massive surge of Asian growth and became its leading performer, bringing about the most dramatic and rapid increase in living standards the world has ever seen. No one who had worked on the opening to China, from Richard Nixon and Henry Kissinger on down, predicted this, much less imagined that nuts-and-bolts economics would become the center of our relationship.

Like most great successes, that Chinese growth created a whole series of new problems. Pressures for personal freedom grew with it. Deng's reforms allowed people to travel and to take jobs in other parts of the country. China opened up internally. The tight, drab, tense society of the Cultural Revolution days was replaced by a brighter, hyperenergetic boom culture, burgeoning prosperity, rampant materialism, and widespread corruption, particularly in the coastal areas, which attracted the most foreign investment. It was the start of what American media began to call the "Bling Dynasty."

At the same time, a middle class was forming, which owned a growing portion of the economy and wanted more consultation on government decisions affecting its interests. The student body, returning eagerly to reopened universities, felt the pressure to learn in order to earn but were confused by the collapse of Maoist orthodoxy, perplexed by the lack of a belief system to put in its place, and revolted by the corruption of their rulers. The wave of democratization in Asia that struck the Philippines in 1986 and Taiwan and Korea in 1987 washed into China.

In the spring of 1989, hundreds of thousands of students converged on Beijing's Tiananmen Square to protest official corruption and the lack of party attention to political reform. The cameras and anchors of world media were already in place to cover the visit of Soviet leader Mikhail Gorbachev, who had come to change the course of confrontation and conflict that had brought China and the Soviet Union near war and driven the United States and China together during the 1970s. They stayed to cover an even bigger story—the mounting crescendo of student protest and the bloody suppression that followed.

In the United States, one night of media coverage documenting the armed brutality of the People's Liberation Army on June 4— perhaps even just one picture, that of a lone unarmed Chinese facing down a huge tank—destroyed the bipartisan consensus in support of our relationship with China, created with such care seventeen years before during the week of live broadcasts throughout the Nixon visit. But, while Deng Xiaoping had snuffed out political dissent at Tiananmen, he held firm to his economic policies of openness and reform. Quietly, the administration of the senior President Bush moved to assure Beijing that U.S. interests required a constructive relationship with China.

In Manila, I discussed the Tiananmen tragedy with President Aquino. Under instructions from Washington, I briefed her on our president's China decisions, emphasizing the carefully aimed and calibrated nature of our measures as well as our desire to keep the U.S.-China relationship intact in a difficult, obscure, and, in many ways, infuriating situation.

President Aquino replied that she deplored the violence of the Chinese military and identified strongly with the students. During her visit to China in 1988 she had sensed that the people were enthusiastic about the new openness and economic opportunities that China's policies provided. Clearly, however, that was not enough. "It's in man's nature to want to be free," she said. The Philippines situation, she continued, required her to adopt a rather cautious public posture that commented only on the evils of the violence. She would work to maintain relations with Beijing while trying to assure the safety of Filipinos there.

I told President Aquino that the political events in China made the Philippines look good by comparison. She and her people had a lot to be proud of after three years of democracy. Several students in Beijing told reporters they had been inspired by television coverage of the 1986 People Power revolution along Epifanio de los Santos Avenue (EDSA) in Manila. They had seen pictures of nuns placing flowers into the barrels of tank guns and soldiers' rifles.

The Philippines, she replied, were fortunate that the EDSA revolution had lasted only four days. Had it gone longer, "people power" might have run out of steam and Marcos might have recovered his resolve to crack down.

At the end of our talk, President Aquino raised the question of possible participation by Taiwan in the international aid program for the Philippines. Taiwanese officials had told her they would be pleased to contribute if asked by the United States. Could President Bush give Taiwan's president Lee Teng-hui a call?

No way, I replied. President Bush had all he could do to keep our lines open to Beijing these days without the complications that would arise from any contact between him and Lee. We had a successful unofficial relationship with Taipei and wanted to keep it that way. Taiwan had prospered under that arrangement and naturally wanted to convert its economic success into political advantage, but we could not play that game. President Aquino said she understood. She would simply tell the Taiwanese that she had raised the issue with me.[56]

# 26

# The "Best Embassy on Park Avenue"

## A Phone Rings in the Himalayas

When the Soviet Union dissolved in 1991, I had been U.S. ambassador to Pakistan for about six months. The powers in the State Department had insisted that my four years helping Cory Aquino displayed a knack for dealing with female heads of government in struggling democracies. This made me just the right person to deal with Benazir Bhutto, they thought. Startled, I replied I was unaware that this knack was a core Foreign Service skill but would be happy to accept the post, whatever the rationale. Pakistan had been close as "lips and teeth" to China for decades and had played a key role in facilitating the U.S. opening to the People's Republic. The Chinese had built the strategic highway paralleling the ancient Silk Route, along the Indus River and up over the Kunjerab Pass into Xinjiang, and continued to maintain it against constant earthquakes and landslides.

As it turned out, there were few reasons for direct dealings with the Chinese in Islamabad. Furthermore, our bilateral relationship was in the dumps since 1990, when the United States had cut off all aid to Pakistan because they developed a nuclear weapon. We had discarded them "like a used Kleenex" once the Cold War was over, the Pakistanis told me. There was not much to do except travel—the Pakistanis loved having the American ambassador show up—and watch with fascination and alarm as the Afghan insurgency next door turned in on itself, and the new countries of Central Asia coped with their newfound and unwanted independence from the Soviet Union. Benazir Bhutto had been turned out of office by the time I arrived, so I passed the time acting as both referee and guidance counselor in squabbles between the prime minister, the president, and the chief of army staff.

That was the scene on a March morning in 1992 when the phone rang as I sat in my office looking at the foothills of the Himalayas. It was Osborn Elliott, former editor of *Newsweek* and a friend since the 1960s, calling to inquire if I would be interested in becoming president of the Asia Society in New York. A longtime trustee and member of the society's search committee, Oz had done his homework. He knew that I was in my thirty-fifth year in the Foreign Service and would have to retire soon or sign on as a political appointee. The job was the best nongovernmental position in the Asia field, he said, and traditionally came open only once every ten years. I told Oz I would call him back.

The society was well known throughout Asia. Most leaders, heads of government, foreign ministers, and U.S. ambassadors in Asia spoke there when visiting the United States. I had given a talk there myself while home from Manila. The Rockefeller pedigree, dating from the society's founding by John D. 3rd in 1956, was important to Asians. It seemed an ideal job for my "afterlife," even more so because all my children, now grown, had settled in New York, drawn by the cultural and financial magnets of the great city. For Sheila and me, it would be a return to New York roots. More important, the opportunity to operate across Asia and reconnect with China was irresistible.

I phoned Oz back, said I really wanted the job, but if the Asia Society really wanted me, they would have to wait seven months until the November elections. I could not tell President Bush I was just downing tools after only a few months in Pakistan; all he could expect of any of his ambassadors was to stay until the first term ended. The deal was done after discussions with Asia Society Board Chairman John Whitehead, whom I had advised when he became George Shultz's deputy secretary of state five years earlier. I left Islamabad the morning of the elections, before the polls had opened, and en route home at breakfast with the Aga Khan (an old Harvard rowing colleague) in Paris watched Bill Clinton announce victory. Two weeks later, I retired from the Foreign Service in the morning and took over at Asia Society in the afternoon. Later when asked if I had done anything between careers, I replied, "Lunch."

## The "Best Embassy on Park Avenue"

Foreign Service friends called Asia Society the "Best Embassy on Park Avenue." It was the best job I had ever had, bar none. I had worked at high levels in the government and at the far reaches of diplomacy, but nothing could touch the presidency of the Asia Society for reach, access, and variety. I had all of Asia to work in, from Persia to Perth. The society's goal was to teach Americans about Asian culture, politics, business, and finance, the "nuts and bolts" that I now knew fastened countries to each other.

I stayed twelve years. We did our educating through programs—exhibitions, performances, seminars, conferences, conversations public and private, teacher training—organized at our headquarters in New York and presented throughout the United States and Asia. Compared to our elephantine government, the staff was small and nimble. I could shape programs as I saw fit, as long as the board approved and funds were available. That was the big "if."

I had had no experience with America's unique not-for-profit world and was stunned to learn that the sector represented 8 percent of our entire economy, a figure close to the size of our two-way foreign trade or our entire national budget. I found out the hard way that NGOs are businesses, requiring the best management techniques, attention to detail, and balanced budgets. Ambassadors get good training in leadership and the management of relationships, but not numbers.

The Asia Society trustees wondered what I knew about fundraising. I told them I had no experience in the private sector but had raised hundreds of millions for aid to the Philippines and Zambia. If fundraising meant persuading authorities with money to back particular programs, I had done well with congressional committees and agency heads. Asia Society donors might be difficult, but no one could be more cantankerous than David Obey, who then chaired the House Appropriations Committee. The answer satisfied them.

I turned out to be good at raising money, and I had to be. The Rockefellers' legacy notwithstanding, we had a tiny endowment and a burgeoning budget at the Asia Society, most of which came from private foundations, companies, and individuals. By the time

I left in 2004, we had raised over $100 million in operating grants, and $67 million in capital resources. I found that substance was what pulled money. Donors would give if the programs excited them. The backing of three strong board chairmen—in turn, John Whitehead, Maurice R. "Hank" Greenberg, and Richard Holbrooke, big donors and/or ace fundraisers in their own right—was crucial.

### Riding the Asian Wave

My years at the society coincided with what Henry Kissinger and other strategic thinkers called a "global shift in the balance of power from the Atlantic to the Pacific."[57] Those of us who had lived U.S.-Asian relations had felt the shift coming for a long time, but the evidence had become overwhelming. Asia's weight in the world economy had grown rapidly, approaching 40 percent. U.S. interaction with Asia economically, politically, and culturally was exploding. Trade relations were robust. Roughly 40 percent of our imports came from Asia; 30 percent of our exports went there. The influence of Asia pervaded our visual arts, film, fashion, food, and photography. The Asian American minority grew, too, and came into its own, culturally, politically, and financially. My challenge was to position the society to catch this wave, and then to ride it for all it was worth.

When I arrived in 1992, the Asia Society was prestigious and austere, proud of its Rockefeller legacy, a superb private collection of traditional Asian art, and a reputation for excellence in cutting-edge programs involving politics, business, and the arts. It was also clear that people in Asia knew more about the society's work than Americans did. Attendance was low despite the quality of the programs. The "best embassy" building on Park Avenue did not function very well. The galleries were tiny, and the lack of a freight elevator meant that caterers had to drag carts of steaming food through the middle of receptions in the lobby. The solemn aura of the main entrance hall, its design informed by a famous tomb in India, mystified the neighborhood. Old ladies would wander through the revolving door, ask, "What is this place?" and wander out again. We had a network of regional centers in the United States and a fledgling Asian foothold in Hong Kong, but our methods for reaching out and interconnecting were primitive.

During the next decade, our reach expanded dramatically. The revolution in information technology struck early in my tenure. We bought the best technology available. As the Internet came into its own, we grabbed hold right away and hung on for dear life. The result was a group of pioneer Web sites that reached millions of new users and provided the best curriculum materials on Asia available in America, profiles of society activities, and Asian news, food, and developments. Computers also made us more efficient and wove the Asia Society network more tightly. By 2004 we were producing more than 500 programs a year in New York and nine regional centers, with a worldwide staff of only 150 people, not much larger than the numbers in 1992.

Renovating the "best embassy" cost $40 million and turned my hair white. Experts called it the most extensive root canal in the history of New York architecture. But when finished in 2001, we had a building that really worked, a full-fledged museum with four galleries, a cafe, a store, and international teleconferencing facilities—a place people wanted to come to. Attendance tripled, thanks to a torrent of innovative programs. We added the best of Asian contemporary art to our presentation of Asia's traditional offerings. Performing arts and film flourished in alliance with avant-garde institutions like the Brooklyn Academy of Music and AsiaCinevision. Children flocked to the museum and presented works of their own inspired by what they had seen here.

At the same time, working with like-minded organizations such as the Council on Foreign Relations, we drew a steady stream of Asian and U.S. foreign policy figures to speak at the society, concentrating our programs on the issues of the day. Programs on Asian social issues—including women's rights, HIV AIDS, the environment—and a series on the challenges of Islam in Asia that grew out of 9/11 engaged all the disciplines of the society. Behind the scenes, focused Track II–diplomacy initiatives enabled us to study the issues dividing China and Taiwan and India and Pakistan; to explore the potential for relations with Iran and the conflict in Muslim Mindanao; and to make recommendations to the Washington policy community.

Education became the third main pillar of the Asia Society during these years, taking its place alongside the arts and public policy.

The society was the spearhead of a national campaign to give international relations and Asia a larger place in the curricula of America's primary and secondary schools. We helped create new high schools built around international relations themes and promoted the study of the Chinese language in various parts of the United States, as the Asia Society's reach and heft outside the country also grew. The opening in 1998 of a representative office in San Francisco complemented existing U.S. centers in Washington, Houston, and Los Angeles. In Asia, regional centers in Melbourne and Manila expanded the base created by Hong Kong. We established a China presence in Shanghai and helped prepare the way to build permanent headquarters in Hong Kong and Houston.

Society members' insatiable lust for travel took them in carefully organized "caravans" up the Yangzi Gorges, down the Silk Route in Central Asia and China, into Iran, across Mongolia, Siberia, and the length and breadth of India and Japan. Along the way they met political and cultural leaders we had cultivated over the years. Corporate conferences—pioneered by the society in 1989—attracted thousands of executives and leaders to a different Asian city each year. Ostensibly, they came to discuss the rise of China, India, and Southeast Asia and their impact on the world economy. But the hallways were where the real action was, scenes of networking frenzies and private deals. I made a point of attending major meetings in the region, including all the annual APEC Ministerials and CEO functions after President Clinton invited heads of government to Seattle in 1993. Just showing up, Woody Allen style, helped project the image of the society as a player across the region, strengthened our network, and boosted fundraising. As president, I traveled almost a million miles to, from, and within Asia and the United States.

If all this sounds exhausting, it was. By the end of twelve years, I was beginning to burn out. I had loved the opportunity the society gave me to use long-developed diplomatic skills, management techniques, and analytical muscles and to develop some new ones. Important ghosts from my Foreign Service past like Henry Kissinger and Richard Holbrooke came alive again in a new context. I had left New York in 1946 a fat disgruntled eleven-year-old with an allowance of 25 cents a week, vowing never to return. Now, after dealing directly with the inner workings of city politics, business, and culture, my roots were thicker than ever. My family was all around me. Most important, my time at the best embassy on Park Avenue enabled me to step back on the escalator of China's rise and influence our relationship in the process. Working on Asia Society programs in and about China proved the perfect bookend for a career that began and ended with the "nuts and bolts" of foreign relations.

## Deciding to Reengage with China

When I arrived at the Asia Society in 1992, the Cold War was over and the strategic imperative that had driven Nixon's initiative and sustained our ties with China for decades was gone. After a brief pause following Tiananmen, the Chinese economy had resumed expansion at high rates, creating the specter of a major new competitor and, some believed, enemy. Contending concepts buffeted U.S. policy thinking about China. Some said the United States did not need China any more, while others insisted that we maintain close ties with a country that could emerge as a superpower. Political initiative on China policy slipped from the White House to Congress, which, under the leadership of human rights activists like Nancy Pelosi, worked to impose a series of sanctions that would end, for the time being at least, normal Sino-American relations.

President George H. W. Bush had decided that a sound relationship with China was in the long-term interest of the United States, and had taken heat for his views. President Clinton's administration would come to the same conclusion, but only after a zigzag course blown by winds coming from different directions. Everyone wanted to have their say, from multinational corporations dazzled by the business potential of the Middle Kingdom, to Congress and activist organizations intent on punishing massive human rights violations, to farmers lured by the China market. Private institutions that sought to expand ties across the political, cultural, and economic spectrum, including the Asia Society and much of the academic world, pitched in, too. It would take the Clinton administration two years to untangle trade from human rights, and another six to approve China's entry into the World Trade Organization. Tensions over Taiwan almost led to a military confrontation in 1996.

The society was in the middle of a running national debate that continues to this day.

During the 1980s, the Asia Society's track record on China programs had been solid, the work of my predecessor, Robert Oxnam, himself a China scholar. But revulsion against Tiananmen had brought contact and activity to a halt. Program attention shifted to Hong Kong and Taiwan. Realizing that the society could be a vehicle to strengthen links with the PRC at every level, I resolved to act. In 1973 Sino-U.S. relations had resembled a single-line, hand-cranked tactical field telephone, with Zhou Enlai at one end and Henry Kissinger at the other. By 1993, our ties were more like a broadband fiber-optic cable, with a high volume of different messages passing back and forth, many of them outside the purview of either government. Relations were no longer in the exclusive hands of the respective executive branches but represented the interaction of two societies, economies, and bodies politic. This was the new norm during the era of globalization, and I was anxious to play a role.

# 27

# China Boy Redux

## Back to Beginnings

On the way to Beijing in March 1993, after thirteen years away, I checked in with other China Boys I knew. Winston Lord was soon to become assistant secretary of state for East Asian and Pacific Affairs. I called from the Red Carpet Lounge at JFK, briefed him on my itinerary, and asked for his policy guidance. He said we should urge Beijing to make as much progress between now and mid-May on trade, human rights, and proliferation issues to help President Clinton deal with Congress. The annual debate over trade rights for China, or most-favored-nation (MFN) treatment in the shorthand of the day, was fast approaching. While the new administration would be firmer than its predecessor on human rights, it realized the importance of China and did not intend to move either to "isolation or insolence." When I asked if I could portray him as sitting in the corner growling softly, Win laughed and said yes.

In Beijing, I spent hours with Ambassador Stapleton Roy, the most distinguished of America's professional China Boys, a missionary kid who had spent years of his childhood in the country before joining the Foreign Service. He felt that China was succeeding where much of the rest of the world was failing. Its economy was growing at a record rate, and the country was stable. The leadership was engaged in a delicate generational transition and, despite problems, keeping its pact with the people—economic progress in return for political acquiescence.

American visitors to China were astonished by what they found, Stape continued. The openness and the materialism evident everywhere were at complete variance with the Tiananmen tank versus man image they'd brought with them. Eight times more cities were now open to foreigners than had been the case in the mid-eighties, years considered quite liberal. Diplomats could go practically anywhere without sending a note to the Foreign Ministry. The Peace Corps would soon be going into Sichuan Province. Many rural villages now had satellite dishes. There were more TVs in Beijing than households. Thirty thousand Chinese students had been sent to the United States since Tiananmen. Our Congress and administration seemed totally out of touch with Chinese reality. They badly needed an update. Get them here to see, Roy urged.

The next day I got on a bike to visit old haunts, looking for my own evidence of the openness and prosperity he had described. It was there. The old department store on Wangfujing was a madhouse, wall-to-wall buyers snapping up ordinary items, with an entire floor devoted to luxury imports. People dressed like other Asians, in simple, colorful, Western-style clothing. Some of the old proletarian items—PLA sneakers, for example—were nowhere to be found. The city had expanded enormously outward, with satellite towns springing up along two new concentric beltways around Beijing (there are now four). The architecture, boring and stolid, along the patterns set in the early 1970s, just multiplied. The road systems, ramps, and flyovers were much more elaborate now but already inadequate to handle the burgeoning traffic. Cars were taking over from the cyclists. Air pollution was as bad as before and getting worse. The Chinese were then anxious to host the Olympics in 2000, and the slogans one saw everywhere read "A More Open China Welcomes the 2000 Olympics," instead of "Down with U.S. Imperialism."

I spent the rest of my stay in Beijing building the network that would help me organize future Asia Society programs, meeting representatives of China's GONGOs (Government-Owned Non-Governmental Organizations), most of them former officials, retreads like myself. Among them, I made a point of calling on my old PLA colleague Xu Yimin, the first military attaché in Washington. He had become vice chairman of the new Chinese Institute for International Strategic Studies (CIISS), today one of China's most prominent research institutions. I remembered how perplexed the Chinese had been over retirement placements for their officers when we first met in 1980. The PLA had taken a leaf from the U.S. book and established a web of think tanks to catch and use smart, cultured generals like Xu. We made plans for future seminars on strategic issues.[58]

This visit set the pattern for twenty-seven more trips to the Mainland and Hong Kong during my time at the Asia Society. The combination of observing, teaching, traveling, and networking enabled me to keep up with a country that was changing at warp speed, make contact with the leadership, and fashion an active, influential role for the Asia Society in China.

Our first programs were small. We held a pan-Asian policy seminar at a new golf resort in Zhongshan, Guangdong Province, near Macao in March 1993. About fifty participants came from most countries in the region, but Beijing, miffed that we had sponsored the event from Hong Kong without consulting them, sent no one. We still had a lot to learn about how to operate in China. The Asians loved the idea of golfing in the Middle Kingdom. To me, it felt weird and unsettling, a symptom of the massive changes underway.

In May of 1994, the society organized a boatload of members, three generations of Asians and Americans, to sail from Chongqing down through the Yangzi Gorges to Wuhan, before the great Three Gorges Dam was finished. Our travelers were entranced by the scenery, shocked by the poverty of central China's cities, intrigued by lectures afloat documenting the cultural losses and ecological damage to be caused by the dam (all proved true), and appalled when the dining room wait staff took our leftover food and simply threw it out the cabin window into the river. The tight belt of Mao's China was no more.

Later that month, Secretary of State Warren Christopher chose the society's Park Avenue headquarters as the location for a major speech on U.S. policy toward Asia, following President Clinton's decision to extend most-favored-nation treatment to China. Describing the society as "America's pre-eminent organization devoted to forging links across the Pacific," he announced that trade levels with China would no longer be contingent on human rights behavior. We were making headway in the national debate.

We started planning early for a 1995 corporate conference in Beijing. Interagency coordination was always a special obstacle in

China, because lower levels of the bureaucracy did not talk to each other. The only way to assure cooperation between the Ministry of Foreign Affairs, which invited Asian leaders to attend, and the Ministry of Foreign Trade, which owned the hotel and was responsible for business relations, was for me to call separately on each of the responsible vice premiers a year in advance.

China was ripe for a big international business meeting. As the global economy boomed during the 1990s, government leaders and private corporate executives developed avid interest in direct contact with each other. CEOs and their companies would pay handsomely for the chance to rub shoulders with officials, particularly those from authoritarian systems like China, where access was extremely limited. For the Asia Society, corporate conferences became arenas of communication as well as rich cash cows. The field would soon be overcrowded and overused. But in 1995, China was the place Americans and Asians wanted to be, and the Chinese wanted them there.

The Corporate Conference in Beijing put us on the map in China once and for all. The society's convening power and organizing skill was on display, as several hundred business and government leaders from across Asia gathered to discuss "China and its Neighbors—Economic Relations in a Region of Rapid Growth." Vice President Rong Yiren opened the three-day affair. The prime ministers of Korea and Singapore, among others, described for their hosts the benefits and drawbacks of living so close to such a big neighbor. Vice Premier and Foreign Minister Qian Qichen and Foreign Trade Minister Wu Yi, the government's top foreign policy figures during the decade, responded with assurances of China's benevolent intent. The pace of networking and deal making in the halls was a sign of solid success.

For me and the Asia Society, discovering Freda Wang Yixun was the most important outcome of the conference. She worked for Dow Jones, a regular cosponsor of our business meetings, which saw this conference as a way to strengthen its foothold in China. Freda had been the bilingual star of the staff we put together to organize the event. She came up to me after it was over, revealed that she had been an intern at the Asia Society galleries in 1980, and offered to be our volunteer resident representative in China.

I agreed immediately, thus beginning a close cooperation that remains crucial to the society and to me. Freda had lived through the Cultural Revolution, then resumed her education early and won a scholarship to study in the States. Her contacts and savvy would drive our programs and understanding of events in China over the years. We went straight to her native Shanghai after the conference, where she introduced me to important academics, business leaders, and municipal party officials. Her boss, Jim McGregor, offered to contribute space in Dow Jones's office and provide a part-time staff assistant. The society now had a base of operations on the ground in China.

## The Friendly Fossil

I found myself thrust into the rough and tumble of relations between China and the United States. The think tank and business channels I used had become respected supplements to discourse between governments. Access was no problem for me. The number of Americans still standing who had been in Beijing with Nixon, and kept coming back, was small and shrinking. Chinese saw me as something of a friendly fossil. Though they bent my ear with constant complaints about U.S. policies, they listened when I explained our positions. So it was when I found myself at Shanghai's Fudan University in May 1995 on the day the Clinton administration decided to grant Taiwan's controversial president Lee Teng-hui a visa to visit the United States after months of assuring Beijing it would do no such thing. In fact, Win Lord had made the same assurance to me just as I left for China. The scholar-officials I met were in shock, and my explanation that our president had no choice when confronted with a massive congressional majority in favor of Lee's visit made little impression. What upset the Chinese the most was the flaky suddenness of Clinton's change of course and the sense of instability that went with it.

The crisis continued for the next several months, leading up to Taiwan's presidential election in March of 1996. Days before the poll, the PLA fired missiles into the sea near Taiwan in an effort to scare people away from electing Lee. Lee's majority increased in the panic that followed. Tension in the Taiwan Straits grew, with the United States sending a carrier task group close to the area in our own show of force. The situation cooled soon, as the economic imperative that now ruled U.S.-China ties kicked in, but it was clear that the Taiwan issue, so skillfully sidestepped in the Shanghai Communiqué and subsequent declarations, still lay unresolved and dangerous at the heart of our relationship.

In May of 1996, my old colleague General Xu Yimin of the China Institute for International Strategic Studies, fulfilling an old promise, invited me to Beijing for consultations with leading PLA officers and analysts and then took me on a trip to his native Shandong Province. In our talks, China's military intellectuals held the United States responsible for the current deterioration of relations caused by Lee's visit. The reversal of our decision to prevent Lee from coming was incomprehensible, evidence that American leaders had forgotten the strategic value of cooperation with China and the meaning of the three communiqués that governed our relationship. Attitudes in the PLA had hardened accordingly. My assertions that China's March missile exercises had been unnecessary and counterproductive went without rebuttal, suggesting tacit agreement.

Nevertheless, good relations with the United States remained important and desirable to my PLA contacts, which hoped for progress in military-to-military ties after the U.S. elections in November. My consultations took me also to the PLA Academy of Military Sciences in Beijing's Western Hills, long a holy of holies off-limits to foreigners. There, a group of generals and colonels provided their strategic overview of Asia as stable for now, with the worry that an expansive U.S. global strategy could move toward confrontation with China in the future. Younger PLA officers I talked to admired the United States but perceived a pattern of purposeful U.S. measures designed to obstruct China's emergence as a great nation. They said they would fight and die if need be to secure their country's rightful place in the world.

General Xu and I continued our conversations during three days on the road in Shandong Province. Sheila was with us. The ancient sites were special. Confucius's graveyard, a grassy forest of more than 300 hectares devoted to providing burial places for one family over a period of 2,500 years, is unique in the world, and very moving in a gentle way. The sweep of history was palpable here and in the family temple and feudal residence. Premier Zhou Enlai is said to have forbidden Red Guard activity at any of the Confucian sites.

Modern Shandong took our breath away, literally. The air was as thick as Pittsburgh's in the 1940s. We climbed legendary Mount Tai with thousands of others but could see nothing from the top through the haze. The pace of development was furious, with construction sites dotting the cities and the rural landscape. Farm fields were rich with crops and well tended, but the fall in the water table was alarming. The provincial capital, Jinan, boasted a park with 170 natural springs, all but two of which were dry. The Yellow River was a series of shallow, unconnected pools, a forceful reminder that China started its major industrial revolution bumping up against the limits of land, water, and air. The United States had the benefit of a half-empty continent. Something will have to give, I thought. Meanwhile, all the mayors and provincial vice governors we talked to, banquet after banquet, voiced China's determination to grow now and cope later.[59]

## Hong Kong Handover

When we lived in Hong Kong during the Cultural Revolution years, return to the Mainland was inconceivable. But the economic gap between the sleek, booming British territory and the country that loomed over it had narrowed in the decades since the British agreed in 1980 to hand over the territory in 1997. In fact, Hong Kong took over the economy of South China during those years, providing management and marketing talent, insurance, and shipping services in return for plentiful, cheap, and increasingly skilled mainland labor. By the time reversion occurred in 1997, the integration of the two economies was an accomplished fact. Five million people worked for Hong Kong companies, but only 750,000 lived in the territory. The international media did not understand this and moaned about approaching doom when the bamboo curtain would descend upon the bastion of free enterprise.

Asia Society had had a center in Hong Kong since 1990 and had emerged as the foremost private organization linking the territory with the United States. I had kept close ties with the leaders there ever since I took over. A year before reversion, I called on C. H. Tung, the man picked to lead the new special autonomous region. He asked me what it would take to make the more than 8,000 international media representatives scheduled to descend on Hong Kong for the handover go away. They were his major worry, not whether China would leave him alone to govern Hong Kong, even less whether he had the ability to do the job. I answered that three things had to happen before the press would depart: (1) a dignified farewell for the British; (2) a genuinely joyful celebration of the reunion with China, credible to the people of Hong Kong; and (3) the smooth handling of a major demonstration. I noted that the media had the attention span of a nine-year-old and were expensive to move and maintain. Their managers would pull them out once the three events had occurred.

And that was the way it turned out. As a guest of both the British and the Chinese governments at the handover ceremonies on June 30, 1997, I reported to Asia Society colleagues that the most disruptive "demonstrator" was the weather. The British farewell ceremony at HMS Tamar—the naval base on the harbor—was a drown-out. The ten thousand umbrellas issued to the invitees only succeeded in directing the torrential rain down the backs of necks and onto the shoulders and knees of those sitting behind and in front. Tycoons, dignitaries, and luminaries alike melted in their finery. Prince Charles told one of our British friends, "It's the first speech I've ever given under water."

The British farewell was truly moving. As the Union Jack came down and "the last post" was played, and the lone Black Watch piper skirled his sad Scottish tune, there was not a dry eye, or any other part of the body for that matter, among the spectators. Governor Chris Patten gave an elegant tribute to "Hong Kong, a very Chinese city with British characteristics" and then sat down and wept.

Spectacular, deafening fireworks broke out and reflected off the shiny skyscrapers along the waterfront as we made our way to the British reception and banquet at the new Hong Kong Exhibition Center. History, adrenaline, and wine dried me gradually as I worked the daunting dinner—four thousand damp people seated at tables of twelve. This was the first opportunity for British and

Chinese to appear together, and it was done with dignity, if not warmth. The Chinese had loathed Patten's populist political style. I met many British officials who had worked with the Chinese to fashion the Joint Declaration and Basic Law, all China Boys I knew from the U.K. Diplomatic Service in Beijing. I also connected with many private Asia Society regulars from Japan, Korea, Hong Kong, Australia, and the Philippines.

The handover ceremony was brief, solemn, and heavy on the symbols of sovereignty—language, flags, soldiers, anthems. What TV viewers missed was a marvelous duel between the British and the Chinese military bands that preceded the ceremony, with each alternating numbers, clearly trying to outdo the other. Both were excellent, but the Brits had a long edge on material, from Handel to Colonel Bogey to an exquisite Charpentier overture. Prince Charles and Jiang Zemin gave their brief speeches, the Chinese flag went up, and all over Asia Chinese began to celebrate wildly.

In the hour between the handover and the installation of the new Hong Kong Special Autonomous Region government, I found a small balcony of the convention center with a clear view of the royal yacht *Britannia* and the shining city in the background. I watched her pull slowly from shore and sail majestically by beneath us and out of the harbor, with faint puffs of music coming from a military band playing busily on the top deck and a small knot of observers—Patten and Prince Charles among them—watching the receding skyline from a darkened stern.

Sharing the balcony with me were three chefs from the convention center, their work now done, and two policemen, also taking time off for a smoke and a moment of history. All were Hong Kong Chinese, and I asked them what they thought about the event they had just seen. One chef replied, "Old boss go, new boss come. I work all same. If I don't like new boss, I quit." A classic response, but still possible in Hong Kong, where it will remain much easier to quit than in other parts of China.

The swearing in of the new government was blessedly short (it was close to 2 A.M.). With the ceremonies over, a small unit of the People's Liberation Army forces marched quietly into Hong Kong, arms swinging, hands encased in white gloves.

At a celebration the next morning, President Jiang Zemin reviewed in detail the rules agreed with the British to make "One Country—Two Systems" work. Sternly, he forbade any "central department or locality to interfere in the affairs which, under the Basic Law, should be administered by the Hong Kong SAR on its own." He threw a small but unexpected bouquet to the British, thanking them for their contribution to the smooth transition and successful negotiation of the historic issues between the two countries.

C. H. Tung followed with his own "State of the SAR" speech, outlining in detail his objectives of improving education and housing and reducing the price of land. I had a chance to talk briefly with Chinese Vice Premier Qian Qichen, whose prominent role as MC in the handover events suggested that he would be the senior Beijing official responsible for relations with Hong Kong.

The serious stuff then gave way to a Chinese version of halftime at the Super Bowl. A gigantic orchestra of Western instruments, Shang dynasty (2400 B.C.) gongs and bells, Chinese flutes and drums, two children's choruses, and Yo-Yo Ma playing an electronically enhanced cello belted out a weird but joyous oratorio written especially for the occasion by Tan Dun. They were then joined by a horde of tiny girls in pink tutus and every major rock singer in Hong Kong bellowing a propaganda hymn expressing pride in their return to the motherland.

The Chinese were serious about their promise to leave the place alone. The first PRC commissioner to Hong Kong, Ma Yuzhen, was an old contact from liaison office days who had served as ambassador to the United Kingdom. When I called on him a year later, he told me, "My instructions are to do as little as possible, and I am following them to the letter. The fact is that we do not know how to run Hong Kong. I am here solely as a symbol of Chinese sovereignty."[60]

## A Two-Way Bridge

By now, the Chinese regarded the Asia Society as a reliable bridge between China and America. Months before President Jiang Zemin's visit to the United States in November 1997, an advance team led by his close confidant, party elder Wang Daohan, sought me out for advice. I had met Wang in Shanghai through Freda Wang. I told him that how Jiang came across as a person would be as important as what he said. As the first Chinese leader to visit since Tiananmen, Jiang had to present himself to Americans as a warm human being, not the bloodless cardboard cutout cadre they thought him to be.

Jiang outdid himself, startling the media when he first arrived by appearing on the beach at Honolulu for a swim in a pink bathing cap. While he stuck to orthodox policy lines, he spoke some English during every speech and earned respect for doing something no Chinese leader had dared before: He took questions from the floor. This was brave and dangerous, particularly at Harvard University, where five thousand demonstrators, both pro and con, milled in the streets. His answer to a question on Tiananmen—"We have made mistakes in our work"—became famous. The Tibet issue was a running sore throughout the visit. At the White House joint press conference, Clinton told him he was "on the wrong side of history" in Tibet. Jiang offended everyone in a speech to foreign affairs organizations, including the Asia Society, by comparing the Chinese takeover of Tibet to the emancipation of slaves during the Civil War in America. But the Chinese leader's willingness to take on tough issues in the open projected confidence and made a difference to Americans.

The White House also recognized Asia Society's role, choosing us to organize the venue in Washington for President Clinton to make a policy speech on the eve of Jiang's arrival and letting me do the introduction. Clinton was balanced and constructive, setting just the right tone. Days later at the state dinner for Jiang, I told him I had waited for years for a president to make this statement. The dinner was a huge affair, following an arrival ceremony earlier in the day on the White House lawn, with the same ruffles, flourishes, and trumpets that had greeted Deng Xiaoping seventeen years before. This was crucial to Jiang, who wanted to project himself as a leader of Deng's stature. Sheila remembers sitting next to ultraconservative Senator Jesse Helms at the dinner. He seemed to hate being there and had little to say.

The Asia Society center in Los Angeles sponsored Jiang's last event, which featured seven hundred of California's rich and famous stuffed in a hotel ballroom at lunchtime on the most beautiful Sunday of the year. He pulled them in off their farms and golf courses and made them put on suits and place little pins with Chinese and American flags in their lapels. They loved it. As demonstrators roared and chanted outside, Governor Pete Wilson introduced Jiang, hosing down his introduction with references to the "elixir of freedom," a powerful tonic to progress of all sorts. He also documented honestly the shame of California's history of discrimination against Chinese, as well as its current performance as China's sixth largest trading partner and first home for Chinese Americans. Wang Daohan, during a chat in Shanghai two months later, judged Jiang's visit a success, though he said honestly that reaching the goal of a "constructive partnership" had a way to go.

During the years that followed, the pace and depth of Asia Society interaction with China intensified. We organized a corporate conference in Hong Kong in 1998, followed by an all-day flight across China to the fabled Sunday market in Kashgar, and then by caravan across Central Asia to Samarkand, Bukhara, and Khiva. In September 1999, we brought the best of our Rockefeller Collection of outstanding Asian art to the new museum in Shanghai, whose multitudes broke all our records for exhibit attendance. Though it was the first pan-Asian art shown in China, with exquisite pieces from Japan, India, Korea, and Cambodia, Shanghai viewers spent most of their time in front of the Chinese ceramics in the collection. I gave lectures on U.S.-China relations and foreign affairs at Fudan University and the Shanghai Academy of Social Science. We lobbied municipal and party officials hard in favor of Shanghai as the site for our corporate conference in 2000, touting the meeting as a dry run for the huge APEC Summit China would host in Shanghai in 2001. They agreed, and the conference turned out to be our most important ever in China, with Premier Zhu Rongji opening the meeting, introduced by his friend, Maurice R. "Hank" Greenberg of AIG, Asia Society chairman during these extraordinary years and a driving force behind our China programs.

## A New Ball Game

George W. Bush came to power in 2001 with a neoconservative chip on his shoulder, determined to treat China as our major competitor. But the crisis early in his term caused by the collision of a Chinese F-8 fighter and a U.S. intelligence plane forced down at Hainan Island gave both sides a chilling look at the potential consequences of armed conflict. Reason and professional competence on both sides prevailed.

The APEC Meeting in Shanghai in November 2001 was destined to be significant even before the events of September 11. The Chinese had planned for years to stage a gigantic coming-out party to celebrate their entry into the World Trade Organization, which had finally occurred in April 2001 and symbolized their emergence on the world scene as a major economic power. Rather than "hijack" the conference, as media commentators forecast, the September terrorist attacks lent intensity and focus to the proceedings, engendering a sense of a real turning point in history at which participants felt fortunate to be present. The huge gathering of top officials and CEOs (some 11,000 in all, counting hangers-on, the media, and me) were united in the desire both to counter terrorism and to get on with the regular-life tasks of expanding trade and investment, long-term antidotes to gloom over current trends in the world economy. As a result, an unusual sense of community marked this first major international meeting since the September tragedies.

The events of 9/11 gave the Chinese an opportunity to put relations with the United States back on a positive track, and they jumped at it. Jiang had been one of the first world leaders to telephone Bush after the World Trade Center attack. The two men met face to face for the first time during the APEC Summit and got along fine. Bush took care to avoid the kind of expansive assessment that followed his first meeting with Putin ("I looked into his soul and found trust."), which had caused such ridicule. They discussed the whole range of issues and continued to disagree on the contentious ones (Taiwan, proliferation, human rights) while cooperating on measures against terrorism, including intelligence sharing. References to "strategic competition" and other abrasive formulations were gone, and a new tone of bilateral cooperation was established that was to last for the next four years.

Always looking ahead, the meeting in Shanghai gave the Chinese an opportunity to show how they might manage a future Olympic Games. The weather was clear and free of pollution, making the city look like a huge stage set. A sense of magnificent unreality was enhanced by the almost total absence of Shanghai's fifteen million residents, who had worked throughout the weekend before but were given five days off from Wednesday through Sunday and told to stay off the streets. Security was drum-tight, with empty streets lined with public security police, who barked sharply at stray pedestrians and taxis. George W. had not seen the city for more than twenty-five years and declared himself amazed. He told the audience at the CEO Summit, "I was here in 1975 with my mother. Shanghai has finally recovered."

Beneath the preoccupation with international terrorism at APEC ran a strong current of concern among Asian participants that the Chinese economy had become a giant vacuum cleaner, sucking away their trade opportunities and investment partners. The Chinese kept their ears open and adjusted their policies during the following years, making sure that their Asian neighbors received a significant and increasing share of China's trade and investment.[61]

**Life of the Party**

One of the authors of this policy was a man named Zheng Bijian. I had met Zheng through Freda Wang in 1998 when he was running the CCP Communist Party School, Beijing's main leadership training institution. I found him a sophisticated, broad-gauge thinker who understood that China's upcoming officials had to work with the rest of the world. He had visited the States a number of times and spoken at Harvard's Kennedy School. The curriculum he had developed for the Party School contained strong doses of international economics, foreign policy, and technology. At the end of a long discussion on U.S. relations and governance in China, he invited me to lecture at the Party School during a future visit to Beijing. I finally did this in 2004, a mind-blowing event for a China Boy whose first conversations with Chinese began furtively on a bicycle thirty years before.

By then, Zheng had retired from administering the school to chair the China Reform Forum, a super think tank personally tasked by Hu Jintao to map out a course for China during the coming decades. Over the previous twenty-five years Zheng had been the theoretician of change in China. He and his staff were the ones who wrote the endless leadership reports to Party Plenums that provided the ideological justifications for new policies, in language often as obscure as they were politically acceptable. Decisions to open the economy, protect private property, include capitalist entrepreneurs in the party, elect party politicians, village leaders, and low-level municipal officials by democratic vote had all been introduced and justified in words crafted by Zheng. It was he who framed the catchphrase "China's Peaceful Rise."

In November 2003, Zheng invited me to take part in a conference at the BoAo Forum for Asia on Hainan Island to discuss China's rise. Anxious to establish a firm tie between his Reform Forum and the Asia Society, I readily accepted. Arriving at the conference site, Freda and I had a long lunch with Zheng and his staff. The main subject was his upcoming visit to the United States. He was to visit Washington in a few days (November 8–10), talking to the very top of the administration. He wanted me to tell him the intellectual backgrounds, mindsets, roles, and relationships of the president, vice president, national security advisor, secretary of state, and secretary of defense. He wanted a context for a conversation with each one, should he need it. I told him what I knew and thought.

The next day I went to hear Zheng's speech to the BoAo plenary session. I arrived ten minutes ahead of time and was immediately waylaid by his staffers. Zheng wanted me to introduce him to the plenary, sit on the stage while he talked, and ask the one question he was permitted to take after the speech. Knowing how rare and how significant such last-minute protocol improvisations were for Chinese, I shook off a brief spasm of terror, gathered my wits, read his speech, crafted an introduction and a question, and then went onstage.

The speech was classic Zheng, anodyne and weighty at the same time. China's big problems involved multiplication and division. Every tiny economic or social development, multiplied by 1.3 billion, and some day 1.5 billion, people became huge. Every gain in financial and material resources divided by 1.3–1.5 billion people became tiny in per capita terms. Yet China had added significantly to its weight and wealth over past decades, not by walling itself off but by taking part in the globalization process, the result of major strategic decisions by its leaders. China would continue to rise and to add wealth to its own people and its Asian neighborhood, and would do so peacefully, taking whatever strategic decisions were needed to make this happen.

For the record, my one question was also about math. It dealt with the change in the shape of China's population in the coming decades, with a smaller proportion of younger workers supporting a much larger proportion of older people. This would require the development of modern pension plans, financial markets, and investment devices. How was China going to deal with this? Are there opportunities for closer investment ties with Asia and the West? Answer: We're thinking about it.[62]

The following November, Zheng convened foreign policy intellectuals from China's major think tanks, the United States, Japan, Southeast Asia, and Europe to continue the discussion. It was clear that the "Peaceful Rise" formula had been controversial in China. Hu Jintao's measured address laid out all the elements of the policy but did not mention the word "rise." Zheng Bijian's statements at the conference contained defensive passages clearly aimed at domestic audiences, which justified the policy as a continuation of the path set by Deng Xiaoping and Jiang Zemin. There were passages of assurance for foreigners as well, expressing the need for a new framework for security consultations and economic interdependence. In the course of the daylong roundtable, the outlines of concern and debate began to emerge.

Domestic critics objected to the Chinese term Zheng had chosen for "rise" (*jueqi*), which struck them as too aggressive. Hardliners in the PLA thought the policy sounded too soft, seeming to rule out the use of force, especially where Taiwan was concerned. The Ministry of Foreign Affairs had problems primarily because they did not coin the terminology in the first place.

Foreigners, on the other hand, were delighted with the "peaceful" thrust but much more concerned about the implications of China's "rise." How, some asked, could China reach its goal of quadrupling its GDP by 2020 without starting a worldwide competition for resources. The Chinese economy was already absorbing most of the world's steel production, scrap metal, and container ships and driving up the prices of raw materials across the board. Energy was a particular issue. If the billions in China and India consumed energy at the same rate as Americans and Europeans, the world would run out of fossil fuels long before the end of the century, as currently estimated.

Zheng Bijian sat through all this, a silent, congenial sphinx. He was using the conference as a policymaking vehicle, responding to domestic debate by bouncing ideas off the foreign intellectual community. He was also using his Reform Forum as a mechanism for cross-communication between Chinese think tanks and ministries. It took years of talk to get his earlier policy initiatives through the Chinese body politic. I felt we were part of a huge and important process, and was glad I came.

Asia Society also got some valuable, if fleeting, national visibility at the big conference. BoAo organizer Long Yongtu (the man who negotiated China's entry into the World Trade Organization) asked me to open the discussion period after Hu Jintao's speech with a question about how the Chinese president planned to slow a hot economy without forcing a hard landing that would hurt the world economy. It was a plant, but a good question that was on everyone's mind. Hu's answer was about what one would expect, namely that the economy had to continue its growth path, though with better-enforced controls of irresponsible and redundant capital formation (read: bad loans). The whole exchange was televised nationwide to an audience of several hundred million viewers.[63]

That was my last act as Asia Society president. In fact, I had formally retired in July of 2004. But I have continued my dialogue with Zheng and other leaders during regular visits to China in later years with luminaries from my past like Henry Kissinger and George Shultz. I helped Zheng place an article in *Foreign Affairs* on China's "Peaceful Rise" in September of 2005.

My twelve years at the Asia Society confirmed the organization's role as a trusted and objective channel of interaction between China and the United States. They filled the gaps created by the painful interruptions of my Foreign Service career. Ironically, I never succeeded in getting the society formally registered under China's new regulations governing nongovernmental organizations. The rules for registration tightened significantly after the "color revolutions" in 2003–2005, in which NGOs played a role in overthrowing established governments in Georgia, the Ukraine, and Kyrgyzstan. The Chinese were content to keep our status influential though unconfirmed, a constructive ambiguity any China Boy would understand.

# 28

# Safe in a Clinch

## The Triumph of "Nuts and Bolts"

President Nixon and Henry Kissinger cut the State Department out of their balance of power diplomacy with the Chinese in the period leading up to the Beijing breakthrough and during the Liaison Office years that followed. Kissinger's anger when he learned that I had taken the notes during David Bruce's first conversation with Premier Zhou Enlai showed how tight he wanted the compartments to be. We were relegated to deal with the "nuts and bolts" of the relationship—trade, investment, sports, culture, education, and scientific exchange. In fact, my colleagues and I were happy to be in Beijing at all, fascinated with domestic Chinese politics, life in China, and the dynamics of the first interactions between Americans and Chinese, whether Olympic athletes, orchestra maestros, members of Congress, airplane manufacturers, bankers, scientists, or inner city youths.

Over the years, our "nuts and bolts" fastened together the structure of U.S.-China relations, in the process creating an economic imperative that replaced the original strategic rationale after it collapsed. The size of the structure became enormous. Trade in 1972 was $92 million both ways. Now it is close to $400 billion, with a huge, troublesome surplus in China's favor. As late as 1982, U.S. direct investment totaled $1.8 million. Today it is at least $60 billion. The year Nixon went to Beijing perhaps 1500 Americans visited China, as opposed to over a million now. Nowadays 5000 people are in the air traveling to and from China every day. There were close to 100,000 mainland Chinese attending U.S. universities in 2008. When we normalized relations in 1979 there were 1,300.

After Beijing's triumphant close of its Olympic Games in 2008, I realized how well Chinese athletes had followed the advice on how champions are produced provided by our swimmers in 1973. Our modern basketball relationship began in June 1973 with the Beijing games that Madame Mao attended, and used to kick off her public campaign to succeed the chairman. When Shanghai's Yao Ming joined a National Basketball Association (NBA) team in 2002, his debut in Houston was watched on television by nearly three hundred million Chinese (a number nearly equaling the entire population of the United States). In 2004, I led an NBA leadership group to China for games between the Houston Rockets and the Sacramento Kings and felt firsthand the mania shared by Chinese and Americans for this game first brought to China by YMCA missionaries in the 1890s.

Successful management of the nuts and bolts is the key to the future, and will be a complex task. Old China watchers like me have had to learn from the ground up the ways of the modern Chinese business community, which are evolving rapidly. These days, an absence of more than six months from China is a ticket to disorientation for Chinese and foreigners alike. Every spring and fall since leaving the presidency of Asia Society, I have found a place as a visiting lecturer at different Chinese universities, mainly to find out what is new and what is not. Those most interested in what I have to say are the younger generation, who fill university lecture rooms to hear first hand about historical figures Zhou Enlai, Henry Kissinger, Richard Nixon and Madame Mao, tales no one else will tell them. A speaking tour in the fall of 2009 celebrating thirty years of U.S.-China relations took me to six cities and eleven universities. The more than two thousand students I addressed had two things on their minds at every stop: Zhou Enlai's role in the opening between the United States and China, and the emerging shape of President Obama's China policy today.

Some contemporary issues are familiar to old China Boys. For example, it is harder than ever for the central authorities to govern the provinces. The heavens are higher and the emperor further away, to paraphrase the old saying, now that municipal mayors and provincial governments have been let loose to compete in the race for rapid development. And the pace of growth has brought back a gap between rich and poor that resembles to many the inequality in old China that the Communists sought to change in the first place. An emerging new political left and right now argue about development policy in terms different, but still quite familiar to those who followed the old debates pitting the "Red" against the "Expert." Western suits and ties have replaced Mao outfits, but the old Middle Kingdom bureaucrat flourishes in modern China at all levels, lining his pockets and watching his back, free of the idealism that steered his forebears.

Once beaten and often killed by peasant and Red Guard mobs, successor generations of capitalists and entrepreneurs are now welcomed into party ranks where senior officials and their children busily enrich themselves through real estate deals and insider relationships. The party is now working to co-opt the private sector by setting up its own committees in the big new firms. The rules of engagement change every day. Newly trained accountants, lawyers, judges, bankers, engineers, and managers learn Western techniques but insert themselves into a uniquely Chinese system that favors relationships over rationality and control over independence. The legal system is modernizing slowly, but Chinese are just as leery of going to court as they were under imperial Mandarin judges, who levied ruinous fines and penalties on everyone, plaintiffs and defendants alike, who had the temerity to disturb their busy schedules. Instead, extralegal arbitration and mediation practices, perfected over centuries, continue to serve society quite well. Neither the Chinese masses nor the international community will trust the court system until it is independent of party control, but the party is as reluctant to let go as the emperors were.

"Nuts and bolts" are also a key factor in cross-straits relations, given Taiwan's de facto economic merger with the mainland economy over recent decades. The rapid growth of trade, investment, travel, and cultural exchange is bringing the mainland and Taiwan inexorably together. Younger Taiwanese tell me during recent trips that they have three main aspirations: an education in the United States, a job in the mainland, and a home in Taiwan. More than a million Taiwanese, or almost 5 percent of the island's population, live and do business in the mainland. The return to power in Taiwan of the Nationalist (Kuomintang) Party in 2008 has seen practical ties improve further. Direct charter air travel has become a fact. The time to get from Taipei to Shanghai is a few minutes more than a shuttle ride from New York to Washington. Tourism in Taiwan from the mainland is on the rise.

The Chinese are just as interested in our nuts and bolts as we are in theirs. They are in learning and listening mode, for their own benefit. They sell off bits of their economy, though not cheaply, in exchange for the know-how the foreign buyers will bring. They are interested in creating connective tissue with the rest of the world and are using the trillions of dollars in foreign reserves gained through massive trade surpluses to buy into other economies, including our own. They know that the United States and China will have to re-balance their economies, with Chinese spending more and saving less, and the United States saving more and spending less. But they prefer to adjust slowly while still learning the ropes of the global business world. The China chief of the consulting firm McKinsey & Company told me in 2005 that the firm had bought the former CIA headquarters in Frankfurt for use as a training school for fifty Chinese students at a time, teaching them how to be worldly, how to order wine, dress properly, behave internationally. More training centers are planned, as Chinese confidence grows.

## The Generations to Come

Throughout history, Chinese have measured time by reference to the reigns of their rulers. Periods of the Communist era are divided into generations of leadership. Those who ran China under Mao and Zhou are the First Generation; Deng Xiaoping, the Second; Jiang Zemin the Third; Hu Jintao, the current leader, the Fourth. And then comes the Fifth Generation (*wu dai*), whose leader will soon be chosen. All were children of the Cultural Revolution—some as Red Guards—who lived the turbulence of the late sixties, were sent to labor reform in factories, farms, and mines, and who then returned to resume their interrupted educations after Mao's death in 1976. The most talented received training abroad during the eighties. They are the best and the brightest, know each other, and represent the bridge between China's past and future.

One of them recently told me that they are similar to our generation of World War II veterans—molded in a time of terrible trouble, short-changed on education, eager for knowledge, and determined to make up for lost time. The Cultural Revolution shaped their outlook. They have no doubts about the evils of political extremism. At the same time they have gained from the opportunity to travel and from learning how to manage people and organizations. Lasting friendships and key contacts were the product of shared hardship and uncertainty during this time.

Now mostly in their fifties the members of the Fifth Generation who entered government are emerging as national leaders, government ministers, and provincial leaders. Two of them, Vice President Xi Jinping and Vice Premier Li Keqiang, are members of the all-powerful Politburo Standing Committee and appear to be in line to replace both President Hu Jintao and Premier Wen Jiabao when they step down in 2012. Fifth Generation figures in the cultural field, movie makers like Zhang Yimou and Chen Kaige, composers like Tan Dun and Bright Sheng, painters like Xu Bing and Cai Guo-Qiang , have already arrived and earned worldwide reputations.

My experience covering the Cultural Revolution from Hong Kong, and living in Beijing during the 1970s, gives me insight and entrée to the Fifth Generation. The ones I know are surprised to find a foreigner who studied the sequence of events during the Cultural Revolution, and they will open up about their experiences.

At an Asia Society interview in 2004, I gossiped with composer Tan Dun (*The First Emperor*) about Madame Mao's imperious behavior over Eugene Ormandy's Philadelphia Orchestra concert in Beijing in 1973. Tan said he had heard that concert on the commune radio in the peasant village where he had been sent. Broadcast throughout the country, it had transformed his whole concept of music and set him on a career of fusing Western and Chinese musical traditions. I told him I had also attended the Hong Kong hand-over ceremonies in 1997, where he had been commissioned to compose and conduct a grandiloquent celebratory oratorio. Tan decided that we must be soul mates, whose meeting had been foreordained.

Bright Sheng premiered his opera *Madame Mao* in Santa Fe in 2005. He invited me to give a lecture on Mao's controversial wife, to provide context for the music. The Fifth Generation blames her, not her husband, for their suffering. Accordingly, the music was harsh.

In the audience at a 2007 Northwestern University program on Nixon in China, I found Zhao Jia, the interpreter who had translated at the Foreign Ministry meeting in 1973 where I learned that I must leave China "of my own accord." When the date for Nixon's visit was set for 1972, many young English language specialists were released from farm labor in the countryside and brought to Beijing to work on the preparations. She was one of them, and now manages, from Chicago, the China practice of the major law firm Baker and McKenzie.

Many Americans who work in China now are dealing with members of the Fifth Generation every day. They know that those who have risen to the top are superbright survivors who have Western contacts and training. As government and party members, think tank intellectuals, and private sector entrepreneurs they have excelled in an environment of rapid growth, intense competition, and profound change.

Digging deeper, one finds signs of self-doubt and concern that contemporaries in the Fifth Generation will not be able to make much impact on the future. Surviving the contrary pressures of the Cultural Revolution and the opening of the economy, some generation members think, has made many of them two-faced and unsure about what they believe. Others in positions of responsibility now realize that the gaps in their education have deprived them of basic knowledge needed to govern. Those who went abroad to study in the early eighties are educated but also mildly tainted by foreign associations. Within the government and party system, the "returned turtles" (*hui gui pai*) are seen as less politically reliable than the "local tortoises" (*tu bie*) schooled at home. The majority of "returned turtles" feel most comfortable in modern China's vastly expanded private sector, where they have room to maneuver. Looking ahead a decade, we have a pretty good idea what we are dealing with but must wait to see how the Fifth Generation manages at the helm of the Middle Kingdom.

But what of the sixth, seventh, and eighth generations? They will be something else again. My experience with Chinese twenty–year-olds in the work force has been mildly alarming so far. Known in their society as *ba ling hou*—born after 1980—they are conspicuously laid-back. During a 2006 tour of Jiangsu Province, the young assistant of the secretary general of the Wenzhou Industrial District greeted me in the staid marble headquarters foyer dressed in low-cut jeans with tummy showing, green satin slippers with white pom poms, and a blue sateen sports jacket. Her cell phone was on a key ring festooned with miniature fuzzy animals. She was pretty in a doll-like way and flirted with all the males who accompanied us.

According to slightly older, and clearly disapproving, young Chinese in their thirties, the *ba ling hou* don't live at home, change jobs frequently, and spend all their money immediately (*yue guang zu*—the nothing-at-the-end-of–the-month gang). They shack up with each other early and often (*shang hun*—"flash marriages," or *shi hun*—"trial marriages"); are fond of pop music and Korean and Japanese TV dramas about young adult love; and vote for their favorites in pop music contests by cell phone SMS.

The authorities are quick to point out that this is *not* democracy; but the question remains, what will the party do with this age group? The emerging Chinese younger generation resembles that in other countries of Asia, but other Asians have more outlets for political expression. Graduate students in recent Chinese audiences of mine seem more straitlaced, disciplined perhaps by the fierce competition they face in China's post–2008 crisis job market. What they will turn into if jobs do not materialize is a question that preoccupies the leadership.

## China in the Twenty-First Century: The Dilemmas of Growth

How should future generations of Americans position themselves to deal with their opposite numbers in China? Will China be our enemy or our friend? Where should investors put their money? Will China keep on growing? Will it rule the world? What form of government will it have? These are the questions I am asked most often by American audiences.

To find the answers, I have asked China's top planners where they want their country to go in the decades ahead. What intellectual leaders like Zheng Bijian have told me is that, having expanded fivefold in the last three decades, China's new goal moving forward is to quadruple the gross domestic product by the year 2020. China's impact on the twenty-first century, good or bad, as well as the very survival of Chinese Communist Party rule, Zheng believes, will depend on meeting three challenges: resources, environment, and coordination between economic and social development, meaning narrowing the gap between rich and poor.

The statistics are daunting. China supports 20 percent of the world's population, but has only 7 percent of the world's arable land, 7 percent of the world's fresh water, 3 percent of the world's forests, 2 percent of the world's oil, and 1 percent of its natural gas. Planners know that the country must grow at 7 percent a year to absorb new arrivals in the workforce.[64] Resources must come from elsewhere. By 2008 the booming Chinese economy absorbed 47 percent of the world's production of iron ore, 32 percent of its aluminum, and 25 percent of its copper.[65] The pace has only gotten hotter each year since. Prices of raw materials have gone through the roof.

International competition for energy is already ferocious, if peaceful, and a source of political friction. The weapons are financial and economic, pipeline deals, and purchases of energy properties throughout the world, including from pariah regimes in Sudan, Somalia, and Iran. Friction between Japan and China has risen recently over competing claims to offshore islands and supplies of energy from Russia.

Like the rest of us, the Chinese are just becoming aware of the urgent threat posed by climate change and the dangers of reliance on fossil fuels. So plans to develop alternative energy sources, nuclear power, wind, solar, geothermal, hydrogen technology, and hydroelectric power are being addressed right now and backed with massive investments. For example, China currently gets less than 2 percent of its power-generating capacity from eleven nuclear reactors but plans to build dozens more by 2020, bringing the sector's share to 5 percent of its generating capacity. In twenty years national energy planners expect to have more than 100 nuclear reactors, matching the current level in the United States They will need many more to deal with energy demand and the need to curb carbon emissions. The implications for international security are high. China could become a destructive force in the twenty-first century, planners tell me, if energy needs are not met. International cooperation will be essential.

Current rates of growth are creating unsustainable pressure on the environment. Three hundred million Chinese do not have access to clean drinking water, while 400 million live in areas with dangerously high levels of air pollution. One third of the land is affected by acid rain.[66] I rarely return from a visit to China without a respiratory problem. The Chinese are spending more and more on the technology to clean up the air, spurred on by the pressures of the Olympics in 2008.

Water is an even more serious problem, one that could put sharp brakes on China's rate of growth. With the rapid pace of urban development, the water table throughout China has been dropping each year. The Yellow River, whose floods were once called "China's sorrow," is now dry downstream for parts of the year. Water levels behind the gigantic Three Gorges Dam on the Yangzi River have failed to meet target heights. Consequently, construction of a massive system of pipelines and aqueducts to transport water from the Yangzi River to North China is now on hold.

Looking further ahead, China's population growth will hit a great wall between 2010 and 2040, the abrupt result of the one-child policy instituted a generation ago. The portion of people 65 and older will rise from around 7 percent to somewhere between 25 percent and 30 percent of the population. In some cities, the elderly could make up 33–50 percent of the population. The slide in fertility rates, combined with improved medical treatment and longer life expectancy, will confront China with a problem that governments in Europe, Japan, and the United States already face. But these societies got rich before they became old. Measured per capita, China will still be quite poor when it gets old.

Glaring inequalities have emerged in society as a result of rapid and uneven economic growth—between rich and poor, between city and countryside, and between various regions of the country, notably the prosperous coasts versus impoverished interior areas. The resultant flows of migrant labor between city and countryside, a floating population estimated at 200 million, adds to instability, particularly during times of recession.

The Third Generation leadership under Jiang Zemin emphasized economic growth above all else. Fourth Generation leaders
under Hu Jintao are seized with the fairness issues caused by the
gaps and with controlling rampant official corruption, which threat-
ens the underpinnings of the political structure as well as social order. They are calling for the creation of a "harmonious society."

And with good reason. In 2008, according to reliable sources,
100,000 disturbances occurred in Chinese towns and cities—riots,
demonstrations, and acts of group civil disobedience, aimed mostly
at corrupt or overbearing local officials. That is about 275 incidents
a day spread across a large country and population. So far, these
have been local and unconnected, but they remain a deeply wor-
risome preoccupation for party authorities all the same. Any time
an opposition organization such as the Falun Gong, show signs of
developing a national network, the authorities come down hard.
There have been no published statistics in recent years, but analysts
conclude that the disturbance rate continues. More recent bursts of
tension and violence between Han Chinese, Tibetans, and Uighurs
in Xinjiang add to the pattern of disharmony.

During the decades since the Tiananmen incident, the government has invested heavily in the Armed Public Security Forces and
equipped them with sophisticated crowd-control techniques and
improved electronic intelligence to spot and manage disturbances.
To deal with the root causes of unrest, the party is aware that they
need to deliver not only continued economic growth, but also a bet-
ter-distributed prosperity. The rapid growth of the Internet—China
now has 340 million users—has created new sources of information
for Chinese society, and new freedoms of expression for the people;
but it has also inspired major efforts at government censorship and
control.

Finding a balance between the requirements for control and
stability and the freedom that propels growth is the monumental
management dilemma that consumes China's central and provincial authorities. The most sophisticated planners realize that the
Communist Party will need to share power in order to keep it.
They pay lip service to creating a system that is more transparent,
participatory, and responsive than it is now. Ironically, as China's
economy and world stature grow, its internal policies become more

restrictive and less confident. During my professional lifetime, Chinese leadership performance has evolved from the erratic and destructive mood swings of Mao and his Cultural Revolution to the much more measured pace of technocrats who operate as a collective under President Hu Jintao and Premier Wen Jiabao. These men are not charismatic. They are well trained, politically shrewd, exceptionally competent, and increasingly cautious and risk-averse.

Faced with conflicting pressures, the leadership is focusing on what it has done best, stimulating economic growth. It knows a lot about the hardware—roads, bridges, airports, urban housing projects, and dams—and all are under construction at a rapid pace for all to use. The software of a developed economy is harder to create. The leaders realize that a solid banking system, reliable, working capital markets, and a judiciary that is seen as competent, fair, and reasonably independent are needed to sustain foreign investment and domestic growth and reach their long-term goals. In the meantime, most foreign investors try to bypass China's weak domestic capital markets by working through offshore entities and the Hong Kong Stock Exchange. They make every effort to avoid the Chinese courts.

Hong Kong, which got its software from the British, is a discreet role model for the rest of the mainland. The Beijing government has allowed Hong Kong to operate pretty much on its own in these areas and is wooing democracy advocates there in an effort to promote stability.

How do ordinary Chinese confront their panoply of problems? With an "unmistakable air of optimism," knowledgeable visitors report. In places as disparate as Beijing, Chongqing, and Shanghai, Chinese feel their country is hurtling toward a future that will be very different, and probably better. My own soundings match these. At the same time, China's problems will preoccupy its government and inevitably slow its rate of economic growth. To succeed, Premier Wen Jiabao told recent visitors, China will need "peace, friends, and time." Its influence in Asia and the rest of the world will continue to expand. It has already become a major global player. But will it rule the world? My answer is no.

## China and the United States in the Twenty-first Century

Not everyone is so sure that China's intent is so peaceful. They point to rising Chinese defense expenditures and missile deployments along the Taiwan Straits. Unquestionably, small but vocal schools of foreign policy thinking exist, both in Washington and Beijing, which argue that the United States and China are inevitable adversaries, in addition to being competitors. Xenophobia and nationalism in China match latent "yellow peril" fears in the United States and lie just below the surface in both societies.

If we want China as an enemy, that can be arranged. If we want China as a friend or, more likely, a constructive competitor, we can have that, too. To deal successfully, we need closer contact between the peoples and the governments. Americans know very little about China, much less than the Chinese know about us. The Internet, travel, student exchanges, and trade and investment contacts are teaching us more about each other all the time, but we need to increase the pace and the density.

U.S.-China relations were comparatively simple in the early years. Nixon, Kissinger, Mao, and Zhou, like national security managers for centuries before them, sought stability through a balance of power, measured in hard physical terms—geographical location, numbers of tanks, ships, men under arms, production of steel, oil, chemicals, treasury reserves, and the like. The forces of globalization, which took hold late in the twentieth century, replaced the traditional balance of hard power with a more complex, composite balance of influence, combining economic strength, intellectual weight, cultural creativity, and the military muscle needed to deter attack, project power, and deal with natural disasters.

Furthermore, the forces of globalization changed the way the nations of the world interact to preserve stability. Governments now have to share power with corporations, nongovernmental organizations, terrorist groups, drug cartels, regional and global institutions, and banks, private equity funds, and hedge funds. Sovereignty has been affected by the powerful and accelerating flow of people, ideas, greenhouse gases, goods, dollars, renminbi, viruses, emails, and weapons within and across borders. One of the fundamentals of sovereignty—the ability to control what crosses borders—has been challenged.[67]

Chinese planners embraced globalization, and their economy grew accordingly. U.S.-China relations expanded in every way, and became increasingly complicated. The "triumph of nuts and bolts" in the 1990s made trade, investment, and technology transfer the new drivers of our dealings, sources of both cooperation and competition in our ties.

Looking ahead, we need to address vigorously those issues that threaten our economic ties—market access, outsourcing, the growing trade imbalance, exchange rates, and intellectual property. Strategies to rebalance our economies must be found over time if we are to build a stable future together.

What will our relationship look like a generation from now, after China has achieved the growth and stature it desires? Sovereign states now measure their vulnerability not only to one another but increasingly to forces of globalization beyond their control. In response, twenty-first century policy thinkers are calling urgently for a concert of power, rather than a balance of power, to deal cooperatively with the global threats of climate change, terrorism, radical Islam, proliferation of weapons of mass destruction, environmental degradation, and medical plagues. In addition to the nuts and bolts, our political leaders, diplomats, businessmen, and military officers will be spending more and more time together on these issues.

In May 2008, I laid out the advice I would have for the next president of the United States in a keynote speech at Fudan University's Shanghai Forum. The key points represent an appropriate ending for this book:

Dear Mr. or Mrs. President,

The world balance of influence is shifting toward Asia. . . . China and India have gained considerable weight in the balance of influence during their decades of peaceful development.

The United States will remain strong and influential, and the key to maintaining stability in this region, but we will have to share power with the rising nations of Asia. We have been the military power of choice here for decades, and we must upgrade our capabilities and presence, not only to preserve balance but to help with a rising tide of natural disasters.

Be careful about protectionist sentiment in Congress. Trade is what ties the Asian region together, and the United States with Asia. Under free trade policies we have all prospered during the past decades. Moves to limit trade may have been popular during the campaign but will harm economic growth rates in the United States and Asia and reduce our clout.

Our alliances and bilateral relations in Asia are in sound shape, but our preoccupations in recent years with the wars in Iraq and Afghanistan and instability in the Middle East have led us to neglect the rapidly growing web of multilateral arrangements that are linking the region together. This has led to a perception that the United States does not care about Asia. You should lead a concerted effort to refocus and enhance U.S. engagement with APEC, the Asian Regional Forum, and ASEAN and welcome a constructive Chinese role.

The most severe challenge to Asian stability during your administration, recent studies agree, is likely to come from climate change. Rising sea levels, food shortages, mass migrations, widespread disease, drought, flooding, and political unrest stem from global warming and already threaten the countries of Asia and the rest of the world. The challenge of climate change—described by some as the ultimate weapon of mass destruction—will alter the way we manage regional stability in Asia during your term of office and, in fact, the rest of this century. The growing impact of global warming will force a much greater emphasis on collaboration and a concert of power, even as it exacerbates competition between nations for supplies of food, water, and energy.

A new level of consultation between the political and military establishments of the region, particularly the United States and China, will be essential. Your administration will have to take the lead in shaping new mechanisms for controlling carbon emissions and developing sources of clean energy, including nuclear power.

Your most complex single Asian relationship will be with China. Look beyond the arguments of those who see China's rise as a threat to the United States. China faces formidable challenges, particularly regarding resources, environment, and coordination between economic and social development.

All of the challenges arising from China's peaceful development represent dangers and opportunities for U.S.-China relations during your administration. The United States has nothing to gain if China fails. It will be your task to turn China's challenges into areas of cooperation and opportunities for investment. ....

Our economies will become more intertwined, as the foreign direct investment of today expands in both directions, and as China invests the proceeds from its trade surplus with us in U.S. bonds and equities. Many of the thousands of Chinese who have been studying in the United States are returning to put to use the contacts and knowledge they have gained. This does not necessarily mean that they will love the United States. They will, however, understand better the needs and techniques that make Western civil society operate, and the forces that move the world economy and financial system.

They will be needed. A pension system large enough to take care of the rapidly aging population can only be based on direct participation in the global financial system and the development of sophisticated investment and insurance instruments at home. China and the United States are fast becoming the largest investors in each other's economies.

In addition to working together on alternative energy, the banking system, and financial services, we can help China deal with its health problems. We know a lot about water and water management, and are suffering from our own major drought. Water is big business in China, and bound to get much bigger. U.S. experience in housing, construction, and city planning can also be helpful as the Chinese economy becomes urbanized. Permanent population shifts from countryside to city have already totaled 211 million; 100 million more are to come as China urbanizes, with 400 new cities to be built.

To achieve a harmonious society, China will have to set new standards for representative, responsive, and accountable government under a credible, and ultimately independent, rule of law.

You and your administration should not try to tell China how to do this. We have no idea what it is like to govern a population of more than 1.3 billion people. But the United States is already engaged in providing legal and judicial training to those Chinese who want it, as well as advice on how to establish accounting procedures and regulatory institutions and systems that will work for them.

Taiwan has always been the most delicate and dangerous issue between us, one that could trigger a war. With the new leadership in Taiwan, both Taipei and Beijing are embarked on a cautious process of further economic and cultural integration leading in the future, one hopes, to a cessation of hostilities and more lasting political arrangements. Without seeking any direct U.S. role, your administration should encourage the two sides to find their own path to better cross-straits relations.

Secretary of State Alexander Haig once told me, "In the boxing ring, the safest place is in a clinch." Since 1972, the United States has worked its way into a clinch with China. Your goal should be to stay there. You want the economies, political systems, and societies to become so closely connected that conflict and confrontation are no longer even thinkable, much less doable. The relationship, while certainly not friction-free, and surely not without competition, should be free of the dangers of the great power rivalry which once threatened the world.[68]

The advice still stands.

# Notes

**3 Learning the Chinese**
   [1] Letter from Taichung, January 27, 1963
   [2] Letter from Taichung, February 8, 1963.
   [3] Letter from Taichung, April 7, 1963.
   [4] Ibid.

**5 The Cultural Revolution**
   [5] The analysis based on this and other interviews was published in *Current Scene*, a United States Information Service magazine, and was part of the raw material on which Ezra Vogel based his book *Canton under Communism: Programs and Politics in a Provincial Capital, 1949–1968* (Harvard University Press, 1969).

**6 Signs and Signals**
   [6] Marshall Green, John Holdridge, and William N. Stokes, *War and Peace with China: First-hand Experiences in the Foreign Service of the United States (DACOR Press, 1994)*, p. 178.
   [7] Reported by Stewart E. Hoyt, *Milwaukee Journal*, September 14, 1969.

**10 Trouble in the U.S. Delegation**
   [8] John H. Holdridge, *Crossing the Divide: An Insider's Account of Normalization of U.S.-China Relations* (Rowman & Littlefield, 1997), p. 93; Marshall Green et al., *War and Peace with China*, p. 162.

**11 The Birth of the Bruce Mission**
   [9] Holdridge, *Crossing the Divide*, pp. 112, 152, passim.

**12 The Liaison Office Starts Work**
   [10] *Window on the Forbidden City: The Chinese Diaries of David Bruce, 1973–74*, Priscilla Roberts, ed. (University of Hong Kong Press, 2001), pp. 97, 98.

[11] Bruce's six hundred–page *Beijing Diaries* provided a detailed description of his activities each day.

[12] Bruce's full account of the meeting, based on my notes, is carried in his *Beijing Diaries*, pp. 70–73.

### 13 Shepherd of Sports

[13] Quoted in David Bruce, *Beijing Diaries*, pp. 122–23.

[14] Bruce, *Beijing Diaries*, p. 108.

[15] Bruce, *Beijing Diaries*, p. 133.

### 14 Family Liaison (Sheila Platt's diaries are quoted throughout this chapter in passages identified as such in the text.)

[16] Nicholas Platt, China Diaries Vol 2.

[17] Bruce, *Beijing Diaries*, p. 171.

[18] Ibid., p. 173.

[19] Platt, China Diaries, vol 2.

### 16 Watching, Waiting, Welcoming

[20] Ibid., p. 12.

[21] Ibid., p. 20.

[22] Holdridge, *Crossing the Divide*, p. 147.

[23] Ibid., p.148.

### 17 The Politics of Music

[24] Holdridge, *Crossing the Divide*, p. 148.

### 18 Kissinger Comes

[25] Bruce, *Beijing Diaries*, p. 317.

[26] Ibid., p. 283.

[27] Ibid., p. 345.

[28] Platt, China Diaries, vol. 3.

### 19 Death and Departure

[29] Ibid.

[30] Bruce *Beijing Diaries*, p. 398.

[31] Ibid., p. 399

[32] Ibid., p. 421.

### 20 Renewal in Japan

[33] Letters from Japan, March 15, 1974.

[34] Platt, Japan Notes, p. 9. The entire chapter draws on pp. 1- 9 of Japan Notes.

## 21 Becoming an Asia Hand

[35] In document A-163, May 4, 1976, "Some Observations on Power Relationships in Southeast Asia."

[36] Japan notes, pp. 17.

[37] Ibid., p. 14.

[38] Ibid., p. 15.

[39] Ibid., p.17.

[40] Letters from Japan, February 8, 1977.

## 22 The Pentagon Meets the PLA

[41] The best description of these is in James Mann, *About Face: A History of America's Curious Relationship with China, from Nixon to Clinton* (New York: Knopf, 1998), pp. 70–100.

[42] Members of the group included: State—Assistant Secretary Richard C. Holbrooke; Arms Control and Disarmament Agency—General George M. Seignious; National Security Council—Michael Oksenberg; Department of Defense—Under Secretary Robert Komer (Policy); Assistant Secretary Gerald Dineen (Communications, Command, Control, and Intelligence); Assistant Secretary for International Security Affairs David McGiffert (my immediate boss-to-be); Deputy Assistant Secretary for East Asia and Pacific Affairs Michael Armacost; and Admiral Thor Hansen, joint staff; Central Intelligence Agency—David Gries, DDO (Operations Directorate) and Charles Neuhauser, DDI (Intelligence Directorate).

[43] Mann, *About Face*, p. 111.

[44] Platt, notes, p. 13.

[45] Platt, notes, p. 14.

[46] Platt, notes, p. 39.

## 23 America Greets the PLA

[47] Platt, notes, pp. 51–53.

[48] Platt, notes, p. 62.

[49] Platt, notes, pp. 61–62.

[50] For the record, Geng Biao's delegation consisted of:

> Chai Zemin, Chinese ambassador to the United States
> Liu Huaqing, vice chief of general staff
> Chai Chengwen, director of Foreign Affairs Bureau, Ministry of Defense
> Chen Lai, deputy chief of staff, General Logistics Department
> Han Xu, director, Department of American and Oceanian Affairs, Ministry of Foreign Affairs
> Huang Zhengju, deputy director, Intelligence Department, General Staff

Xu Yimin, defense and military attaché, Chinese Embassy
Zhang Zai, chief of the United States Division, Department of
American and Oceanian Affairs.

Among the Chinese along for their language skills were some old friends and people who became important later. One was Ni Yaoli, a Foreign Affairs Ministry interpreter who helped Geng Biao specifically, and Zhou Wenzhong, Ambassador Chai's interpreter, later ambassador in Washington.

On our side listed after me were :
Rear Admiral Samuel W. Hubbard, Jr., assistant deputy under
secretary (international programs and technology)
Colonel William Webb, air attaché, Beijing
Colonel Monte Bullard, air attaché, Beijing (designate)
Darryl Johnson, State desk officer, later ambassador to Thailand
James Brown, interpreter, now interpreter for the U.S. ambassador in Beijing

[51] Pentagon Notes, pp. 62–68, cover Geng Biao's tour of U.S. facilities.

## 24 The Perry Mission
[52] Platt, notes, pp. 72.
[53] Ibid., pp. 87–91.
[54] Ibid., p. 95.

## 25 Change and Move On
[55] Platt, notes, p. 100.
[56] Manila Diaries, June 8, 1989.

## 26 The "Best Embassy on Park Avenue"
[57] See Nicholas Platt, "1992–2004: The Beginnings of a Global Role," in *A Passion for Asia: The Rockefeller Legacy* (Asia Society and Hudson Hills Press, 2006), pp. 138–41.

## 27 China Boy Redux
[58] Asia Society Trip Notes, Beijing March 18–20, 1993.
[59] Asia Society Trip Notes, Consultations: China Institute for International Strategic Studies (CIISS)–Beijing, Shandong, Shanghai, May 20–25, 1996.
[60] Asia Society Trip Notes, The Handover of Hong Kong, July 7, 1997.
[61] Asia Society Trip Notes, APEC, Shanghai 2001, October 30, 2001.
[62] Asia Society Trip Notes, BoAo Forum for Asia, Nov 1–3, 2003.
[63] Ibid, BoAo Forum Revisited—Hainan, April 23–25, 2004.

**28 Safe in a Clinch**

[64] These statistics are drawn from *Assessing the Next Phase of a Rising China* by Brookings Institution chairman John Thornton. It is his report of a Brookings delegation he led to China in 2007.

[65] *The Times* of London, January 28, 2008.

[66] Thornton, *Assessing the Next Phase.*

[67] Richard N. Haass, "Sovereignty," *Foreign Policy*, September/October 2005, #150, p. 54.

[68] Nicholas Platt, keynote speech, Gala Dinner, Shanghai Forum 2008,Fudan University, May 26, 2008.

# Index

Huang (madame). *See* Zhu Lin
	(Madame Huang)
Huang Hua, 66, 67, 183, 255
Huang Zhen, 109, 122, 123, 125,
	191, 215
Hummel, Arthur, 110, 111, 201

Imperial Hotel (Tokyo), 22–23
Ingersoll, Robert S., 201, 224
Intelligence and Research, Bureau
	of (INR): NP's assignment at,
	53–61
Iran-Iraq war, 282
Iran, U.S. embassy hostage crisis
	in, 243, 251, 254, 255, 256, 267–
	68, 269, 270
Ivey, Mitch, 128

Japan: emperor's role in, 231;
	energy resources and, 336;
	Ford visit to, 225–31; Foreign
	Ministry of, 222, 225; foreign
	policy issues in, 225, 233–35,
	236; and Korea, 225, 233, 239,
	241, 245; MiG-25 crisis and,
	236–38; Mondale visit to,
	239–40; NP's boyhood ties
	to, 4–6, 30, 105–6, 222–23;
	political-economic status of, 61;
	in relationship with U.S., 225,
	230–31, 233–34, 238, 241–42, 265.
	*See also* Tokyo
Japanese language: NP's training
	in, 217, 219–21, 224
Jenkins, Alfred L.: Nixon visit
	preparations and, 68, 71, 73, 75,
	76, 77, 78, 79; in Nixon's PRC
	visit, 81, 83, 85, 89, 96; at USLO,
	61, 109, 119, 120–21, 123, 124,
	148, 150, 151, 152–53, 177, 198,
	211, 212, 216
Ji Chaoju, 110, 111, 185

Ji, Emile, 185
Ji Pengfei, 83, 89, 90, 93, 97, 98, 99,
	**173**, 183
Jiang Qing (Madame Mao):
	Cultural Revolution and, 33,
	34, 44, 49, 50, 119, 190, 195; in
	Gang of Four, 97, 119, 143–44,
	145, 235–36; NP's encounters
	with, 30, 91, 142–45, **174**, 191–
	92, 330; NP's lectures on, 330;
	Philadelphia Orchestra tour
	and, 187, 189, 191–92, 194, 195,
	333
Jiang Zemin, **286**, 319, 320–22, 323,
	332, 338
Job, Brian, 128
Johns Hopkins School of Advanced
	International Studies (SAIS),
	8–9, 11, 55
Johnson, Lyndon B., 51, 132
Johnson, Peter, 72
Johnson, U. Alexis, 75
Jones, David, 271, 294–95
Jones, Don, 296
Jones, Edward, 54
***
Kamman, Kurt, 50
Karnow, Stanley, 35, 89, 114
Kaunda, Kenneth, 298
Keatley, Bob, 89, 92
Kennedy, John F., 21, 22, 51
Kennedy, Robert, 22, 51
Kim Dae Jung, 265
Kim Kyong Won, 246
King, Micki, 128, 132, 138
Kirkpatrick, Jeane J., 297
Kishi, Nobusuke, 230
Kissinger, Henry A.: and Asia
	Society, **285**, 308, 327; at Bruce
	dinner for PRC Liaison Office,
	110, 111; distrust of State
	Department and, 65–66, 87,

of Intelligence and Research
(INR), 53–61; on Mainland
China desk, 51, 53; and Nixon
visit to PRC, 68, 71–103, **172,**
315; on Secretariat staff, 62,
63–69, 73–103, 105–9, 263–64
——————, at U.S. Consulate,
Windsor (Ont.), 11–12, 13–17
——————, at U.S. Embassy
Tokyo as first secretary, 216–17,
221, 222–23, 235
Platt, Nicholas Jr. ("Sanhu"):
arriving in PRC, 148, **173;** in
Beijing, 151, 155, 157, **175,** 198;
birth of, 39; on family trip in
PRC, 160–64, 166, 167, 168; and
nickname, 39, 122; and NP's
collision with cyclist, 207, 208,
217; in Tokyo, 223
Platt, Oliver ("Erhu"): arriving
in PRC, 148–49; in Beijing,
151, 157, **175;** birth of, 16, 21;
boarding school and, 153–54,
181–82, 217; en route to Taiwan,
22–23; and family trip in PRC,
160–64; in Hong Kong, 39,
41; nickname and, 24, 122; in
Taiwan, 23–24; in Tokyo, 223;
and Wuhan finger injury, 165–
67, 168, 169
Platt, Sheila Maynard (NP's wife):
at Alsop dinner for JFK, 21–22;
at Alta Lodge, 103; at Asia
Society dinner, 321; at Ban
Xi restaurant, **173;** as Beijing
hostess, 198; at Chiang's garden
party, 28–30; and children's
births, 10, 16, 39; Chinese
language study and, 22, 26, 39,
157; and family move to Beijing,
147, 148–51, 153–58, **175;** and
family move to Tokyo, 217,

223; and family travel within
PRC, 160–67; in Hong Kong,
**v,** 38–41; and marriage to NP,
6–7, 8; in New York City, 6, 304;
Nitze family and, 9; and NP in
Nixon's PRC visit, 66, 73, 81,
89, 99, 102; and NP's collision
with cyclist, 207, 208–9, 212;
Philadelphia Orchestra tour
and, 191, 192, 193, 194; social
work career and, 39, 147, 164,
217, 223; and sons' departure for
boarding school, 182; Taiwanese
reaction to, 23–24; and Windsor
consulate, 13–15, 16
Pol Pot, 255, 268, 269
pollution, as PRC concern, 337
Powell, Colin, 264, **288,** 296
Power, Steve, 128
POWs, as defectors to PRC, 36–38
PRC. *See* China, People's Republic
of (PRC)
Putin, Vladimir, 323

Qian Dayong, 88, 89, 94, 110, 111
Qian Qichen, 214, 320
Qiao Guanhua: Bruce and, 122,
123, 183; Kissinger visit and,
201; at Philadelphia Orchestra
concert, 191; Shanghai
Communiqué and, 83, 97, 122;
at USLO July 4th party, 151, 152

*Ranger,* USS, 272
Raymond, Ed, 136–37
Reagan, Ronald, 282, 283; China
policy and, 293–95, 297
Red Ass Saloon, The (U.S. Marine
bar), 125–26, 157–58, 197
*Red Detachment of Women, The*
(ballet/opera), 34, 91, 103, 268
Red Guards, 43–44, 45–46, 50, 59,